ARCHITECTS OF CHARLESTON

Architects *of* Charleston

by Beatrice St. Julien Ravenel

Photographs by Carl Julien

University of South Carolina Press

*Published in Association with the
Carolina Art Association, Charleston, S.C.*

Published in Columbia, South Carolina, by the
University of South Carolina Press

Manufactured in the United States of America

Library of Congress Cataloging-in-Publication Data

Ravenel, Beatrice St. Julien, 1904–1990
     Architects of Charleston / by Beatrice St. Julien Ravenel ;
photographs by Carl Julien.
          p.   cm.
     Originally published : Charleston, S.C. : Carolina Art Association,
1945.
     "Published in association with the Carolina Art Association,
Charleston, S.C."
     Includes bibliographical references and index.
     ISBN 0-87249-828-X
     1. Architecture—South Carolina—Charleston. 2. Charleston
(S.C.)—Buildings, structures, etc. 3. Architects–South Carolina—
Charleston—Biography.   I. Carolina Art Association. II. Title.
NA735.C35R3 1992
720' .92' 2757915—dc20
     [B]   91–34126

PREFACE

BEATRICE ST. JULIEN RAVENEL (1904–1990) WAS AN architectural historian and native of Charleston who lived through the era when Charlestonians first became active in preserving their rich historical legacy. She witnessed the establishment of the city's first historical district and the founding of the Historic Charleston Foundation and the Preservation Society of Charleston and was an active member in each of these organizations.

Architects of Charleston was first published in 1945 by the Carolina Art Association as part of a group of publications and exhibitions on the city's cultural heritage. Through extensive use of the city archives, private papers and letters, wills, writings, and secondary sources, Beatrice St. Julien Ravenel provides a detailed examination of the lives and accomplishments of Charleston's builders, engineers, and architects, from the famous, Robert Mills, to the favorite sons, Gabriel Manigault and William Drayton. The book spans the period from the Colonial era to the end of the antebellum era. Over one hundred photographs by Carl Julien emphasize the architectural details of the structures.

The Carolina Art Association gratefully acknowledges the assistance of the University of South Carolina Press in reprinting this classic volume.

TO MY MOTHER

BEATRICE WITTE RAVENEL

ACKNOWLEDGMENTS

BOTH FOR INFORMATION and valuable suggestions I am deeply indebted to Albert Simons, Samuel Lapham, Miss Anna Wells Rutledge, Miss Alice Huger Smith, Miss Helen Gardner McCormack and Samuel Gaillard Stoney of Charleston; Clarence McK. Smith, of Newberry, South Carolina, and Dr. Charles Anderson, of Johns Hopkins University.

For their unflagging kindness and assistance I wish to express my gratitude to Miss Ellen FitzSimons and her staff of the Charleston Library Society; Miss Virginia A. Rugheimer, of the College of Charleston Library; Miss Eva Wrigley, librarian of Furman University; Miss Elizabeth H. Jervey, librarian of the South Carolina Historical Society, and to the staffs of the Charleston Free Library, the Library of the University of South Carolina, the New York Public Library and the Library of Congress.

My thanks also are due to the D. Appleton-Century Company for permission to quote the excerpt from *A Diary from Dixie* by Mary Boykin Chesnut, which occurs in the chapter on Hugh Smith.

While information has been collected from a variety of sources, the most valuable were found to be old newspaper files—the "Pompeii of the press," as an editor has termed them—stretching from 1732 to 1861.

BEATRICE ST. JULIEN RAVENEL

Charleston
May, 1945

For additional information included in the revised edition, I am grateful to Charles E. Peterson, F. A. I. A., and Thomas J. Tobias. Gratitude is due also to Henry P. Staats, president of the Carolina Art Association, and to his associates. Most especially am I indebted to those persons who aided with the first edition and whose interest has remained constant throughout the years.

Charleston
February, 1964

INTRODUCTION

C HARLESTON was never a "housing project." Rather, when the
English colonists who settled on the west bank of the Ashley in 1670 moved ten years later to the peninsula between
that river and the Cooper, it was a defense project, and the city,
about 1730, entered upon the enjoyment of riches and attendant
culture. Marquis James relates that when Andrew Jackson, youth of
fifteen, veteran judge of horse flesh as well as of military prowess,
came to Charleston from the Waxhaws in 1783, he found that "the
late fight for freedom loomed merely a vexatious interruption to the
historical progress of affairs on the Charleston turf." And Charleston, gaining negligibly in population, grew in the stature of wealth
and in the texture of gentle living until the downfall of the Confederate States of America.

History is written by men in wood and bricks and stone while
flesh and blood are making it. Many a book has told of the soldiers,
statesmen, poets of Charleston, and what they did and said subtly
found its way into the buildings they worked and lived in. So, architecture reacted upon and influenced them.

With the fall of the Confederacy came poverty and with it brave,
new effort to restore or to create fortunes. In the engrossment of
commercial tasks art for long years was neglected, its existence in
Charleston almost was forgotten, and if a building in the grotes-
querie of the late Victorian period was erected, to it the Charlestonian of the middle 'nineties pointed with pride as evidence of
progress.

In 1906 a book was published that re-introduced Charleston to
the world and to Charlestonians as well. It was Harriott Horry
Rutledge Ravenel's *Charleston, the Place and the People.* From that
time forward what was always Charleston has been again in the
hearts of its men and women. They value their houses, and *Architects of Charleston* is valuation of men who designed and built them.

In the preface to Mrs. Ravenel's book about Charleston, she said:
"The writer has simply chosen from the story of its 250 years such

[ix]

events as seem to her to have had most to do in shaping the fortunes of the men who made the town, or best to illustrate the character of their children who lived in it."

The author of *Architects of Charleston* has written to inform of men and commemorate them who in a literal sense "made the town".

WILLIAM WATTS BALL

Charleston
May, 1945

CONTENTS

ILLUSTRATIONS

ARCHITECTS OF CHARLESTON

Gates, St. Michael's churchyard, 80 Meeting Street, made in the early nineteenth century by Iusti, an ironworker from Central Europe.

MEN AND TRENDS

MUCH HAS BEEN WRITTEN ABOUT THE ARCHI-
tecture of Charleston, South Carolina, but the architects
who brought it about have remained largely neglected,
although information about them often can throw additional, sometimes even unexpected, light upon their work. The majority of them
were hard-working and conscientious men, and the best were decidedly gifted. As a rule, they were young (Drayton, the amateur,
being an exception), and something of the force of youth went into
their buildings. In other respects, they were a diversified lot. They
sprang from all ranks of society from that of the indentured servant
to that of the planter, and—to the honor of Charleston—seem to
have received patronage based on the merit of their work. A goodly
percentage were native-born Charlestonians, but the stranger was
welcome, so that there were also Northerners, Britons, Irishmen,
Frenchmen, Germans, and one Swede. Their abilities ranged from
the genius of Robert Mills to the mediocre talent of men who, perhaps, do not deserve inclusion, but have been considered in the hope
that they may have done better work in some other city, in which
case this mention of them may prove useful to students of architecture there.

Charleston, under its early name of Charles Town, was founded
in 1670 on the west shore of the Ashley River, on part of the plantation now known as Old Town. As early as 1672, a few colonists had
moved to the present site, a tongue of land between the Ashley and
Cooper Rivers, and in 1680, the town was transferred there.

Barely two or three country houses built prior to 1700, and
scarcely a town house built before 1730, remain. But after 1700, a
few names appear which one may connect, with varying degrees of
plausibility, with architecture—John Fitch and Thomas Rose,
"supervisors" of St. Andrew's Church, Samuel Holmes, Peter Chassereau, and John Wood, servant and soldier, besides several contractors who owned architectural books. Coeval with them were the

military engineers, Gabriel Bernard, uncle of Jean-Jacques Rousseau; Othniel Beale, adventurous Peter Henry Bruce, scholarly William Gerard de Brahm. In the middle of the eighteenth century came Dudley Inman, Joseph Fournier, William Axson, the Villepontouxs, uncle and nephew; A. Howard, Samuel Cardy, indissolubly associated with St. Michael's Church; the Horlbeck brothers from Saxony, and Cardy's son-in-law, William Rigby Naylor.

As a rule, these Pre-Revolutionary men are shadowy figures, but they and their nameless contemporaries worked with accuracy and distinction, at first in Georgian baroque, and later under the influence of Chippendale. To these early architects, England was all but everything. Dutch influence, barely traceable, came mainly via England, following the accession of William III; French influence was to come later; Spanish influence was nil.

Certain houses which rear, shoulder to shoulder, on lower East Bay are startlingly reminiscent of part of the Cadiz waterfront, but the resemblance is greatest in the contrast between sun and salt water outside and the dark, huddled rooms within. A Mediterranean flavor, which will not be gainsaid, springs from the climate and the harbor, aided by the presence of garden walls and ironwork (incidentally, *not* of South-Europe design), but the architecture is not responsible.

The eighteenth century architects, for all their preoccupation with English design, did make two concessions to the Charleston summer. They developed the piazza from small beginnings, and the Charleston "single house." The piazza is sometimes said to have been introduced into South Carolina from the West Indies, but its growth seems to owe as much to Charleston as to the islands. As early as 1700, the word appeared in "An Act to prevent the Sea's further encroachment upon the Wharf of Charlestown," which provided that owners of front lots "that hath or shall hereafter build a brick house at least two stories high, are hereby permitted and impowered to build piazzas, not exceeding six foot, in the said wharff or front lots, with steps in the said piazzas up to the said house." Only after 1750, however, do references to piazzas become frequent, but from then on they are numerous. A Hessian soldier of fortune, Captain Johann Hinrichs, who came to South Carolina during the Revolution, wrote of "palaces" in Meeting and Church streets and on East Bay, of which everyone was surrounded (*umgeben*) with porticoes having Ionic and Doric pillars. Not until the end of the century, however, is there definite mention of the two-storied variety.

St. Michael's Church, completed in 1761, and a single house, 76 Meeting Street, built about 1800.

A double house. The Gibbes House, 64 South Battery, built by 1779.

Old houses on East Bay below Elliott Street. "Rainbow Row".

As for the single house, the name has reference to the width, that of a single room. The building stands with its gable-end to the street and consists, typically, of two rooms on a floor, with a hall between, containing the stair case, while a piazza runs along one side of the house (generally the south or west) to shelter it from the sun as well as to provide out-door living space. Entrance usually is through the piazza. Although one would give much to know who first designed the single house, this form was not, in later years, an architect's house. As a practical solution of the problem of keeping cool, before the invention of artificial ice, electric fans, and air conditioning, it offered little room for improvement, and therefore, little scope for the imagination. The nineteenth century enlarged the scale and played tricks with the piazzas, but the plan, being complete, remained unchanged. Few architects are content with repetition. Consequently, this most characteristic of Charleston dwelling forms will be mentioned seldom in the following pages.

Unlike the single house, the "double house" was familiar to England and America alike. With its hall running through the middle from front door to back, it offered more opportunity for variation, yet even it belonged more to the builders than to the architects. The Miles Brewton house is a superlative example of a dwelling on this plan.

The Post-Revolutionary period (1783-1835) in Charleston saw the domination of two very different styles, the Adam and the Classic Revival. The first was made popular about 1800 by Gabriel Manigault, long after it was known in England. It had an amazing success, being found, at least as regards the superficials of decoration, in dozens of houses. Adam fundamentals of plan, with easy intercommunications, curving rooms, and generous closet space, are confined almost entirely to Manigault's own work. In fact, much of the popularity of this style in Charleston was probably due to the presence in 1802-1803 of an able stucco worker, William Purviss, examples of whose craftsmanship can be seen in the Dock Street Theatre today. The Adam influence lasted through the 1830's, though the later work degenerated into mere carpenter's detail. Sometimes, too, it mingled strangely with a Federal influence, though this was often no more serious than an outburst of plaster eagles. The Classic Revival, so far as Charleston was concerned, was hardly under way before the 1820's, and stemmed from Robert Mills, an architectural giant. Like Manigault, he was a native son.

Also practicing in the Post-Revolutionary period were James Hoban, the Irish-born architect of the White House at Washington; William Drayton, Thomas Bennett, the younger Horlbecks, Hugh Smith, the Gordon brothers, who reared massive churches; and Joseph Hyde, architect of St. Philip's Church, all of whom did noteworthy work. Russell Warren, from Rhode Island, worked in two manners, switching from his early style to that of the Greek Revival. Frederick Wesner and the Englishman, William Jay, were both exponents of the Classic Revival, although their work shows wide dissimilarities. Others of this time were David Burn, Depresseville, Emes, Hope, Magrath and Nicholson, Thomas Walker, John Bruton Rickets, Cox, Colonel Senf, the engineer; Augustus de Grasse, John Baptiste Aveilhé, Daniel M'Giverin, F. Gabriel Paque, Joseph Jahan, James Dupre, Ready or Reedy, Abraham P. Reeves, and the earlier members of the Curtis family. Charles Fraser, an amateur, gains interest from his associations with his own province, that of painting. Both William Strickland and Thomas U. Walter, of Philadelphia, sent plans for buildings which still stand.

The date assigned here to end this period and to begin the Ante-Bellum era, 1835, is somewhat arbitrary, since no distinct cleavage in style was visible until after 1861. However, about the mid-thirties, a new manner became apparent, manifested in lavishness of decoration and an increase in scale, which became more evident as time went on. The Greek and Classic Revivals had lost their bloom, though one forgets this in seeing the hotel by Charles F. Reichardt, and the Market Hall by Edward B. White. No one or two styles were sufficient any longer. Charleston, like the rest of the world, was already wandering happily in a maze of eclecticism, which became most pronounced in the 1850's. Her architects, who included several of talent, White, George E. Walker, Edward C. Jones, and the latter's pupil and partner, Francis D. Lee, designed in a variety of styles, Lee even venturing into the Moorish. All four of these men worked in both the Classic Revival and the Gothic Revival styles, while Jones and another pupil, Louis J. Barbot, designed largely in that of the "Italian villa." Outside influences came from the work of "Mr. Young of Boston," architect of the Classic Revival Custom House; Patrick C. Keely, of Brooklyn, responsible for the Gothic Revival cathedral; and the cotton mill builder, Charles T. James, of Rhode Island. Also practicing were P. H. Hammarskold, Edward B. Bryan, John E. Earle, John H. Seyle, William Bell, Longley and Long, C. C. Trumbo, William Jones, Louis F. LeBleux, John A.

Adam style stucco work by William Purviss, now in the Dock Street Theatre, formerly in the demolished Ratcliffe House, built by November, 1802. *(Frances Benjamin Johnston)*

Adam style stucco work by William Purviss from the Ratcliffe House.

(Francis Benjamin Johnston)

Michel, Edwin J. White, William M. Ramsay, Justice Wuhrmann, and James Kenney, while John H. Devereux, of Post-Bellum days, was commencing his studies in Jones' office.

Meanwhile, side by side with the fashionable styles of the leading architects of the 1850's, existed two distinct and contrary trends, inconspicuous and generally anonymous. The mass of would-be householders still patronized builders who continued to raise the traditional single and double houses. At the same time, the roots of modern household engineering and building construction were feeling their way. Plumbing no longer was an oddity (one Broad Street dwelling in 1850 had a private bath for each bedroom), and steam heat was increasing in use. Francis D. Lee employed castiron pillars in a warehouse in 1853, and in another structure combined iron and concrete. Iron fronts, strange to view but significant in the history of structure, were made by a Charleston foundry in 1854. These new growths were destined for fruition elsewhere, however. It probably is more than a coincidence that iron and steel construction assumed so much prominence toward the end of the last century in St. Louis, where Lee was then practicing. Nor should one forget Christian Edward Detmold, who worked in iron and glass as supervising architect and engineer of New York's Crystal Palace, which opened in 1853. Detmold, a Hanoverian by birth, gained much of his experience in South Carolina, where he superintended the laying of the foundations of Fort Sumter.

If emphasis seems placed unduly upon these structural matters, it is by way of reaction to the general conception of Southern architecture as concerned entirely with the many-columned portico. South Carolinians were cognizant, from the 1820's on, of the trends of their days, and sometimes were in advance of them. They erected a building with furnace heat in the 1820's, worked in iron and concrete, as has been shown, in the 1850's, used the Romanesque style before Richardson, and produced buildings with exteriors stripped of unmeaning ornament before Functionalism. They were derivative in so far as it suited them to be, working in the prevailing style of the moment but brashly individualistic in regard to planning, conscious of the demands of climate.

To quote Mills:

"Utility and economy will be found to have entered into most of the studies of the author, and little sacrifice to display; at the same time his endeavors were to produce as much harmony and

Federal eagle, on a ceiling in the Southern Railway Building, formerly the William Aiken House, 456 King Street at Ann, built between 1807 and 1811.

beauty of arrangement as practicable. The principle assumed and acted upon was that beauty is founded upon order and that convenience and utility were constituent parts. . . . His considerations were—first, the object of the building; second, the means appropriated for its construction; third, the situation it was to occupy; these served as guides in forming the outline of his plan."

THE EARLY MEN

THE EARLY HISTORY OF ARCHITECTS IN CHARLES-ton and its neighborhood consists largely of blanks, most of which can be filled only with question marks. Carpenters and bricklayers were abundant, even in the seventeenth century, but not until after 1700 can one hazard a possible connection between any building and the name of an architect.

Where their work was poor, these men are well lost in their anonymity, but frequently structures arose whose designers deserve to have been remembered, and were not. These unknowns built the beautiful "robust" Georgian houses of the Low Country, in the style then prevailing in England. On the other hand, they developed the piazza from the short and shallow porch of 1700,[1] to the multi-storied affair characteristic of Charleston. All through the first half of the eighteenth century, a valuable and distinctive architecture came into being, but of the individuals who made it little is known.

It is true that documents in the State Paper Office, at London, show that on August 16, 1698, the lords proprietors wrote to the governor of Carolina that one Mr. Johns, a master builder, was leaving for that province by the same ship which carried the letter. Johns, they wrote, would be of service in repairing the damage made by a recent fire and would contribute to the regularity of the new building. One would give much to know more of Mr. Johns.

However, a few names afford clues. The Act of November 4, 1704, provided for building, in the Low Country, six churches and their parsonages and gave the "several Supervisors for the building the several Churches, houses and other works" ample powers to impress labor and materials. Nothing, unfortunately, was said as to plans. On St. Andrew's parish church, built under this act in 1706, appear the initials of its supervisors, J. F. and T. R. Samuel Lapham, F.A.I.A., has observed that these are the initials of two members of the vestry, John Fitch and Thomas Rose.[2]

Old inventory books show that a John Fitch, dead by 1745, and a Thomas Rose, dead by 1733, both made bricks,[3] and that Fitch was due payment from a customer for bricklaying and plastering work. It seems likely that he had done at least part of the job with his own hands, for he owned only one negro man, unlike Rose, who was master of nine. Whether these supervisors drew, or even selected the design of the church, is not known.

Both Fitch and Rose owned books, though nothing shows if any of them dealt with building. "Books of Architect" figure in various old inventories, generally builder's manuals, though some may have been more elaborate. Their value (second-hand) ran, in the examples discovered, from seven shillings, threepence, to three pounds each, Carolina currency, worth only from one-fifth to one-seventh of the pound sterling.

Farmer Bull, dead by 1729, left sundry tools and an architectural library consisting of one volume.[4] Thomas Bless or Bliss, of Georgetown, South Carolina, who died in 1735/6, owned one such book,[5] and John Rich, dead in 1744, had five.[6]

John Fowler, who was in Lisbon in 1733, but died in South Carolina the following year, left lumber, tools, and three architectural books. He owed money to Joseph Mackey, a joiner, but Jacob Motte, and the estate of Motte's uncle, Charles Hill, were indebted to Fowler.[7] May one surmise that Fowler built houses for Motte and Hill and hired Mackey to work on them? This is guesswork with a vengeance.

Meanwhile, however, had appeared Samuel Holmes, who may have been Charleston's first architect. A series of curt advertisements in the *South-Carolina Gazette* tell his story, beginning February 2-9, 1733/4:

> "Samuel Holmes of Charlestown *Bricklayer* undertakes and performes in workmanlike manner all sorts of Brickworck and Plastering at reasonable Rates: He likewise if required draws Draughts of Houses, and measures and values all sorts of Workmanship in Houses or Buildings."

"If required"—but was he required? His further advertisements do not mention plans and throw no light on any architectural activities, though they add to our knowledge of him in other ways. He had imported from London two indentured bricklayers, Richard Dearsley and Thomas Cawood. White indentured servants and black slave property worked side by side in eighteenth-century Carolina, and were equally apt to take to their heels. Masters advertised then

St. Andrew's Church, St. Andrew's Parish, built in 1706. J. F. and T. R., "Supervisors".

for runaway human belongings (servants or slaves, apprentices, or even wives) as they do now for lost dogs. Off went Dearsley and Cawood. After seven months, Holmes inserted a notice in the *Gazette*.[8] It must have borne fruit, for a few months later, the following appeared:

> "Any person that is disposed to buy two white Servants as good Bricklayers and Plaisterers as is in this Town and Country, who have above 5 years to serve, may have them cheap by
>
> *Samuel Holmes."* [9]

Nothing about a propensity to scamper! Shortly after, Holmes let the public know that he was still performing his trade, "(God willing) in workmanlike manner and with Expedition." [10]

But building was not his only stand-by, as this advertisement, published early in 1735/6, shows:

> "Samuel Holmes of Charleston, designs to leave this Province some time this next Summer, and to sell his house, and Outhouses and Garden, well planted with Orange Trees and Grape vines, and all his utencils fit for brewing of Beer, he likewise selleth at his Store on Mr. Elliott's wharf, fine pale Beer at 12s. 6d. per Gallon, and Sider at 6s. 3d. per Gallon, and good Chester Cheese at 3s. per pound all for ready Money, and by the Barrel some allowance will be made to the buyer." [11]

This house stood on Tradd Street.[12] Elliott's wharf was at the foot of Elliott Street, then a shopping center.

In 1737, Holmes was still trying to sell his house, and was offering to take in horses to graze at the New-market Plantation near Charlestown.[13] His story ended in 1740, when his widow and administratrix, Elizabeth Holmes, addressed a notice to the creditors of his estate.[14]

Contemporaneous with Holmes was Peter Chassereau, whose advertisement in January, 1734/5, nearly a year after Holmes' first notice, was more professional in tone:

> "Mr. Peter Chassereau, newly come from *London,* surveys Lands, and makes neat maps therof, draws Plans and Elevations of all kinds of Buildings whatsoever, both Civil and Military, likewise perspective Views or prospects of Towns or Gentlemens

Houses or Plantations, he calculates Estimates for Buildings or Repairs, inspects and measures Artificers Work, sets out ground for Gardens or Parks, in a grand and Rural manner, and takes Levels; young Gentlemen and Ladies will be attended at their own Houses to be taught Drawing. To be heard of at Mr. *Shepherd's* in Broad Street, or at Mr. Lawrence, Saddler." [15]

This advertisement, which appeared twice, is the sole scrap of evidence about Chassereau, who may have succumbed to the "climate" or left on the next ship, for all that is known.

John Wood is noteworthy, not because he bore the same name as the well-known architect of Bath, but because he seems to have been the first person in Charleston to whom the word *architect* was applied. Whether he deserved it, one has no means to determine, but the appearance of the term has its interest. It occurred in the *Gazette* of July 4, 1744:

> "To be sold on Thursday the 12th Instant, by publick Vendue, at the House of Mr. Rice Price on the Bay, the Effects late of Mr. *John Wood*, Architect, deceased, consisting of great variety of choice Tools for Carpenters and Joyners, with sundry other Goods. The Sale to begin at 11 o'Clock in the Forenoon."

But the inventory of Wood's estate termed him *joiner*. Included in his property was a "parcel of Books," valued at ten pounds Carolina, instruments, and a "Draw^g board T.s & bevil." [16]

He was probably the same John Wood who was in South Carolina by 1737. His beginnings were inauspicious. Samuel Holmes had owned indentured servants; but Wood was an indentured servant. To pay the passage-money of his family in coming to this country, he and another member had sold their time. Then, without leave of his master, he enlisted in the "publick Service." The matter was arranged, however, for a sum of money which was remitted partly by the treasurer of the province and partly by a colonel, to compensate for Wood's lost services. [17] Fortune must thenceforward have smiled on Wood, to enable him to amass tools and other goods, as well as a *Mr.* before his name.

FOUR ENGINEERS

GABRIEL BERNARD. In Charlestown by 1735/6. Died 1737.

CHASSEREAU, IN STATING THAT HE WOULD DRAW plans for buildings "both Civil and Military," was not alone in combining the two fields of endeavor. In 1800, de Grasse was to advertise in much the same way, and later on, Edward B. White and Edward B. Bryan, educated as engineers, were to become civil architects, while George E. Walker, an architect, was to design a Confederate battery.

The presence in Charlestown of military builders must have influenced its domestic architecture, making for more scientific and substantial work. Apart from the churches, successive watch houses, State House, and Exchange, Charlestown's important public works in colonial days were military, consisting of barracks, powder magazines, and fortifications.

The town had defenses of a sort by 1700,[1] but the first extensive works were the bastions and half-moons with connecting curtain lines commenced in 1703 under the superintendance of Colonel William Rhett (1666-1722), later to become known for his capture of the pirate Stede Bonnet and his crew.[2] Where Rhett obtained the plans does not appear. In 1707, he was replaced by one Captain Thomas Walker.[3]

The town soon spread beyond these early confines, and in 1717 the north, south, and west walls were leveled,[4] leaving only the east side (toward Cooper River), ending on the north at Craven's bastion and on the south at Granville's bastion, on the sites of the present Custom House and the Shriners' Temple, respectively. Tinkered at whenever war seemed imminent, the defenses were neglected in peacetime. They were in poor shape when Gabriel Bernard appeared in South Carolina.

Bernard is familiar to students of literature as the uncle and guardian of Jean-Jacques Rousseau. Most of the information about him, apart from that concerning his stay in Charlestown, comes from Rousseau—unfortunately, for the source is by no means reliable.

Bernard, the son of a Huguenot minister, was a native of Geneva. On the same day that his sister, Susanne, married Isaac Rousseau, Bernard married the latter's sister. A few years later, he served as an engineer in the Holy Roman Empire and in Hungary under Prince Eugene, and distinguished himself at the capture of Belgrade in 1717. On his return to Geneva, he was employed on fortifications there. About 1724, he took charge of his nephew, Jean-Jacques Rousseau, whose mother was dead and whose father had absconded. Bernard had children of his own too, a daughter who died young and a lank, well-mannered son who was Rousseau's favorite schoolfellow. After four years, however, Rousseau ran away, to commence the wanderings related in the famous *Confessions*.[5]

This happened about 1728. By 1735/6, Bernard was in South Carolina. According to Rousseau:

> "Mon oncle Bernard étoit depuis quelques années passé dans la Caroline pour y faire bâtir la ville de Charlestown dont il avoit donné le plan. Il y mourut peu après."[6]

Much of this statement is, of course, absurd, Charlestown having been laid out many years before. However, Bernard did work there. By 1735/6, he petitioned the authorities to employ him, producing papers to show that he had served as an engineer in Europe.[7] A "Letter of recommendation from the Honrble. Coll. Schutz" seems to have obtained the position for him.[8] As a result, the Act of Assembly of 1736 decreed:

> "That Mr. Gabriel Bernard shall and he is hereby appointed Chief Engineer, who shall constantly attend direct and inspect the raising and repairing such fortifications as the same commissioners" (those in charge of the fortifications) "shall think fit and shall be allowed at and after the rate of £700 per annum nevertheless subjected to be displaced and the said salary taken away by vote or order of the General Assembly."

In June, Bernard advertised that persons who wished to furnish materials and work to "rebuild the Battery before Johnson's Fort" could have the "Perusal of the Plan, and be better informed of the Particulars by Mr. *Gabriel Bernard* Engineer, who will give Attendance at his House every Day from 7 a Clock in the Morning to the Hour of Twelve."[9] This must have been the sea battery which in 1741 mounted thirty guns.[10] Johnson's Fort, or Fort Johnson, stood opposite the city on James Island, where its ruins are still seen.

Bernard is next heard of in command of the forces at Port Royal, South Carolina.[11] He can hardly have built much, for he died in July, and was buried in St. Philip's churchyard in Charleston, July 19, 1737.[12] His executor was Samuel Prioleau,[13] a fellow Huguenot, and a member of the committee which had recommended his appointment.[14]

The inventory of Bernard's estate has been preserved. Its contents indicate that, when not drawing plans, he may have gone fishing, and that, like other gentlemen of the day, he wore silk stockings and used a "Tooth Picker." [15]

Bernard's son, who had entered the Prussian service, died at nearly the same time. The engineer's wife, thus doubly bereaved, remained at Geneva, where Rousseau saw her not long after, and amused himself by going through his uncle's books and papers.[16]

OTHNIEL BEALE.   Died March 22, 1773.

Othniel Beale, a son of John Beale of Marblehead, Massachusetts,[1] was both merchant and engineer.[2] Tradition says that while he was on a voyage the ship was captured by Algerine pirates, and that Beale, under pretense of steering them to Africa, headed instead for England, and brought the vessel safe into the Thames before the Algerines knew what was happening.[3] If true, this story justifies the opinion which de Brahm, a fellow-engineer, entertained of Beale as "a gentleman of great ingeniousity and judgement." [4]

In 1735/6, Beale was a member of the Commons House of South Carolina and one of the committee on whose recommendation Bernard was appointed Chief Engineer.[5] In 1742, Beale was himself placed in charge of the new fortifications.[6] By November of that year, the *Gazette* could boast that "we shall in a short Time be in a Condition to beat off any Enemy." [7]

In 1744, when news came that England and France were again at war, additional works were contemplated, and Beale advertised thus:

"CHARLES-TOWN,
Tuesday June 19th.

Whereas I have received from His Excellency the Governor, the Sum of *Two Thousand* and *Five Hundred* Pounds, current Money, to enable me to carry on the Fortification Works in *Charles Town*, such Labourers and others employed by me on the said Works, may therefore be assured of immediate Payment.

And as it may be expected, that great Numbers of Negroes will be sent by their Masters voluntarily to assist without Pay, I give Notice that the said Works will be begun on *Thursday* next.

Othniel Beale." [8]

So far, so good. But these works were termed unsatisfactory, according to Peter Henry Bruce, chief engineer of the Bahamas. Bruce wrote that the South Carolina authorities alleged in 1745 that Beale had run the colony into great expense by erecting works "of no signification." [9]

Even Bruce believed, however, that Beale was competent to carry out the designs of others. Having himself provided a plan, Bruce gave "full instructions to Colonel Baile (sic) how it was to be performed, and recommended him . . . . . for the execution of it" . . .[10] Bruce's spelling of the name may be a clue to the pronunciation.

Beale had a brother, William, a sea captain, who is buried in the Circular Church graveyard.[11] The engineer married Katherine Gale in Charlestown in 1722.[12] They had a son, John,[13] and a daughter, Hannah, who married Lieutenant-Governor William Bull, but left no children.[14] Beale died March 22, 1773, aged eighty-four.[15]

PETER HENRY BRUCE. 1692-1757. In Charlestown,
1741 and 1745.

Peter Henry Bruce's visits to Charlestown were only episodes in an adventurous life, but the space which he accorded the second one in his memoirs indicates that he attached importance to it, and to his plans for the fortification of the town.

Three-fourths German, for all his Scotch name, Bruce was born in 1692 at Detring Castle in Westphalia, the son of James Bruce and his wife, Elizabeth Catherina Detring.[1] He entered the army in his teens and became an engineer, fighting in several battles, and successively serving Prussia, Russia, and Great Britain. Able to land on his feet anywhere, he traveled in Tartary, Turkey, the West Indies, "&c." Whether Charlestown was included in the West Indies or in the &c. is not clear. Hard-bitten and generally objective, he wrote of his experiences in a matter-of-fact way—"we saw twelve men broke alive upon the wheel" at Riga,[2] or, crossing the Atlantic, "the distemper began to rage more and more among us." [3]

About 1724, he married in Great Britain, and for sixteen years lived quietly on a farm. Then, in 1740, to provide for his family, who were "pretty numerous," he obtained the office of chief engineer for the fortification of the Bahamas.[4]

On his voyage thither, in company with their governor, the ship touched at Charlestown in February, 1741.

Bruce found the place devastated by the fire of 1740, ("the ruins were still smoaking"), yet attended a round of entertainments, Charlestown refusing to let disaster interfere with hospitality. Bruce saw and praised a review of the militia, followed by a ball, and spent agreeable days at the Vanderdussen plantation on Goose Creek. He inspected the defenses which did not impress him. Then, on April 10, he sailed for Providence in the Bahamas.[5]

There, three years later, he received a letter dated June 22, 1744, from Lieutenant-Governor William Bull of South Carolina, requesting a plan "in brick building" for a magazine to hold 500 barrels of gunpowder, and promising remuneration. Bruce sent a plan and a profile (a section?).[6] This magazine evidently was built by 1749, with a few minor changes, but stands no longer.[7]

Later in 1744, Bruce received an invitation from Governor Glen to visit Charlestown. Though the engineer does not mention it in his memoirs, his presence there was desirable for business reasons of his own—he was being sued in the court of common pleas at Charlestown by two merchants, George Philp and Alexander Livie, causing the provost marshal to attach a sum of money and some mahogany plank, Bruce's property.[8] How this affair ended is a mystery, but it as well as the governor's letter probably had a share in bringing him again to Charlestown.

He was nearly wrecked at the harbor mouth, when the ship "thumped eighteen times," but landed safely, January 21, 1745. He has left a long account of this visit, mentioning rice and indigo, live oaks ("preferable to English oak" for ship-building), "tame and familiar" mocking-birds, and Cherokee Indian guests, with faces daubed in four colors. He saw too, a captured French ship, which held so much treasure that the shares of prize money were delivered by weight "to save the trouble of counting it". It should be noted that his arrival and the public events he mentions are corroborated by the *South-Carolina Gazette* of the time.

Kindly received by governor, council, and assembly, Bruce was asked to survey the place and give his opinion as to what more was necessary for defense. His report is worth quoting in part as showing the dangers which threatened the colony from within and without. Bruce's advocacy of a "fort or citadel" curiously foreshadows the erection of the State Arsenal (now the Old Citadel), built after the abortive slave insurrection of 1822.

"The more I consider the situation and circumstances of the place, the more I am confirmed in opinion of the utility and necessity of a fort or citadel, as the town is quite open on that side" (the north or land side) "to the incursions of the Indians; two hundred of whom, by approaching in small parties through the woods, might do great mischief in one night. Your country negroes are quiet at present, but they have not always been so; and their late attempts at Antigua, New York, and Jamaica, may be sufficient warning to any country, where they are so numerous, to provide against accidents, and consider of a force that may be turned against them; the town negroes also will be more faithful when they know it is impossible for them to escape if they should misbehave." [9]

As a cheap alternative for the fort, Bruce advised running a moat and a curtain line of sods, strengthened by a bastion and a demi-bastion, across the undefended land side of the town. This second plan was chosen by the authorities, who urged Bruce to stay in order to superintend the work, but he persuaded them to let Beale carry it out. He also advised them to build two batteries to command Hog Island Channel, one of which was to be placed on "Rahte's point" (Rhett's point) near "Anson's house". This had been the dwelling of Captain (later Lord) Anson, the circumnavigator, who was stationed at Charlestown, 1723/4—1730, and gave his name to Ansonborough, now a part of the city.

For these plans, Bruce received fifty guineas, less than he had hoped for, but as he was told, all that could be allowed him since he was not to supervise the work. He sailed for England, June 1, 1745, on the *Flamborough* man-of-war.

The new works, including a powder magazine, were under way by July.[10] Their completion is doubtful. Probably the news of the treaty of Aix-la-Chapelle in 1748, which established peace between England, France, and Spain, caused them to be neglected.

As for Bruce, he arrived in England in 1745, in time to aid in putting down the Jacobite Rebellion. That over, he rejoined his family, wrote his memoirs in German, translated them into English, and finally died in 1757.[11]

The book appeared posthumously in London in 1782, and was praised for "originality and authenticity" by the *Monthly Review* of December. Another edition (pirated?) appeared at Dublin in 1783.

Strangely enough, in 1757, the year of the engineer's death, a marriage took place at Charlestown between a Peter Henry Bruce and one Elizabeth Fitchett, widow, on April 10.[12] Whether relationship or coincidence was responsible for the sameness of name is not known.

WILLIAM GERARD DE BRAHM. 1717—c. 1799.

William Gerard de Brahm is both well-documented and mysterious. He wrote at length on intellectual matters but briefly of himself, leaving us uninformed of his early life, even of his exact place of birth. His given names themselves are uncertain. At one time he signed them John Gerar William, later they became William Gerard, and sometimes were hyphenated.

After his arrival in America, his outer activities were chronicled by various sources, so that one catches glimpses of him—with a dark bay horse in the Carolina upcountry;[1] wrangling with the commissioners for fortifying Charlestown;[2] or, in old age, wearing a long beard and puzzling over alchemy.[3] Scientifically, he planned forts, mapped land and water, worked out nautical tables. But another side of his mental life remains half-hid, even from the few who open his almost-forgotten books—his philosophical, perhaps mystical, beliefs.[4]

Two affections are apparent, love of his work (he resented the American Revolution because it interrupted his map-making),[5] and love of Charlestown, where he found the citizens "renound for concord, compleasance, courteousness, and tenderness towards each other, and more so towards foreigners, without regard or respect of nation or religion."[6]

De Brahm is said to have been Dutch, and his spelling of certain words, such as "didges" for *ditches*, indicates that his tongue never forgot its gutturals. He claimed to have served as engineer in the army of Charles VI,[7] Holy Roman emperor who died in 1740. In 1751, de Brahm came to America. He told his story succinctly in the preface to his *Philosophico-Historico-Hydrogeography of South Carolina, Georgia, and East Florida:*

"The author begins his Remarks in the year 1751, when with a number of 160 German colonists, reinforced in eleven months after by a like number (the relations and acquaintances of the former), he established the florishing settlement of Bethany, in

Georgia, during the reign of his Majesty, of most glorious memory, King George the Second; and he made a general survey of the frontiere, or eastern part of that Province, to which joining the surveys of William Bull, Esqr, Lieu^t Governor of South Carolina, he delivered to the public in 1757 the first map of South Carolina and Georgia. In the year 1755 he fortified Charlestown, in South Carolina; in 1756 erected Fort Loudoun, on the west side of the Apalachian mountains, on Tanessee, one of the Mississippi branches; in 1757 he fortified Savannah, and erected a fort at Ebenezer, in Georgia; in 1761 he directed the construction of Fort George, on Coxpur Island, in the sound of Savannah River; from 1765 to the present time he is employed in measuring the western Atlantic coast, the Martiers at Cape Florida, and the eastern coast of the Gulf of Mexico".

To this account a few details may be added.

The Bethany settlers were protestants who came from Salzburg in southern Germany by way of England.[8]

The fortifications at Charlestown consisted mainly of an extension of the curtain line south from Granville's bastion to connect with a detached work, Broughton's battery (at or near the present park known as the Battery), and thence west along the south waterfront to a wharf near the present corner of King Street and South Battery.[9] Quicksands added to the difficulties, but "In ten months, with 300 men, all the ramparts was raised." [10]

De Brahm had more plans for Charlestown than came to completion. Like Bruce before him, he advised digging a canal across the land side of the city,[11] and again the scheme came to naught. The writer of A Short Description of the Province of Carolina, published in 1770, could say:

> "The old fortifications on the land side, is in ruins; a new work was begun in 1757, a little without the other; the plan was a hornwork, to be built with tappy, and flanked with little batteries and redoubts, at proper distances; the whole to extend from one river to the other, but a stop was put to this likewise, after a considerable progress was made in it, either from want of money, which is probable, or from an opinion that it was unnecessary." [12]

Not until the American Revolution was a continuous fortified line to defend the land side of the city.[13]

The extension of the waterfront ramparts was directed by de Brahm during 1755 and part of 1756, but in the latter year, as he tells us, he went to the mountains to build Fort Loudoun, intended as a bulwark against the French in the Mississippi valley.

De Brahm has left a hair-raising account of his ride through the Cherokee country, across narrow ridges between precipices.[14] The problem of transportation was enormous; nevertheless, the fort was built. It was to surrender to the Indians in 1760, but its fall was due to the starvation of the garrison.

Early in 1757, de Brahm again visited Charleston, on his way to Georgia.[15] In Savannah, he built himself a dwelling with a piazza (the description sounds Charlestonian, though it was not a "single house"), but its chief feature was a ventilated cellar for wine-making.[16]

In 1764, having fortified Georgia, de Brahm was appointed surveyor-general for the southern district of North America.[17] He was living in St. Augustine about 1766. He acquired 10,000 acres of Floridian land.[18]

But in 1770, when again in Charlestown, he learned that Governor Grant of Florida had suspended him from the surveyorship in that province, alleging overcharging and obstructing applicants for lands.[19] In the *South-Carolina Gazette,* de Brahm challenged the governor's authority in the matter, and a few days later, again in the *Gazette,* he forbade "any Person or Persons, of any Rank whatsoever, in St. Augustine or in the Province of East-Florida, to meddle in settling his Affairs, under any Pretence whatsoever." [20]

De Brahm's son-in-law, Captain Frederick George Mulcaster, was appointed in his stead,[21] but in 1774 de Brahm was reinstated, probably as a result of a trip to London.[22]

The engineer's difficulties with the Floridian authorities resemble those of William Drayton (qv) whose brother-in-law he became in 1776. De Brahm's first wife had died in 1774 at Charlestown, leaving him with a family of daughters,[23] and he now married Drayton's sister, Mary, the widow of Edward Fenwick.[24]

Meanwhile, the American Revolution had broken out. De Brahm's part in the struggle is obscure; however, in 1783, the British saw fit to grant him £1,138 6s 8d in compensation for his lands (lost when East Florida became Spanish), but no further funds.[25]

His last years seem to have been spent in Philadelphia, where he published several short works. He was alive in 1798, aged eighty-one,[26] but his will was proved July 3, 1799.[27] His widow died in 1806.[28]

SOME MID-EIGHTEENTH CENTURY NAMES

FOLLOWING ON THE HEELS OF HOLMES, CHASSE-reau, and Wood, but belonging to the second half of the eighteenth century, came another group, of whom the earliest, as well as the most voluble, was Dudley Inman.

Inman's assertion that few Charleston houses were supplied with "all the conveniences necessary to remove the disadvantages" of the climate would be of greater interest if one knew, first, exactly what he meant, and, secondly, whether his word could be relied on. His advertisement appeared in the *Gazette* in May, 1751.[1]

"DUDLEY INMAN,

CARPENTER and Joyner, lately arrived from *London,* in Capt. *Crosthwaite,* who now lives next to Mrs. Finlay's in Church-*street, Charles-Town,* undertakes all sorts of carpenters and joyners work, particularly buildings of all kinds, with more convenience, strength and beauty, than those commonly erected in this province, in which he will closely adhere to either of the orders of architecture: He likewise gives designs of houses, according to the modern taste in building, and estimates of the charge: And hangs bells, in the best, neatest and least expensive manner.—A good taste in building is a talent (as all others) brought into the world with a man, and must be cultivated and improved with the same care and industry as such others: But a structure, tho' ever so beautiful, cannot yet be perfect, unless supplied with all the conveniences necessary to remove the disadvantages proceeding from great heat and cold, or, the country wherein it is built: Of such there are but few in or near this town, tho' put up and finished at a greater charge than if they had all the conveniences and beautiful proportions of architecture.

"All these shall be done to the entire satisfaction of all gentlemen that shall be pleased to employ *Their most humble Servant,*
Dudley Inman."[2]

Later we learn of Robert Kirkwood, who advertised in the *Gazette* of February 2 to 9, 1765.

"Robert Kirkwood, Carpenter, Carries on his business at his house on Tradd Street, opposite to Mr. Wainwright's, and is ready to undertake building and finishing of houses and other buildings on the most reasonable terms. He likewise draws plans, elevations and sections of buildings; and will be obliged to such as will be pleased to employ him in any part of his business."

Another advertiser was Joseph Fournier, who appeared briefly in Charleston in 1770 and 1771, at a time when the city was prosperous and in the mood for building. Primarily a miniature painter and drawing master, he may have been more draughtsman than architect. All that is known surely is that he advertised in March 1770. "Plans of Architecture drawn." [3] Again, in September, after stating that he had been "prevailed on by his friends" to remain during the winter, he thanked the public for their patronage, and added, "N.B. He continues to draw plans for architecture." [4] Later he became ill, but was sufficiently recovered by February, 1771, to resume work.[5] No more was heard from him.

Between Inman and Fournier were several men who should be mentioned. The name of William Axson, together with Masonic emblems, is found incised on both Pompion Hill Chapel, built 1763, on Cooper River, and on St. Stephen's Church, built 1767, at St. Stephens, South Carolina. Zachariah Villepontoux, who made excellent brick at his plantation, Parnassus, on Back River, carved his initials on Pompion Hill Chapel, also. Francis Villepontoux, Zachariah's nephew, and A. Howard were the supervisors for building St. Stephens, and placed their names upon it.[6] Dalcho, historian of the Protestant Episcopal church in South Carolina, writing in 1820, termed them the architects, rightly or wrongly.[7]

Meanwhile, several master builders of merit, Cardy, Naylor, and others, were working in Charleston. They deserve to be considered separately.

ST. MICHAEL'S AND SOME NEIGHBORS

SAMUEL CARDY Died January 24, 1774, and
    MR. GIBSON Died 1799?

SAMUEL CARDY SEEMS TO HAVE BEEN AN IRISH-
man, probably from Leinster, since his will mentions relations, "next akin which may be found in Dublin." [1] The earliest record discovered of him in South Carolina (or anywhere) is in
connection with another son of Erin, Andrew Rutledge, whose will
Cardy witnessed, June 8, 1752. [2]

Rutledge had been the speaker of the Assembly of South Carolina which passed the act of 1751 authorizing the erection of St.
Michael's Church, and also was one of the building commissioners
of that structure. [3] One wonders if he was responsible for Cardy's
becoming the builder of St. Michael's.

Was Cardy also the architect? On several indentures for the sale
of pews in the church, dated 1760, his name appeared as a witness,
signed "Sam¹ Cardy, Archᵗ." [4] But the meaning attached to the
word in Charlestown at that time is uncertain. The earliest evidence
is against him. In describing the laying of the cornerstone, February
17, 1752, the *South-Carolina Gazette* said, in part:

> "This Church will be built on the Plan of one of Mr. Gibson's
> Designs" . . . [5]

Who was Gibson? The theory has been advanced that James
Gibbs, the English architect, was intended. [6] This idea is rendered
the more plausible in that Gibbs had published in 1728 *A Book of
Architecture, containing Designs of Buildings and Ornament,* showing not only plans he had used but also alternative designs, including the rejected steeples for his famous church of St. Martin-in-the-
Fields. This volume was a godsend to colonial builders.

However, one cannot overlook the fact that a John Gibson, architect and master builder, died in South Carolina in 1799, [7] although
no evidence has been found to show that he was the Mr. Gibson
mentioned in the *Gazette.*

[29]

St. Michael's Church, 80 Meeting Street, built 1752-1761.

Another early source is the account of the Rev. Charles Wood-mason, an English clergyman for some years resident in South Carolina. He wrote in 1765, only four years after the church was opened:

> "St. Michael's. Is a New Built Church from the Model of that of Greenwich being Truss'd—Roofd and no Pillars. Is 80 feet by 60. Has a Tower and Steeple 196 feet high" . . . . .[8]

The church at Greenwich is St. Alphege, and its architect was no one less than Nicholas Hawksmoor. He had died in 1736,[9] fifteen years before the Charleston church was contemplated, but there was no reason why his work should not have been copied. But was it? Anyone who seeks in St. Michael's for a trace of Hawkmoor's luxuriant and highly individualistic treatment of the baroque is doomed to disappointment. St. Michael's has a definite flavor of Gibbs; it lacks that of Hawksmoor. Evidently all that Woodmason meant was that both St. Michael's and St. Alphege's are trussed and lack interior pillars to support the roof. The structural resemblance is true enough, but it goes no further.

As first planned, St. Michael's would have lacked even this structural likeness to the Greenwich church. Its first design called for precisely those interior supports, the absence of which is necessary for the resemblance. Foundations for interior columns actually were laid, some 25,000 bricks going into them, but in 1753, these were taken out.[10] Obviously, the first plan had been scrapped and a new one substituted. There is also mention in the vestry minutes of "the foundation of the Portico Originally intended," [11] showing that there too, a change had been made.

No matter whose the plans, they were not followed slavishly. Cardy may have been the architect of the church as truly as is possible with a building, the type of which is academic. Following the custom of that day, many contractors as well as amateur architects planned structures, since recognized as derived from plates in architectural books.

Work on the church went rapidly at first, but a hurricane in 1752, financial difficulties and a shortage of workmen who became busied with other projects caused delays.[12] The first divine service was not held until February 1, 1761.[13] The pews had been distributed the previous year, Cardy receiving No. 89.[14]

Soon after the completion of the church, Cardy engaged in a law suit with the building commissioners, and was paid 8000 pounds currency of South Carolina to settle his bill for building St. Michael's.[15]

A few years later, Cardy appeared as architect of the lighthouse on Middle (now part of Morris) Island, at the south side of the entrance of Charleston Harbor. This early tower no longer stands, but in 1876, laborers digging brick from its foundations discovered a small copper plate, with an inscription stating that the first stone of the structure was laid May 30, 1767. A list of local dignitaries follows, but near the end "Samuel Cardy, arct." is mentioned, as is "Adam Miller, Brick layer". The plate itself is certainly the work of "Thomas You, engr." (engraver), as is probably another plate found at the same time, which bears what seems to be a cross-section of the building.[16]

Nothing more is known of Cardy's work. For the rest, he had various transactions with Thomas Elfe, Charleston's best-known cabinetmaker, buying a coffin, coffin plates, handles, and brass nails [17]; he leased lot No. 1 of St. Michael's glebeland in 1771 (Bennett School owned the ground later), and assigned the lease to someone else the following years;[18] and he had a wife Ann and a daughter Margaret. Ann was an Englishwoman, who had come out in her youth to Georgia when it was settled under Oglethorpe in 1732.[19] She was to survive her husband twenty-four years, dying in 1798, aged eighty-three.[20] Margaret (her father called her Peggy), married William Rigby Naylor, (qv) architect and surveyor. Cardy's will mentions "my Grand Children Sons or Daughters of M[rs] Peggy Naylor".

In 1773, Cardy offered for sale the house and lot where he lived, a few "valuable Slaves, House-Carpenters, House-Wenches, &c.", and his pew in the south gallery of St. Michael's.[21]

He died the following year. The *South Carolina Gazette* of January 31, 1774, said:

> "The same Day" (January 24) "died, very suddenly, Mr. Samuel Cardy, the ingenious Architect, who undertook and compleated the Building of St. Michael's Church in this Town, and the Beacon or Light-House on Middle-Island, near the Bar."

His estate bought from Elfe "a full trimm'd cover'd Coffin", costing eighty-five pounds currency.[22] Cardy was probably buried in St. Michael's graveyard, but neither stone nor document confirms this belief.

St. Michael's Church.

St. Michael's churchyard.

St. Michael's is accounted Palladian. Its nicely-graduated steeple lacks any elements of surprise whatever, with a resultant bland beauty which remains singularly consistent whether seen from near or far. It rears 185 feet, seven inches—eight inches less than before the earthquake of 1886. Now the oldest steeple in Charleston, it stands much as it did when built, except that the lower of two rustic courses has been smoothed, while the other has been pierced by additional windows; clock dials have replaced festoons on a higher course; and the dragon weather-vane has been succeeded by an arrow. Parapets which once edged the roof of the church are gone. In the body of the building, the side door at the north has been walled up, and the cross aisle between it and the south door has been filled with pews. Gone is the splendor of the painted sun which once shone near the altar. The interior suffers from conventional stencilings in the apse, decorated by a fashionable New York firm in 1905, and from stained glass, but the day has vanished when altar-rail, pulpit, and reading-desk were hidden by swathes of crimson rep. In restoration after the tornado of 1938, many coats of paint were removed from the cedar woodwork, which was then waxed and polished, while the plaster pilasters of the chancel were painted to match. No more stained glass is to be admitted, and in time the church may regain its original simple dignity.

WILLIAM RIGBY NAYLOR. Died October, 1773

William Rigby Naylor was one of the builders and, possibly, the architect of the old Watch House or guard house, built 1767-69; he advertised that he would teach architecture; and he was termed architect as well as surveyor in his obituary. He may have designed the Old Exchange.

He was probably related to Henry Rigby who came to South Carolina in 1744 under circumstances reminiscent of John Wood's.

"Hen: Rigby,
House Carpenter and Joiner, his Wife & a Daughter, are brought over into this Province, in the Snow *Loyalty, John Fowler*, Master from Liverpoole; They say they have a Relation in the said Province named *Thomas Rotball.* This is therefore to give Notice to the said *Rotball* (if he is in this Province,) that unless their Passages from *Liverpoole* is immediately paid, the said Rigby will be sold as a Servant for the same, by *John Fowler.*" [1]

A "Mr. Rigby" worked in 1749 on the stairs, balcony and other things at Goose Creek Mansion, (later called Yeamans Hall), a Low Country plantation.[2]

But to return to Naylor. His guard house, which stood at the southwest corner of Broad and Meeting Streets, was contemporary with the Old Exchange, built by the elder Horlbecks, (qqv) which still stands at the foot of Broad Street. The two buildings were provided for in the same act, the same commissioners supervising their erection, and £60,000 current money of South Carolina was appropriated to pay for them.[3]

By October 12, 1767, the contract had been awarded to Naylor and James Brown, for £5,500, and work had begun.[4] It was completed by October, 1769.[5] Besides being the police station, it held other public offices. To quote Charles Fraser:

"Opposite to the State House stood the old Guard house, in the upper story of which was kept the offices of Secretary of State, Register of Mesne Conveyance, and Surveyor General. It was a two story building, on a foundation a little raised. It faced north on Broad-street, with an imposing pediment, supported by four massy pillars of the Tuscan order. But they, projecting over the pavement and obstructing the passage, were taken down. A fine cornice, or entablature, that surrounded the building, was also removed, and another story added, which made it a very shapeless structure. But it accomodated sundry public officers, which was paramount to all considerations of taste. The whole building was afterwards taken down, and the present one erected in its place." [6]

By the present one, Fraser meant the guard house designed by Reichardt (qv) which was built after Naylor's guard house had been torn down in 1838. This was destroyed in its turn, and the post office building occupies the site today.

Naylor also had a connection, it is uncertain how important, with the Exchange. Recent discovery of plans of this imposing building, signed by Naylor, prompts one to ask just what his share in it was. The question of the authorship of the Exchange has never been settled. Could Naylor have been its architect or was he merely employed as a draughtsman? The Exchange will be discussed in the chapter on Peter and John Horlbeck who built it and may also have designed it.

St. Michael's Church.

In his capacity as surveyor, Naylor subdivided the glebeland then held in common by St. Philip's and St. Michael's Churches, in December, 1770.[7] This seventeen-acre tract, then on the edge of the town, is now in the heart of Charleston.

On March 3, 1768, while the guard house was being built, Naylor was married by the rector of St. Philip's to Margaret Cardy,[8] daughter of Samuel Cardy. A child, Elizabeth Ann Naylor, was baptized January 10, 1771.[9]

In 1772, Naylor advertised:

"The Subscriber

Being frequently solicited to teach Drawing, proposes, the Evenings of the ensuing winter, to instruct in the Art of Drawing Architecture, provided he can get a select number on or before the First of November.—His Proposals may be known, by applying to him in Harleston.

William R. Naylor.

Who has to dispose of, some neat white and Vein Marble Chimney-Pieces, and Carpenters Tools." [10]

His death occurred the following year. The *South-Carolina Gazette and Country Journal* of October 19, 1773, said simply:

"Died Mr. William Rigby Naylor, Architect and Surveyor."

MILLER AND FULLERTON. Working in 1766

Miller and Fullerton, partners, together built in 1766 and 1767 the brick single house, now 39 Meeting Street, as a parsonage for St. Michael's Church. The vestry minutes tell the story of its erection, but unfortunately omit to state whether or not the plans were drawn by the builders.[1]

John Fullerton is said by Johnson's *Traditions and Reminiscences of the American Revolution* to have been a Scot—Johnson believed him to be related to the historian Hume.[2] We know that Fullerton was one of the "Liberty Tree boys" who met in 1766 to congratulate each other on the repeal of the Stamp Act.[3]

About 1773, Fullerton built, apparently for his own use, the charming wooden single house, now 15 Legare Street. The account book of Thomas Elfe, Charleston's best-known cabinet maker, shows transactions with Fullerton, and the decorative cornices and richly ornamented chimney pieces of this house probably were obtained from Elfe.[4]

Stair window at 39 Meeting Street, completed in 1767.
Miller and Fullerton, master builders.

Miller, in his turn, is associated with a group of excellent dwellings. His grandson, William Simmons, in applying for a position in 1822, gave a brief sketch of his family in order to establish his Charleston background, and thus described his mother's father, the builder. According to this letter, which is now in the collections of the South Carolina Historical Society, Miller built "some of the best old houses" in Charleston—"Governor Edward's, I think, Ash's, E. Rutledge's, Dr. Ramsey's, &c." [5]

The "I think" after the first listed probably meant that Simmons was uncertain of the name; at any rate, South Carolina has had no Governor Edwards. Governor Mathews may have been meant—he owned a large cypress double house which still stands at the corner of Rutledge Avenue and Wentworth Street.

The others are easily identified. All three are wooden double houses, large and well built. The Ashe house (to spell the name correctly) now is 32 South Battery. It was mentioned in an advertisement of 1784 as "that large, genteel and pleasant situated House, on the South Bay, the property of Mr. John Ash" . . .[6]

The Edward Rutledge house, now 117 Broad Street, at the corner of Orange Street, has suffered changes and additions. It was described in 1787 as "That well built elegant HOUSE, No. 55 in which Edward Rutledge, Esq: now resides" . . .[7] Rutledge, it will be remembered, was a signer of the Declaration of Independence.

Dr. David Ramsay (again to give the correct spelling) lived in the three-story building, now 92 Broad Street. The ground floor has been changed into offices, but retains a remarkable amount of old woodwork, with bolection moldings. A fairly advanced physician for his day, who sometimes advised his patients to boil their drinking water, Ramsay wrote a history of South Carolina, and other works. His pious wife, Martha Laurens, we shall meet again in considering the career of Robert Mills.

Miller, according to his grandson's letter, was born in America and came to Charleston from New Jersey. He lived and died in a small house with a Dutch roof at the corner of Meeting Street and South Battery. He married twice and left a son by each marriage, one of whom was named after his partner, John Fullerton Miller. He also had a daughter, the mother of the letter writer.

In placing Miller among the architects, one is confronted by two questions. Did his grandson recall correctly the houses he built? If so, did Miller design as well as build them? The houses have a certain similarity, in materials and design, and it is not difficult to believe that the same man was responsible for them all.

PETER AND JOHN ADAM HORLBECK

Died October, 1797   February 11, 1729—April 1, 1812

ETER HORLBECK AND HIS BROTHER JOHN ADAM
Horlbeck were partners, and as the latter came to Charleston in 1764, it is reasonable to suppose that Peter came at or
near that time also. John had been born near Plauen in the Vogt-
land, Saxony, on February 11, 1729.[1] After learning the mason's
trade under Christian Buckholtz in Berlin, John worked in Copen-
hagen, Riga, St. Petersburg, and Woolwich,[2] at length becoming a
master mason.

In 1767, within three years of John's arrival, the brothers were
contracting to build the Exchange, which still stands, though shorn
of much of its magnificence, at the east end of Broad Street. The
architect of this building is unknown.

William Rigby Naylor (qv) drew plans for the Exchange and
signed them, giving rise to the question as to whether he did so as
its architect or merely as a draughtsman.

The belief has long been held that the Horlbecks developed the
plan of the Exchange after the building commissioners had given
them the dimensions and a general idea of what was wanted. However, a recently discovered notice in the *South-Carolina Gazette* of
September 7-14, 1767, shows that a plan for the building existed
before the contract with the Horlbecks was made.

"Charles-Town, Sept. 9, 1767.

Notice is hereby given, to any person or persons, who are
willing to undertake the building the intended Exchange in
Charles Town, and to furnish materials for the same, agreeable
to a plan thereof, which is to be seen in the hands of the subscriber; that they do give in their proposals, on or before the
first day of October next, to

Tho. Farr, jun."

The *Gazette* of October 5-12, 1767, stated that:

"Last Tuesday . . . there was a full board of commissioners
for building the new Exchange and Custom House, when the

majority preferred the proposals of Messrs. Peter and John Horlbeck, with whom they accordingly agreed for compleating that edifice, for the sum of *forty thousand, nine hundred* and *thirty six pounds,* by the beginning of the year 1770."

At the same momentous meeting, the commissioners agreed with William Rigby Naylor (qv) and James Brown, for building a new Watch House, and with Timothy Crosby and Anthony Toomer, for building a stone bridge over the creek which then crossed East Bay at the present corner of Market Street. Of these three works, only the Exchange remains.

The October agreement was followed on December 1, 1767, by the signing of articles whereby the brothers contracted to finish the building on or before January 1, 1771 (not 1770, as the *Gazette* had stated in October), furnishing the materials, and following specifications which were carefully set forth in the document. The contract has been printed in full,[3] but is well worth quoting in part again.

 —"The foundation to be built or made with good Brick and Mortar Ninety two feet from North to South, and Sixty five and one half feet from East to West . . . The Steps to be made of Solid Portland Stone, Handrail and Banisters of Portland Stone, and under the said Steps and Platforms, to be Brick Walls and Arches to support the same . . . The Piazza fifteen feet in the clear from the Stone Pavement to the Ceiling. The Piazza Floor to be paved with good Perbeck Stone, the Parapet Wall to be One Brick and a half lengthways thick round the Building Coped with good Portland Stone, the Rustick Work to the Center of the East and West Fronts with Block and Architraves to be of good Portland Stone, Two Venetian Windows to the Stair Cases of the intire Ionick Order . . . . Four Columns and Twenty-four Pilasters of the Ionick Order . . . . Twelve Arches . . . . The Covering of the Roof to be of Welch Carnarvan Slate. The Roof of the Cupelo and the Bed of the Entablature to be covered with Lead . . . . All the rooms and Passages to be Wainscotted Chair high with proper Base and Sur Base, Eight Folding Doors to one of Stairs . . . . and Folding Doors to the two Stair Cases, Double Architraves to the same. The Large Room Wainscotted Fourteen feet high with eight Columns and twenty Pilasters and Entablature of three feet high of the Ionick Order, a Cove Ceiling to the same six feet high, two neat Chimney Pieces and Pediment to the Doors, sixteen square windows and two Blank Windows . . .

The Old Exchange, 122 East Bay, completed 1771.
Peter and John Adam Horlbeck, master builders.

Two Venetian Sashes Glazed with London Crown Glass two circular Windows in Pediments, four neat Chimney Pieces with Caps to the other Rooms . . . . Block Cornice to the Piazza and Stair Cases, two Stair Cases Steps good inch and a half Pine Boards with Strong Mahogany Hand Rail and Bannisters . . . . An Ionick Modillion Entablature round the Building with Four Pediments . . . . A Cupelo in the Center of the Building with four Venetian Windows and eight Columns of the Ionick Order, the Flooring to be of inch and a half thick of good Pine, all the rest of the Timber and Boards to be of good Cypress" . . . .[4]

These specifications give some idea of the elaborateness of the building, and of the consistent and harmonious use of the "Ionick" order throughout. Moreover, they show that one should not be misled by the nationality of the builders into looking for Teutonic elements in the Exchange. It belongs to a time when German architecture had ceased to be German, under French and Italian influences. What the building does indicate is the dependence of colonial America upon the mother country. For much of the material, Portland and Perbeck stone, Welsh slate, the Horlbecks or one of them went personally to England.[5] The "heart pine and black cypress," however, came from Benjamin Waring's swamps at the headwaters of the Ashley River.[6] The brick, also, is almost certainly local, for although at times bricks were brought both from England and from New England, the amount required for the Exchange would have made its importation prohibitive.

Because of delays in obtaining materials, the building was completed only late in 1771. The Horlbecks received £44,016 5s 7d, currency, which was more than the contract provided, but they had done extra work, not called for in that document.[7] To secure the funds for the Exchange and the New Watch House, the authorities had placed duties on wine, rum, biscuits, and flour.[8]

The Exchange originally faced the Cooper and the incoming ships, its portico, since removed, being on the harbor side. . . "The new Exchange which fronted the place of my landing made a most noble appearance," wrote a tourist in 1773.[9]

The Exchange has seen the vagaries of history. Its cellars were crammed with American prisoners during the British occupation in the Revolution. But in 1791, George Washington attended a ball there, "at which", he wrote, "were 256 elegantly dressed and handsome ladies." As a boy, the painter, Thomas Sully, sheltered for a night under its arches while escaping from a brutal brother-in-law.[10] Beside it, generations of slaves were sold by chanting auctioneers.

The Exchange has been plundered of the greater part of its ornaments, partly by natural disasters, but more by the stupidity of officialdom. Alterations began early. In 1801, the wooden railings in the arches seem to have been replaced by iron,[11] a change which was probably an improvement. Later mutations were less fortunate. Some had already occurred when Mills described the structure in 1826:

"The exchange (now the custom-house and post-office) is another venerable building, which proves that the hand of science was engaged in its design. Though its style of architecture is not what we desire to see imitated, it is yet a fine building, and shows in its construction how faithfully public work was executed in 'the olden time'.

"The plan presents a square, opened all round in the principal or first story with an arcade, forming a spacious, airy walk or 'change within for the merchants. The second story is divided into apartments for the various offices connected with the customs.

"The main entrance now fronts Broad-street; its principal facade was originally to the east, or the harbor. Formerly the angles of the west front projected out several feet into the street beyond the main walls, throwing the arcade on this front in recess; but these projections were found to obstruct materially the way of carriages, &c., passing along East Bay-street; they were therefore removed, and the front brought almost to a plane surface.

"The upper story walls are ornamented all round externally with pilasters and columns, supporting an entablature, over which runs an open balustrade.

"Though this building is constructed of brick, and stuccoed, yet, without a close inspection, you would take it for a stone structure. It forms a handsome termination for Broad-street. In the basement story the storerooms of the custom-house are kept. Part of the first story is occupied by the post-office establishment, having still a spacious promenade; on the second floor are the custom-house offices." [12]

Not only were the projections on the west removed to avoid interfering with traffic, but the portico on the east was taken away.

The "spacious, airy walk" was lost when the arches were bricked up, apparently by degrees, those at the north being closed in 1835 to make a reading room.[13] In 1846, new steps were built, and a new iron railing was placed at the west.[14] The original cupola was wrecked by a storm, and was replaced by another designed by Charles Fraser (qv) which also has disappeared. The stone urns which graced the parapet fell in the earthquake of 1886, and today are scattered through Charleston as garden ornaments.

In spite of all, the Exchange is still solid and imposing. It is now the valued property of the Daughters of the American Revolution.

On John Horlbeck's monument appears the statement that "he erected many of the best public and private edifices of the time among them the Exchange."[15] Little, however, can now be identified as his work.

A synagogue on Hasell Street was built in 1792 by Steedman and Horlbeck.[16] The first named was probably James Steedman (1746-1798), or his brother Charles, who together submitted an unsuccessful estimate for the carpentry of the Orphan House in 1792.[17] As to which of the Horlbeck brothers was concerned, John seems the more likely, since by that date, Peter appears to have taken up planting. The synagogue was considered "elegant,"[18] but no good description of it has been found. Happily, however, the congregation owns a painting of the interior, which shows it to have been a typical late eighteenth century building of pleasing design. The destruction of this synagogue in the fire of 1838 was a loss to the city, even though it gave the opportunity for the erection of the present beautiful Greek Revival structure which is on the site.

Two houses, one of which still exists, are credited to the Horlbecks. The Laurens house which stood on East Bay until the early days of the present century was said by the late Yates Snowden, of the University of South Carolina, to have been built by John Horlbeck.[19] If this statement was correct, the staunchly built brick house with its jerkin-head roof and lack of outward display must have been one of the first houses he erected here.

The sturdy, three-story, brick and stucco building, now 54 Broad Street, is reputed to have been put up by the Horlbecks from material left over from the Exchange.[20]

By 1773, Peter Horlbeck was married, and a resident of the parish of St. George, Dorchester, where he became a planter.[21] His wife was Catherine Fillhauer (or Villhour, the name being variously spelled), daughter of George Fillhauer.[22] According to tradition,

54 Broad Street, ascribed to Peter and John Adam Horlbeck.

she planted the beautiful avenue of live oaks at Oak plantation, which Peter bought in 1785.[23] They had several children. Peter died in 1797. In his will, he left a legacy to the Episcopal Church at Dorchester, and directed:

> "Imprimis, My Body is to be kept 'till the fifth day after my decease, and then to be interred in the Church Yard, in Dorchester, without any expence, but what is on the Plantation." [24]

Dorchester, near the present town of Summerville, South Carolina, has long since become a vanished settlement, where broken tombstones lie under the trees by a desolate tower.

John Horlbeck fought in the American Revolution at the battles of Beaufort and Savannah.[25] In the Federal procession of 1788, which celebrated the ratification of the Constitution, he led the bricklayers, who, like members of the other trades, carried tools decorated with ribbons.[26]

John's wife, Elizabeth, was born "at the Congarees," in upper South Carolina, March 9, 1740, and predeceased him in Charleston, November 5, 1802.[27]

Ramsay's *History of South Carolina*, written in 1808, cited Horlbeck among local examples of longevity: "Mr. John Horlbeck, born in Saxony, has lived in Charlestown 44 years, and never took a dose of medicine————80." One wonders if Ramsay approved—he was a physician.

Horlbeck lived on Moore Street, now Horlbeck's Alley.[28] He died April 1, 1812, and was buried in the graveyard of St. John's Lutheran Church.[29] He was survived by his sons, John, Jr., and Henry Horlbeck. (qv)

EZRA WAITE

Died 1769

The eighteenth century abounded with master builders—masons or carpenters—who could and did produce plans. The joiner-architect was rarer but occurred, notably in the person of Ezra Waite, whose specialty was carving.

Waite is heard of first and last in 1769, but may have arrived in Charlestown somewhat sooner. By the end of the summer, he had completed a great deal of intricate work on the Miles Brewton house, now 27 King Street. This building and the Post-Revolutionary Joseph Manigault house are probably the two most important dwellings in point of architecture to be found in Charleston.

In the paper of August 22, Waite published a combined advertisement and warning, which has been reprinted in full and in part several times during the present century, but is worth repeating.

"ARCHITECTURE

"Ut res gesta est Narrabo Ordine

"Ezra Waite, Civil Architect, House-builder in general, and Carver, from London, Has finished the Architecture, conducted the execution thereof, viz: in the joiner way, all tabernacle frames, (but that in the dining-room excepted) and carved all the said work in the four principal rooms; and also calculated, adjusted, and draw'd at large for to work by, the Ionick entablature, and carved the same in the front and round the eaves, of Miles Brewton, Esquire's House on White Point for Mr. Moncrieff. If on inspection of the above mentioned work, and twenty-seven years experience, both in theory and practice, in noblemen and gentlemen's seats, be sufficient to recommend; he flatters himself to give satisfaction to any gentleman, either by plans, sections, elevations, or executions, at his house in King-Street, next door to Mr. Wainwrights' where architecture is taught by a peculiar method never published in any book extant.

"N. B. As Miles Brewton, Esquire's, dining room is of a new construction with respect to the finishing of windows and doorways, it has been industriously propagated by some (believed to be Mr. Kinsey Burden, a carpenter) that the said Waite did not do the Architecture, and conduct the execution thereof. Therefore the said Waite, begs leave to do himself justice in this public manner, and assure all gentlemen, that he the said Waite, did construct every individual part and drawed the same at large for the joiners to work by, and conducted the execution thereof. Any man that can prove to the contrary, the said Waite promises to pay him One Hundred Guineas, as witness my hand, this 22nd day of August, 1769.

"Ezra Waite.

"Veritas Odium Pavit." [1]

As Samuel Lapham has pointed out, Waite did not claim in this statement to have been the architect of the house, but merely to have designed and executed the more important woodwork, "for Mr. Moncrieff," who was probably the contractor.[2] Yet, since persons do not always express themselves fully, and since Waite termed himself architect as well as carver, a slim chance exists that he may have had a hand in the design as a whole.

The plan is the familiar Georgian one of the "double house." On the first floor, a hall runs through the center from front door to back. On each side are two rooms, divided from each other by a chimney flanked by closets. In many such houses, the hall is crossed midway by an arch, but here a beam spans it, ornamented with triglyphs. At the back of the hall, the staircase ascends, lit by a window on the landing. Upstairs, the hall is confined to the back, leaving the front to two rooms, a large drawing-room and a smaller cardroom. The same plan had been used in the Heyward-Washington house, built c. 1770, and was to be popular for years. The arrangement is excellent for a warm climate, because every room has two exposures, and the hall draws a draft through the middle. In the Miles Brewton house, the scheme was elaborated by setting the building upon a high basement, both to add to its appearance and to raise it above storm tides, and by placing a portico at the front for ornament. The plan, though not indigenous to Charleston, suits the climate.

Noticeable in Waite's carving is a restrained Chippendale Gothic influence. Nothing of the bizarre or florid enters, however, in all the rich and varied ornamentation.

The house is said to have cost Brewton £8000 sterling,[3] but this sum probably included the lot (much larger then than now), and the extensive outbuildings.

The Miles Brewton House, 27 King Street, built 1769. Ezra Waite, carver and perhaps architect.

Details of carving in the Miles Brewton House. *(Frank Haskell)*

On October 12, 1769, Waite made his will, adding a codicil two days later.[4] He was buried on November 3, in St. Philip's churchyard,[5] where the location of his grave has been forgotten. On November 10, his will was proved.

The largest individual legacy went to Mrs. Margaret Carpenter, whom he termed a friend, bequeathing her £100 sterling by the will, and by the codicil an additional £50 sterling and a negro girl called Bess. To Alexander Hogg, a merchant, he left a gold watch and £50 currency of South Carolina; to friends John Fisher and Samuel Burn, £50 currency each; and to friend James Johnson, notary public, £100 currency. The rest was to be "collected and sold and to be remitted to Cousin, Mr. Moses Waite" of London, "to be by him paid in such proportions, to my Nearest Relations that may then be alive, as he shall think fit, Trusting to his Justice and Integrity in the disposing of that part of my Estate to my Nearest Relations, or those of them most in need of assistance as I am at present uncertain who of them are alive" . . . . Mrs. Carpenter and Hogg were appointed executrix and executor.[6]

This will, brought forward after Waite's death by Hogg, was promptly challenged by Mrs. Carpenter, who entered a caveat against it, which, however, she was induced to withdraw.[7] She and Hogg set about the disposal of the estate and in November, advertised as follows:

> "To be sold on Wednesday the 6th day of December next, at the House of Mrs. Carpenter on the Green, opposite to the Poor House;
>
> "All the Effects of Ezra Waite, deceased, consisting of two Negro Fellows and three Boys, one of the fellows a Bricklayer; several pieces of curious Carved Work, his Tools, Books, Cloaths, &c. &c."[8]

So ended Waite's story. Six years later, Miles Brewton was drowned at sea with his wife and children. During the Revolution, the house became the headquarters of the British commanders, Sir Henry Clinton and Lord Rawdon. Again, in 1865, it served as Federal headquarters. In spite of these vicissitudes, it has remained remarkably unhurt.

The South Carolina Society Hall, 72 Meeting Street, built c. 1800.
Gabriel Manigault, architect.

GABRIEL MANIGAULT

March 17, 1758—November 4, 1809

G ABRIEL MANIGAULT IS CHARLESTON'S BEST-
known amateur architect. In the open field he ranks next,
perhaps, to Mills the professional, who built, however, in a
very different style. Manigault was an interpreter of the Adam manner. A rice planter, a Huguenot (by descent at least), and according to tradition, something of a dandy, he has caught the popular
fancy. Nor is the public at fault, for his buildings have unassailable
merit.

The Manigaults, of La Rochelle, were a capable stock whose
records went back to the fourteenth century. Near the end of the
seventeenth, two brothers, Pierre and Gabriel, came to Carolina as
refugees from religious persecution. Starting with little, Pierre made
money, married, and became the ancestor of the family in America.
Gabriel did none of these things but (and this is interesting because
of his great-grand-nephew, the architect), he practised the trade of a
builder, and is even said to have died by falling from a scaffold.[1]

Pierre's son, Gabriel, a rich planter, married Ann Ashby, through
whose diary one may, if one wishes, trace the childhood maladies
which beset her "Grandson G.," the architect.[2] Gabriel and Ann's
son was Peter, speaker of the Commons House of Assembly, a prominent man in public affairs, with a taste for drawing.[3] He married
Elizabeth Wragg,[4] and on March 17, 1758, became the father of the
architect.[5] In spite of his French name, Gabriel Manigault was thus
mainly English, both his father and grandfather having married
women of English blood.

So much for his paternal ancestry. On his mother's side, he was
the grandson of Joseph Wragg, member of His Majesty's Council in
Carolina,[6] and owner of the tract still known as Wraggboro', now
part of Charleston. Wragg had more than a passing interest in architecture. The inventory of his estate [7] shows that he possessed among
his books *Vitruvius Brittanicus,* Evelyn's *Architecture,* Perrault's
Architecture, Brittanica Illustrated, and, more practical, *The Builder's Vade Mecum, The Art of Sound Building,* and Pozzo's *Perspec-*

tive.(*) Wragg died before Manigault's birth, else one would think that it must have been he who first directed his grandson's interest toward the art.

In 1774, Gabriel, still in his teens, visited Rhode Island for his health.[8] Here he must have heard of Peter Harrison, "prince of the colonial amateurs" as Fiske Kimball has called him. He may even have met him. If the youth needed an example, Harrison could have furnished one. When Manigault sailed for Europe, a few years later, it was probably with his interest in architecture ready-made.

He studied in Geneva [9] and London. At the latter place, he began to read law at Lincoln's Inn on August 12, 1777.[10] It was no time for quiet study, however. Packing up his books, which constituted an architectural library of some value,[11] he returned to America. He took the oath of allegiance to the crown in September, 1780.[12]

The war over, he settled down to rice planting. Plantations which at various times he owned wholly or in part included the Barony of Auendaw, the Salt Ponds, Pompion Hill (pronounced Punkin Hill and later known as Longwood), the Club House tract,[13] and a plantation at Willtown.[14] His estate at Goose Creek, called Steepbrook, with its white, hipped-roofed house set among oaks, may be seen in a watercolor by Charles Fraser (qv), made in 1802. Manigault also owned a farm on the Delaware River in Pennsylvania.[15]

Rich planting, fortunately, was a seasonal occupation. At times, it demanded every jot of attention and acumen the master possessed; but there were periods during which the fields lay fallow, and others when operations might safely be trusted to overseers and the negro sub-overseers called "drivers." During certain months, moreover, the "climate", or, as we now know, the anopheline mosquitoes, made it dangerous for white men to live on the plantations. There was no need for Manigault to filch time from planting in order to find it for architecture.

Though he did not take the part in public affairs played by his father and maternal grandfather, Manigault was no recluse. He was a trustee of the College of Charleston 1785-93.[16] In 1785, too, he joined the South Carolina Society.[17] In 1805, he served as foreman of the jury which tried a remarkably sordid murder case.[18]

(*) Pozzo's *Perspective*, "At the Request of the Engraver, We have perus'd this Volume of PERSPECTIVE: and judge it a Work that deserves Encouragement, and very proper for Instruction in that Art.

Chr. Wren,
J. Vanbrugh,
N. Hawksmoor."

The Joseph Manigault House, 350 Meeting Street, built c. 1803. Gabriel Manigault, architect. (*Tom Peck*)

His portrait by Gilbert Stuart[9] shows a pleasant if not a hand-some face, with a firm set to the fairly full mouth, and a look of calm interest. In society, he was a favorite, and his obituary mentions his "amiable manners."[20]

He married "the amiable Miss Margaret Izard, daughter of Ralph Izard Esq; of this City," on May 1, 1785.[21] Educated in France, well read in French and English literature, she was accomplished, without being a bluestocking.[22] They had a large family—Manigault's will mentioned two sons and five daughters,[23] but the register of St. Philip's Church shows that there had been more.[24] Emma and Maria, baptized at the same time,[25] may have been twins.

In 1804, Manigault advertised his plantations for sale and his town house for sale or rent.[26] Some time later, he moved to Pennsylvania, though he regarded himself as a South Carolinian still, and in his will, made in 1809, termed himself "of Charleston."[27]

He died at Philadelphia, November 4, 1809, aged fifty-one. The *City Gazette & Daily Advertiser* of Charleston, in announcing his death, not only spoke in true obituary fashion of his "well spent life" and "many virtues, amiable manners, sound judgment and talents both useful and ornamental", but went on to say that "he was remarkable for his taste in the fine arts; and several public buildings in Charleston testify that his talents were judiciously employed."[28]

His widow survived him fifteen years, dying in Philadelphia on May 3, 1824.[29]

Albert Simons, F.A.I.A. and Samuel Lapham, F.A.I.A. have pointed out that Manigault was the first Charleston architect as the term is now understood, in that he drew plans for builders to carry out.[30]

He designed the impressive dwelling house, at the corner of Meeting and John Streets, for his brother, Joseph.[31] This was built about 1803. It was survived vicissitudes in which its coachhouse and stable perished, and lately has been accorded the careful restoration it deserves. Three stories high, it is built of Charleston gray brick, laid in Flemish bond, with a steep slate roof and wooden piazzas. A semi-circular projection at the north contains the curving staircase. The western piazza and the dining room at the east also are bowed. Noticeable are the circular basement windows, reminiscent of those in the terrace of the Petit Trianon. In fact, much about the house has a French air, and the decoration derives from the Adam style in its Louis XVI aspects.

It was a simplified Adam which Manigault used, concentrating its applied enrichment on mantels, doorways, arches, and the like. But the coloring was amazingly rich, and the drawing-room ceiling was painted with a spirited design of cartouches and anthemei.

The garden lodge, a happy adjunct, is a small bell-roofed circular structure with a pedimented portico.

Several singular details, the stone plinths of the piazza columns, the layer of lime (sovereign against insects and decay) between floor and sub floor, show Manigault's interest in enduring construction.

About 1800, he built himself a house which has been pulled down within the present century. It stood on the south east corner of Meeting and George Streets, and was made of cypress on a high brick foundation, and reached by stone steps.[32]

The Orphan House Chapel was his also.[33] In some ways, it was his most successful work. The cornerstone was laid August 18, 1801,[34] and the building was opened for worship, September 19, 1802.[35] The rectangular structure of roughcast brick had round-headed windows in the side walls. Inside, an end-gallery and organ loft faced the reading desk. On the street façade, marked by four engaged columns, the Adam manner was feeling its way gingerly toward that of the Greek Revival. This was Manigault's boldest work. It was pulled down in 1953.

The text carved on this front, "The poor shall have the Gospel preached unto them," strikes the modern observer as a tactless choice. There is no reason to believe that the architect selected it.

In 1800 the South Carolina Society, the second oldest society in Charleston, decided to build a hall in which to meet and to keep the charity school which they supported. They advertised for contractors and for plans as well:

> "The society will also feel itself obliged to any gentleman who will favor the committee with his ideas of a plan suitable to the purpose of the institution. The above dimensions" (34 x 100 feet) "are proposed in order to give an idea of the size necessary, but not to limit the architect to the particular shape which those dimensions would give the building." [36]

The gentleman who favored the committee with his ideas was Manigault,[37] already, as has been noted, a member of the society. He disregarded the suggested dimensions, and designed a T-shaped

The Charleston Orphan House Chapel, 13 Vanderhorst Street, completed in 1802. Gabriel Manigault, architect. *(Tom Peck)* No longer standing.

building, lying with its head on the street. The roughcast brick structure is two stories tall on a very high basement. The first floor was devoted to schoolrooms. The meeting hall itself, with a room which opens into it by means of folding doors, occupies the second story. The most attractive hall in Charleston, it contains a small musicians' gallery, semi-circular and carried by Ionic columns, reminiscent of a piazza, which backs against a Palladian window.

The street façade has been changed by the addition of a portico designed by Frederick Wesner (qv).

Besides these four structures, another, the Bank of the United States building, now the City Hall, has been attributed to Manigault. Though more elaborately decorated outside than any other building ascribed to him, it shows decided resemblances to them. (From the interior, nothing can be deduced, since it has been changed drastically at least twice.) The use of curved lines, the semi-circular projection on the north (suggestive of that on the Joseph Manigault house), the marble trim, the circular basement windows, and the general effect of delicacy and balance seem characteristic of his work. Manigault's grandsons, in their family history, stated that he had designed the City Hall,[38] but whether they relied upon family papers or upon tradition for this assertion is not said. Their attributions of other buildings to their grandfather have remained unquestioned. That respecting the City Hall would be accepted unreservedly, were it not for an item in the *City Gazette* of November 8, 1800, which spoke of "Messrs. M'Grath and Nicholson, the architects and Mr. Andrew Gordon, the builder." Who M'Grath (properly Magrath) and Nicholson were is discussed in the next chapter. *Architect* was a term loosely used in 1800, and may have been intended for *contractor,* though the pair are known to have drawn plans on occasion.

An additional bit of evidence has been cited on Manigault's side of this question, namely, the little marble bas-relief of a winged figure with a trumpet, on the side entablature of the basement door. Is this the Angel Gabriel, and was he placed there as a signature by his namesake, Gabriel Manigault? The theory is attractive. Unfortunately, the figure is female and carries a wreath as well as a trumpet. She is the goddess of victory.

The exterior of this disputed building by being frankly pretty has drawn the fire of critics. It has been termed frivolous, yet it seldom fails to charm. Mills, who had strong prejudices, called it "showy" and "repugnant to good taste", but added, paradoxically, that it was "an ornament to the city".[39] In modern times, it has been contemned for the flatness of its decoration. One should recall, however, that originally the building was not roughcast and that the exterior possessed a depth, as well as a contrast between the marble trim and the Flemish bond of its rich-colored bricks, which have been lost by the senseless addition of stucco.

Perhaps another building should be mentioned, the dwelling at the northwest corner of Amherst and Bay Streets, which is too unsophisticated in plan to ascribe outright to Manigault, but may show his influence. As originally built, it was a rectangle from which jutted a rounded projection containing the winding staircase, one of the most beautiful in Charleston. The location of the stair, and the Adam decoration, are reminiscent of the Joseph Manigault house, but the floor plan is simplicity itself. The first and second stories had only one room on a floor, exclusive of the hall with the staircase, and the third story had only two. Cross-ventilation was the chief, almost the only, point considered. This house stands in the district formerly known as Hampstead, where Manigault owned several lots, though, so far as is known, not this one.

In 1817, a sale of property belonging to Manigault's estate was advertised. The city property (except for bare lots) was as follows:

"A three story Brick House, Lot, and Out-Buildings, No. 245, East-Bay, on the south corner of the street leading to Blake's wharf, occupied by Messrs. Street & Keating.

"A three story Brick House, Out-Buildings and Lot No. 246, adjoining the above, and occupied by the proprietors of the Southern Patriot.

"A range of wooden tenements in Amen-street, No's. 1, 2, and 3—they will be sold separately or together.

"A House and Lot in Amen-street, on the corner of Philadelphia Street.

"One do. on the opposite corner of Philadelphia and Amen-streets.

"A double Tenement, Lot, and Out-buildings, in Cumberland Street, opposite to Mrs. Corbett's. The lot is 32 feet front by 34 feet deep." [40]

In seeking out these buildings, one meets with little satisfaction. None seems to have been important. Most have disappeared. If the East Bay houses are the same which now occupy their sites, they have suffered many sad changes, false fronts among them.

The City Hall, formerly the Bank of the United States, 80 Broad Street, begun in 1800.

Detail of the City Hall, the goddess of victory.

Stair detail in the dwelling at Amherst and Bay Streets.

One of the buildings at the corner of Philadelphia Street and Amen (now part of Cumberland) Street, may remain, if it is possible to identify it with the unassuming two-story brick house at the southwest corner, which is so patched with bricks laid casually in running bond that only a second glance notices the staunch Flemish bond of the older part.

All the rest are gone. Under such conditions, it is impossible even to guess whether or not Manigault had any hand in the design of these buildings.

EDWARD MAGRATH AND JOSEPH NICHOLSON

Working c. 1800-1810 and c. 1800-1803

EDWARD MAGRATH (ALSO WRITTEN McGRATH and M'Grath) and Joseph Nicholson, partners, were both architects and builders.

Their antecedents are unknown. One would like to surmise that the latter was related to Peter Nicholson who wrote the *Architectural Dictionary*, and to T. Nicholson, Esq., builder, of Hexham, Northumberland, Mr. W. Nicholson of Fareham, and Mr. James Nicholson, builder, of Southwell, Nottinghamshire, whose names are set forth among the subscribers to that work; but proof is lacking. Data about Joseph Nicholson are scant, more being known of Magrath, though less than one might wish.

The part they played in regard to the Branch Bank of the United States, now the City Hall, begun in 1800, is the subject of controversy. A newspaper of 1800, in describing the laying of the cornerstone, spoke of their "known abilities" and termed them the architects.[1] On the other hand, Gabriel Manigault (qv) has a strong claim to being considered as its architect—evidence offered by the building itself. But before telling the story of the bank, it seems best to present the other information about Magrath and Nicholson.

At a meeting of the vestry and wardens of St. Michael's Church on August 30, 1801, to quote the vestry book, "Gen¹ Vanderhorst and Mʳ Hazlehurst were appointed a Committee to confer with Mʳ McGrath the Artichect, (sic) on the propriety of erecting two Galleries, one on each side the Organ, for the accommodation of People of Colour, and at the same time to procure a Plan and an Estimate of the Expence for building the same".[2] Vanderhorst and Hazlehurst, besides being parishioners of St. Michael's, were members of the building committee of the bank, and so were well acquainted with Magrath's work.

In 1802, Magrath and Nicholson submitted a plan in the competition for the South Carolina College building, to be erected at Columbia. They were unsuccessful, the premium being divided between Robert Mills (qv) and Clark; but their plan was commended by the committee. The same fate befell a plan entered by Hugh Smith (qv).[3]

The directory of 1803 listed both Magrath and Nicholson as carpenters, at 61 Meeting Street. It should be recalled that an earlier Charleston directory had applied that term to Hoban, and a later one was to use it in connection with Russell Warren. Nicholson vanishes from the directories after this, but Magrath appears in three more. Those of 1806 and 1807 called him architect. That of 1809 termed him carpenter again.

In 1804, McGrath (as his name was spelled in the vestry book) submitted an estimate of $15,406.20 for the workmanship and materials for a contemplated addition to St. Michael's, the enlargement designed by Robert Mills, but never built.[4]

On January 25, 1810, Magrath signed a subscription paper of those who wished to become members of the Second Presbyterian Church, then being organized,[5] but his name is absent from the list of those who actually joined.[6] No later notice of him has been discovered.

But to return to the bank, which would deserve consideration on its own merits, even if no architect could be found in connection with it.

In May, 1800, the following notice had appeared:

"The Branch Bank of Charleston being desirous of erecting a Banking House that shall unite convenience & ornament: have appointed the subscribers a committee for the purpose of procuring a plan & contracting for the building of the said Bank. We will therefore give a gratuity of one hundred and fifty dollars (if required) for an approved plan of the Building to be erected on the site whereon the Beefmarket (corner of Broad & Meeting Streets) formerly stood. The lot is 113 feet front to the South & 86 feet deep. The Building to be so constructed as to admit of a free circulation of air & to have none of the offices under ground.

A. Vanderhorst
Nathaniel Russell
Thomas Simons
Robert Hazlehurst
William Blacklock".[7]

In September came another advertisement:

"CONTRACT WANTED

For the Branch Bank of the United States, and to be delivered at the Old Market-Square, corner of Broad and Meeting streets, viz:

Six hundred thousand Bricks

Twenty thousand bushels of Lime

Seventeen thousand feet of Pitch Pine Timber and Scantling, as per Bill

Seven thousand feet best yellow Pine Boards, for flooring, &c. 1½ inch.

Four thousand ditto of Inch boards.

Fifteen Plank of 17½ by 15 inches wide, and 26 feet long.

Six thousand feet of two-Inch Cypress Plank

Fifty thousand feet of clear White Pine Boards.

The above materials to be of the best quality, and those who wish to contract for the delivery of the said materials, either in whole or in part, will send in their proposals at the cash prices, on or before the 30th inst. sealed up, to the Cashier of said Bank; and in whose hands the bill for scantling may be seen." [8]

Stone, it will be noticed, is not mentioned. Tradition says that the marble which forms so elaborate a trim for the bank was brought, ready-cut, from Philadelphia, where it had been imported from Italy for a house which was never built.

On November 8, 1800, came the mention of Magrath and Nicholson.

"Yesterday, Robert Hazlehurst, esq., as one of the Committee appointed to superintend the building of a National Branch Bank in this city, laid the corner stone of the same, in the presence of the president and directors of the bank, and a number of other citizens. From the plan of the intended building, and the known abilities of Messrs. M'Grath and Nicholson, the architects, and Mr. Andrew Gordon, the builder, we venture to assure the public, that the Bank when completed, cannot fail to prove one of the chief ornaments of Charleston." [9]

As is readily seen, all turns on the meaning of *architects*, as the word was used by the newspaper of 1800. Gordon (father of James and John Gordon, qqv) was a master bricklayer, and the theory has been advanced that he did the brickwork, while Magrath and

Nicholson contracted for the woodwork, a theory rendered the more plausible in that such division of labor was common building practice at the time. It cannot, however, rule out a possibility that Magrath and Nicholson may have furnished the plan as well (since, as has been seen, they did draw plans on occasion), and the use of the words *architects* and *builder,* instead of the more usual *carpenters* and *bricklayers,* may mean just this.

On the other hand, the absence of Manigault's name need not mean that he was not concerned. The reticence of the time which deprecated newspaper mention may have caused him to ask that his name be omitted. Late in the century, his grandsons wrote in a family history that Manigault had designed the City Hall, and although they cited no reference for this statement, they are known to have owned numerous family papers. The building has the characteristics found in Manigault's work.

At least three of the five members of the building committee owned splendid structures, two of them erected that same year. Vanderhorst Row, built in 1800, an early example of the multiple dwelling; the William Blacklock house, dating from the same time, and the Nathaniel Russell house, built shortly before 1811, still stand. The first two, made of Charleston gray brick laid in Flemish bond, with stone trim, pediments, and arched panels pierced by windows, look like stern brothers of the fanciful bank, though they lack its plentitude of curved lines. In the present state of the evidence, it would be a brave man who would decide whether Manigault, Magrath, Nicholson, or Gordon, or any or all of them, were concerned in these admirable dwellings.

WILLIAM DRAYTON
March 21, 1732—May 18, 1790

I DENTIFICATION OF JUDGE WILLIAM DRAYTON AS
the architect of the Charleston Court House rests upon the
statement of Charles Fraser. This testimony—emphatic but un-
supported—appeared in *My Reminiscences of Charleston*, first published by installments in the *Courier* of 1853, sixty-three years after
Drayton's death. Such evidence may seem too late to be thought
conclusive, but it has remained uncontradicted, and therefore is
given here.

Fraser's statement is found in the *Courier* of August 20, 1853.
After describing the fire which in 1788 destroyed the old State
House, on the site of which the Court House stands, he wrote:

> "I do not remember the old State House, but I know that the
> present one was built upon its foundation, and differed but little
> from it in its interior arrangements, retaining the old walls and
> doorways. I have always heard that the plan of the new building
> was furnished by Judge William Drayton, father of the late Col.
> Wm. Draton. (sic) But, without knowing wherein it was superior
> to the former one, I have always thought it one of the best pro-
> portioned buildings in Charleston, and wanting only a back-
> ground to display its architectural beauty to proper advantage.
>
> "Having thus incidentally mentioned the name of Judge Wil-
> liam Drayton, it recalls one of the earliest reminiscences of my
> life. He lived in Tradd-street, in the house now owned by Judge
> Frost, and was a near neighbor of my father. I was playing, with
> other children, on a green opposite to it, when, to my great ter-
> ror, I was sent for to draw a Jury, which I only remember from
> taking some pieces of paper out of a box." [1]

When the reminiscences were published in book form, Fraser
inserted another paragraph:

> "I had, for a long time, in my port-folio, an original draft of
> the present building, with all its measurements set down, which
> differed only in a parapet wall from that which was adopted." [2]

The Blacklock House, 18 Bull Street, built 1800.

The County Court House, 77 Meeting Street, completed in 1792.
William Drayton, architect.

It will be noted that Fraser termed the Court House a state house but as a matter of fact, it was never used as one, being finished only in 1792,[3] while the South Carolina Legislature had already moved in 1790 to the newly founded city of Columbia.[4] The building from its beginning was the Court House, but the name of its predecessor clung to it for years.

The planning of this structure was one of the later acts of a varied life. William Drayton was born March 21, 1732, at Magnolia on the Ashley,[5] a noteworthy plantation though then without the magnificent azaleas which make it a showplace today. He was the son of Thomas Drayton and his first wife Elizabeth, daughter of Lieutenant-Governor William Bull of South Carolina.[6] As a young man, he studied law in London, being admitted to the Middle Temple, October 6, 1750.[7] By 1756, he was practicing his profession in South Carolina.[8]

Three years later, he had a spell of soldiering, serving as one of the aides-de-camp of Governor Lyttleton on the bloodless expedition of 1759 against the Cherokee Indians.[9] This was an eventful year for Drayton, for on October 4, he married. His wife was Mary Motte, daughter of the public treasurer of the province. They became the parents of nine children,[10] one of whom, also named William, was to be well-known as the leader of the Union party in South Carolina during the 1830's.[11]

In 1763, William Drayton was appointed chief justice of the province of East-Florida, which had just been ceded to England by Spain. He held the post until the beginning of the American Revolution, when he made the grave political error of criticizing the administration, although asserting loyalty to the crown. Suspended from office in 1776, he went to England to plead his cause, and was reinstated, but after his return to Florida, was suspended anew.[12] Again he sailed for England. It was a trying voyage, for his wife was ill and died soon after their arrival.[13]

Drayton's second wife was an Englishwoman,[14] Mary Gates, whom he married about 1780.[15] They had one daughter.[16]

Unsuccessful in his efforts to obtain a second reinstatement, Drayton returned to South Carolina, while Charleston was still in the hands of the British.[17] After peace was declared, however, he was entrusted with public office by the state and the Federal government. He served as judge of the Admiralty Court of South Carolina, and as associate justice of the Supreme Court of the state.[18] On November 18, 1789, President George Washington appointed him

first judge of the United States Court for the district of South Carolina,[19] a position he held until his death, six months later.

Besides having a profession, Drayton, like many Charlestonians,
was a plantation owner, having inherited Magnolia from his father.
While in Florida, he sold it to his uncle, John Drayton.[20] He invested
in Floridian lands, and (which sounds modern enough) lost thereby,
for upon Florida's again becoming Spanish in 1783, he was refused
compensation for them.[21]

In 1785, Drayton was chairman of the committee of the South
Carolina Society of Agriculture.[22] He received the degree of LL.D.
from the College of New Jersey, now Princeton University, in
1786.[23] At the time of his death, he was Grand Master of the Frater-
nity of South Carolina Ancient York Masons.[24] His dwelling was
the Humphrey Somers house, now 128 Tradd Street.[25]

In all of this, there is no hint of architecture. But it was the age
of amateurs. Manigault in Charleston, Peter Harrison in Newport,
were two (though a gifted two) among many. And if Drayton
needed a professional adviser on ticklish technical points, he could
consult his brother-in-law, William Gerard de Brahm, (qv) engineer and surveyor-general, who had married the judge's sister,
Mary.[26] Moreover, Drayton simplified his task by following, as
Fraser tells us, the interior plans of the former State House, in part
at least. As for the exterior, it is faintly reminiscent of Derby House,
Stratford Place, built about 1775 by the Brothers Adam, which
Drayton could have seen on his last visit to England. There is a still
stronger resemblance to No. 13 Serjeants' Inn, London, in the style
of Bonomi, but this building may be later than the Court House.
With the rejected parapet, the similarity would be even greater.

In spite of the esteem in which he was held, it was a weary old
man, suffering from gout,[27] and concerned about his children's
future, who designed the Court House. The day before he died, he
wrote that very human document, his will,—"if that can be called a
Man's Will when it depends upon the Indulgence and Disposition
of others, whether it shall be executed or not." He had met with
losses during the war, was in debt, and knew that in the event of his
creditors' demanding prompt payment, practically nothing would
remain. Accordingly, he asked them for "a little Time to work the
Debts out". The bulk of the estate he left in trust, undivided, for his
children, but his wife ("the best Wife in the World") who had
a little property of her own, was bequeathed two hundred guineas

with which to travel, with her daughter, to her own land and relations.

"If, however, the urgent Necessities of my Creditors should be superior to their Inclination for Indulgence I recommend a Family of the most dutiful and affectionate Children that ever Parent was blessed with, to the Benevolence of my Friends and the Protection of God Almighty." [28]

Drayton died on May 18, 1790,[29] too soon to see his Court House completed.

By December 10, 1792, it was sufficiently finished for the United States district court to meet there.[30]

Time and the earthquake of 1886 have had their effect on the building. Windows have been re-arranged, and the courses which once showed at the second and third story levels are gone. In 1941, a fireproof addition, designed by David B. Hyer, was added.

As for the building's merit, most observers will agree with William Gilmore Simms, who wrote:

"It is content to be big, solid, square, and lofty, serving its purposes, and making no fuss, and challenging no man's admiration. And this is no small recommendation in the case of plain fabrics as of plain people." [31]

JAMES HOBAN

c. 1762—December 8, 1831

JAMES HOBAN, IRISH-BORN ARCHITECT OF THE White House and other buildings in Washington, D. C., lived in Charleston for several years, became a householder, and was termed "fellow-citizen" by the local press.

Born in Callan, County Kilkenny, son of Edward Hoban and his wife Martha Bayne, he had studied in schools maintained by the Dublin Society. There he was instructed in architectural drawing by Thomas Ivory (d. 1786), architect of Lord Newcomen's bank, built in 1781, on which Hoban labored, probably as a workman.[1] While at school, he won a premium or premiums, which were to figure in his advertisements later.

He came to America, and inserted a notice in a Philadelphia paper, May, 1785.[2] Within two years, he was in South Carolina. The *Charleston Morning Post and Daily Advertiser* of April 21, 1787, had published:

"A QUESTION.

In an eliptical acre of grass, there is given,
Whose length to its breadth is as 9 to 7;
How long is the cord, and how brought to pass,
That a horse fed no more than his acre of grass.

J. C."

The paper of May 7 contained:

"Answer to the Question inserted 21st April.

An English acre, in proportion as 9 to 7, its transverse diameter

is	207,694
Its conjugate ditto	267,036
Difference of diameter, is	59,342
Which, subtracted from the semi-conjugate diameter, is	74,176

The length of cord necessary, which length being kept equidistant from the outlines of an elipsis, as above proportioned on both its diameters, gives the points to place 4 pins round, which pins said length of line is to traverse, which being equidistant from the outline, confines the horse to the oval described.

April 24th, 1787. JAMES HOBAN."

Hoban designed the State House at Columbia, South Carolina, which was built by James Brown,[3] and was still unfinished when the legislature met in it in 1790.[4] Mills described it in 1826:

"The state-house is a temporary building of wood, neat in its general appearance, and commodious. It produces a good effect when approached from the river, being situate upon the brow of the hill. The several public offices occupy the basement story of this building, which is of brick, including a branch of the bank of the state."[5]

An unkinder critic was to state that it belonged to "that very humble order of architecture, which may be designated as *the squat*."[6] It stood until burned by Sherman's army in 1865.

In January, 1789, Hoban bought half of a lot on the north side of Trott Street (now the eastern part of Wentworth Street), his partner, Pierce Purcell, buying the other half. The half-lot was small, but the price which Hoban paid, £261 10s. 10d. sterling, indicates that it contained a house. Hoban and Purcell, "both of the City of Charleston Carpenters," mortgaged these half-lots on March 17 to Thomas Gadsden, but paid off the obligation in 1791. Hoban kept his Charleston property until 1798, by which time he was an inhabitant of Washington.[7]

The Charleston directory of 1790 listed "Purcell & Hoburne carpenters 43 Trott-street". The Census of 1790 called them "Purcell & Hoburn", and showed that the household consisted of three free white males of sixteen and upwards, one free white male under sixteen, two free white females, and two slaves.

On May 4, 1790, Hoban advertised that he would teach architecture to an evening class of young men, gave Thomas Gadsden, George A. Hall, Roger Smith and Daniel Cannon as references, and stated that plans and carpentry would be executed by Hoban & Purcell.[8] Robert Mills (qv) is said to have studied under Hoban in Charleston.

The only Charleston building in which Hoban is known positively to have had a hand was the theater on Savage's Green (at the present corner of New and Savage Streets), built in 1792. This theater, the actual erection of which began after Hoban had left Charleston, was built under the supervision of Thomas Wade West, a theatrical manager. Anthony Toomer, who did the brickwork for Thomas Bennett's orphan house, was the contractor. In August, the *City Gazette* could write:

"NEW THEATRE.

On Thursday last, the ground was laid off for the new theatre, on Savage's Green. The corner stone of the foundation is to be laid the 20th inst. The dimensions, we are informed, are as follows:—125 feet in length, the width 56 feet, the height 37 feet, with a handsome pediment, stone ornaments, a large flight of stone steps, and a court-yard palisaded. The front will be in Broad-street, and the pit-entrance on Middleton-street. The different offices will be calculated so as not to interfere with each other; the stage is to be 56 feet in length, the front circular, with three rows of patent lamps; the boxes will be constructed so that small parties may be accommodated with a single box; to every box there will be a window and a Venetian blind; three tier boxes, decorated with 39 columns; to each column a glass chandelier, with five lights; the lower tier balustraded; the middle and upper boxes panneled; fancy painting, the ground French white, the mouldings and projections silvered; in the ceiling there will be three ventilators. The frontispiece, balconies, and stage doors, will be similar to those of the Opera house, London.

"The theatre is to be built under the immediate direction of Mr. West. When it is considered, that this gentleman has had near thirty years experience in many of the first theatres in England, and that he is to be assisted by artists of the first class, capt. Toomer and Mr. Hoban, we may expect a theatre in a style of elegance and novelty. Every attention will be paid to blend beauty with conveniency, and to render it the first theatre on the continent. The contractors have engaged to compleat the building by the 10th of January next." [9]

The interior was evidently carried out as planned, but the exterior seems to have been skimped. A drawing of it shows an amorphous barn,[10] while Mills, in 1826, wrote that:

"The theatre is a large building, without any architectural display outwardly, which is rather a remarkable circumstance here, as the citizens of Charleston have been always patrons of the muse of poetry and song. It is in contemplation to add a facade or portico to this edifice" . . .[11]

The portico was added, it is uncertain by whom, and proved handsome. In 1833, the building became a medical college.[12] After some vicissitudes, it was torn down in 1850.[13]

But before the cornerstone of the theater was laid, Hoban, as has been stated, had left the city. On August 8, 1792, the *City Gazette* printed an

"Extract of a Letter from a gentleman in Georgetown (M.) to his friend in this city, dated July 19, 1792.

"Yesterday the president of the United States and the commissioners of the federal buildings, examined the plans for a capitol and president's house, to be erected in the city of Washington. A great number of plans of considerable merit for each building, were presented by architects from the different states; and after an impartial and strict examination of them, a gold medal and premium for the best plan of a president's house was adjudged to Mr. James Hoban from Charleston, South Carolina; and he was accordingly appointed architect for the federal buildings.

"It is remarkable, Mr. Hoban had but 20 days to complete his plan after his arrival here, and that after he explained it to the commissioners, they unanimously agreed that it should be adopted."

On August 9, the same paper said:

. . . "On this occasion, we think it is but justice to observe that Mr. Hoban, as a man of abilities, is unassuming and diffident. When a mere boy, he received a mark of distinction from the royal society of Dublin, which none else could then achieve. We wish him success, and every encouragement the city of Washington can afford.—Mr. Hoban furnished a plan, or was about to do it here, for an orphan-house, but whether adopted or not we will not pretend to assert: certain it is, that he relinquished furnishing his plan, &c. unless he was permitted to work it up himself.—When the President of the United States honored this city with a visit last year, Mr. Hoban was introduced to him, as a man of merit and of genius, under the patronage of general Moultrie, Mr. Butler, &c. And we may safely add, that it is no small matter of universal satisfaction to the citizens of Carolina, that their fellow-citizen, Hoban, has succeeded in this enterprise."

The plan of Thomas Bennett (qv) for the Orphan House was chosen, and Hoban was thenceforth busy at Washington. In a letter to Tobias Lear, dated July 30, 1792, the president spoke of "Mr. Hoben" (sic) "who was introduced to me by Doctr. Tucker, from Charleston, and who appears to be a very judicious man", adding that "He has been engaged in some of the first buildings in Dublin—appears a master workman and has a great many Lands of his own." [14]

As Henry Laurens is generally spoken of as the man who gave Hoban letters of introduction to George Washington, it would seem that a whole group of Charlestonians were determined to further the architect's interests. Had he designed houses for them? Unfortunately, tradition is dumb on this point, linking him with only one building, William Seabrook's house on Edisto, built 1810 and still standing, concerning which no proof has been found.[15]

Hoban's work in the capital is nationally known, every schoolchild recognizing pictures of the White House. Hoban built this edifice twice, for after it had been burned by the British in 1814, he constructed it a second time. His plan for the Capitol was not chosen, but he worked on its erection, and both designed and built others of the Federal buildings. Even-tempered and reasonable, he survived more than one shake-up of the building staffs.

In January, 1799, he married Susannah Sewell, by whom he had ten children. Investing in real estate, he prospered, and died wealthy in 1831.[16]

So far as is known, he had never returned to Charleston, which had served him as a springboard to the Federal city.

THOMAS BENNETT

February 11, 1754—February 16 or 17, 1814

L UMBERMAN, CONTRACTOR, AND DESIGNER OF public buildings and a rice mill, Thomas Bennett is a noteworthy example of the builder-architect, although too prominent to be truly typical.

In his early twenties at the beginning of the Revolution, Bennett fought on the American side.[1] Afterward, he was in partnership with Daniel Cannon, using both wind and tidal power to work large lumber mills on the marsh in the western part of Charleston, known as Harleston.[2]

In 1792, he appeared as an architect, his design for the Orphan House being selected.[3]

Need for this institution had arisen from a series of yellow fever epidemics which left many children parentless. One John Robertson, a city warden but comparatively an obscure man, first advocated the idea. It took the city by storm, and money poured in from sources as different as church collections and gamblers' winnings.

The cornerstone was laid November 12, 1792,[4] and the building was opened October 18, 1794.[5]

At first, it was a simple but sizable brick structure,[6] topped by a small wooden cupola,[7] and roughcast.[8] Bennett's plans called for a foundation 2½ feet high, three bricks thick; a first story of ten feet, a second of fifteen, and a third of thirteen, all with walls 2½ bricks thick, and a fourth story, ten feet high, two bricks thick. The center of the building measured 40 x 40, and the wings each 65 x 30 feet.[9]

In 1854-55, the structure was enlarged and given an Italianate quality by Jones and Lee (qqv). It was pulled down during the present century.

Bennett apparently donated his design, which was chosen from among several submitted.[10] He was no loser thereby, for the building committee awarded Cannon & Bennett the contract for the carpentry, including a large order for lumber, probably the best choice they could have made. Anthony Toomer received the contract for the brickwork.[11]

For bricks, the committee relied partly on those in the west wing of the Pre-Revolutionary Old Barracks, which were pulled down.[12] The Orphan House itself was erected on the site of Revolutionary defenses, and was hailed as a triumph of peace over war.[13]

Glass, paint, oil, nails, and locks were brought from Bristol (either Rhode Island or England), and stone from Philadelphia.[14] The committee furnished roofing also, proposals to slaters stating that "The slate is properly dressed and drilled, and must be put on laths with pegs." [15]

The lot was fenced,[16] a massive wall being built only after 1800,[17] though a wall was projected as 1794.[18]

After his connection with Cannon ended, Bennett took his son Thomas, later governor of South Carolina, into the firm, under the name of Thomas Bennett & Son. This partnership was dissolved August 31, 1802, the younger man continuing the business.[19]

The elder Bennett is known to have built a rice mill by a creek at Belle-Vue, his James Island plantation. The best description dates from 1821:

"THE BELLE-VUE RICE MILL,

Is now ready to Beat Out Rice on Toll. The subscribers have purchased the above Mill, situated on James Island, and immediately opposite South-Bay. It was built by the late Thomas Bennett, Esq. whose skill as an Architect was well known. . . . They will also undertake to Gin blackseed Cotton and Saw Lumber, there being in the Establishment one of the most approved roller Gins, and a Saw Mill. . . .

Wm. Peronneau & Sons." [20]

Bennett belonged to the Congregationalist faith.[21] His connection with the erection of the Circular (Congregational) Church, built 1804-1806, is something of a mystery. This building was designed by Robert Mills (qv). However, an account of the church, published in 1853, spoke of "the venerable Thomas Bennett, deceased, the architect and builder of the Circular Church." [22] Builder is perhaps the true solution.

The esteem in which Bennett was held was so great that in 1804, the vestry of St. Michael's who were considering enlarging their church according to a plan drawn by Robert Mills, consulted Bennett upon the matter.

The Governor Bennett House, 1 Lucas Street, built about 1825.

"On Motion—Messrs. Jenkins, Reid, Potter, and Ward were appointed a Committee to wait on Mr. Thomas Bennett, Senior at the request of the Vestry, and to inform him that they, from the high opinion they have of his public spirit as also of his great, and general mechanical knowledge and experience, have determined to lay before him the Plan offered by Mr. Mills for the enlargement of the Church, together with the different estimates given in".[23]

Unfortunately, Bennett's opinion of Mill's plan has not been preserved.

Bennett's own dwelling, now 64 Montagu Street,[24] may be of his designing, but proof lacks. Like many houses of the time, it consists of two clapboarded stories on a high brick basement.

Bennett married Anna Hayes,[25] two years his senior, apparently an intelligent woman since he saw fit to leave her not only creature comforts but also "Pictures, Ornaments, and Library . . . Philosophical apparatus and Machinery".[26] She died June, 1830.[27] Bennett's will mentioned six sons and one daughter,[28] and it would appear that he had had other daughters.[29]

Bennett and his wife are buried in the graveyard of the Circular Church. A stone to their memory states that he died on February 16, 1814, thus differing by one day from another monument, to Bennett only, which gave the date as the seventeenth. The monument was destroyed by the fire of 1861, but the inscription has been preserved.

"Thomas Bennett, who died on the 17th day of February, A. D. 1814. AEtat. 60. He was an architect of distinguished merit; to the beauty and symmetry of whose designs many of the public buildings of this city bear testimony. In the difficulties and privations of the Revolutionary war he bore an honorable part, and in the councils of his country maintained an influence acquired by the correctness of his perceptions, and established in the integrity of his conduct in private life" . . . . . (Virtues and religion follow.)[30]

One may only guess at what public buildings, other than the Orphan House, he designed.

Both the architect's son, Thomas Bennett (1781-1863), governor of South Carolina, and the latter's son, Washington Jefferson Ben-

Bennett's Rice Mill, east end of Wentworth Street. The newer part was built in 1844. The attic on the older part was added to match that on the newer. Only the façade at the right remains today.

nett (1808-1874), were interested in architecture. Probably one or the other of them was meant in the report of the board of trustees of the Apprentices' Library Society, which stated that their hall, built in 1840, had been "originally designed by Mr. Bennett and drafted by Mr. Richardt" (Reichardt, qv). Washington Jefferson Bennett is said to have planned the Free School on St. Philip's Street, begun in 1855, later Bennett School.[31]

JOHN CHRISTIAN SENF
AND MINOR CONTEMPORARIES

JOHN CHRISTIAN SENF. c. 1754—August 24, 1806

JOHN CHRISTIAN SENF, MILITARY ENGINEER AND canal maker who was praised by Robert Mills, designed a few buildings.

He was a Hessian (his name means mustard in German), a son of one Lucas Senf,[1] and perhaps a relation of the minor German poet, Heinrich Christian Ludwig Senf.[2] He surrendered with Burgoyne at the Battle of Saratoga, October 17, 1777, and was converted to the American cause, apparently without difficulty.

Henry Laurens, president of the Continental Congress, and a Charlestonian, sent him to South Carolina to be state engineer.[3] Senf received the appointment of captain engineer in the Continental army, November 29, 1778, and later became lieutenant colonel. He was an original member of the Cincinnati.[4]

His account of the Santee Canal, of which he was the engineer, has been published by the South Carolina Historical Society.[5] It is possible that he designed some of the buildings connected with the canal, such as the storehouse at Simpson's Lock, which is pictured in the *Sketchbook of Charles Fraser*.

In 1787, Senf designed a fort on James Island opposite Charleston, near the site of old Fort Johnson. The neatly drawn plan was accompanied by a profile of the battery and a "View of the Battery and Barraks (sic) at the Gate." The doorway of the barracks was sheltered by a pedimented porch supported by two columns. This plan came into the hands of Robert Mills and was presented by him to the War Department in 1840. It was published in the *Charleston Year Book of 1883*.

In 1800, Senf was mentioned in connection with a very different building, the little clubhouse of the Black Oak or St. John's Hunting Club, without architectural pretension, but noteworthy from its associations with the sporting traditions of the Low Country. The memorandum book of René Ravenel of Pooshee Plantation records under date of May 6, 1800, that

"The Gentlemen of the Neighborhood met and dined on the Road near my gate and drew up Rules for the forming a Club. Also agreed with Coll Senf to build a House for a Club House."

Senf may have designed the house, but he was not the builder, since the same source states on May 9, 1801, that "Nathaniel Mc-Cants put up a House for a Club House on the Road near the Canal" (the Santee Canal) "for the sum of Twenty Five pounds".[6] If this was the same clubhouse which was standing in 1865, it collapsed after being stripped of its boards by Yankees and negroes.[7]

After Senf's death in 1806, the *Courier* wrote:

"Died, at his Seat in Rocky Mount, South Carolina, on the 24th ult." (August) "of a lingering illness, in the 53d year of his age, Colonel Christian Senf, Chief Engineer, to the State of South-Carolina.

"He was an Officer of merit and information, and served with great applause in the Southern States, as an Engineer, during the Revolutionary contest." [8]

Mills wrote of Senf in a tone which indicated that he may have known him personally. In describing Rocky Mount, he stated that it held

—"the ashes of one whose memory should be cherished by Carolinians, for his devotion to their cause in the Revolution, and his subsequent efforts to serve them in his professional capacity— Col. Senf, the engineer, both of the Catawba company and of the Santee canal. He sleeps, in what was his garden, at Rocky Mount; but no obituary stone records his grave. Col. Senf was a military engineer of considerable talent." [9]

MR. EMES AND THOMAS HOPE.   Working in 1788

Mr. Emes and Mr. Hope walked in a procession—the Federal Procession, held May 27, 1788, to celebrate South Carolina's ratification of the Federal constitution. The marchers were arranged according to their trades or professions, each group led by one or two prominent members, whose names later appeared in the newspaper. Thus one learns of Emes and Hope, who headed the architects. There were also a group of bricklayers, led by John Horlbeck (qv), and one of house carpenters, led by John Clements, so that our architects cannot be dismissed as belonging properly to either category.

But aside from the fact that he marched from Roper's wharf to Federal Green and there ate dinner,[1] nothing is known of Mr. Emes. Fortunately, considerably more is known of his companion.

Thomas Hope was born Christmas, 1757, in Kent, and was trained as an architect in London. He was to work also as a wood carver and cabinet maker.[2] He is termed cabinet maker in the only Charleston directory in which he appears, that of 1790, which gives his address as 15 Friend Street (now part of Legare Street).

According to a tradition preserved in Knoxville, Tennessee, where he later settled, Hope left England for South Carolina to plan and superintend a mansion for Ralph Izard, a prominent Charlestonian, and the tradition gains strength from the fact that Hope named one of his sons Ralph Izard.[3] Whether the house was built or not is unknown. It is not the Ralph Izard house at 110 Broad Street, which dates from before the Revolution.

In 1793, he married, at Cheraw Hill, South Carolina, Elizabeth Large. A daughter was born there the following year, and soon after, the Hopes moved to Tennessee, where the rest of their children were born. In that state, Hope worked on a number of imposing houses and also carved woodwork and made furniture, until his death, October 4, 1820. His buildings included the Francis Alexander Ramsey house, in gothic style, near Knoxville, and several other plantation dwellings.[4]

THOMAS WALKER.   In Charleston by 1793.   And
JOHN BRUTON RICKETS, c.   1775—August 24, 1799.

Thomas Walker from Edinburgh may have been an architect; he was a tombstone cutter. Charleston graveyards still contain his sturdy brownstone uprights, where urns, *memento mori* designs, and somewhat dour cherubs reveal a deft if limited craftsmanship. He signed them "Walker," often adding "sculpt" and "Charleston" or "Cha[n].", so that they are readily identified.[1]

But his architectural endeavors, if there were any, remain unknown. All that is certain is one advertisement:

> "Thomas Walker, Stone Cutter, from Edinburgh, Respectfully informs the public, that he has a few Grave stones for sale, at Duncan & Murdoch's, No. 92, Church-street; also, stone cutting done in its different branches, and orders left there will be punctually attended to.

N. B. He has also opened an evening school for teaching the rules of Architecture, from seven to nine in the evening (four nights in the week) at No. 8 Amen-street. An apprentice wanted to the stone cutting and brick laying business." [2]

One Thomas Walker, stonecutter, who died in 1838, may have been the same man or a descendant.[3] A family of stonecutters named Walker worked in Charleston throughout the Ante-Bellum era.

John B. Rickets (or Ricketts), from Bath in Somersetshire, was likewise a stonecutter, but he was called architect so persistently that one is led to believe that he may have had a claim to the term. In his capacity as a stone mason, he was probably responsible for some of the decorative marble trim found on buildings of the time, but his stay in Charleston was too short for him to have accomplished much in any line there.

During the spring and summer of 1799, he advertised as follows:

"J. RICKETTS,
Architect and Marble Mason
At his Work shop, corner of Governor's Bridge,
Informs the Gentlemen of Charleston, and its vicinity, that he has returned to this city, with a CARGO OF MARBLE, of the first quality, which he is enabled to render on as cheap terms as can be imported.

CHIMNEY PIECES, from 10 to 300 dollars each
TOMB and HEAD STONES, from 10 to 100 dollars
WINDOW HEADS
KEYSTONES and WINDOW SILLS
STEPS, Printers PRESS-STONES,
SIDE-TABLES
WINE COOLERS
Also, ANT TABLES, which are particularly recommended, in a warm climate to keep all kind of provisions in a cool state.

WANTED,
Two COUNTRY-BOYS, as apprentices in the STONE-CUTTING Business March 29." [4]

Rickets' obituary appeared in the *City Gazette* of Monday, August 26:

"Died, on Saturday morning last, after a few days illness, Mr. John B. Ricketts, architect and marble mason. Mr. Ricketts was a native of England, and had established here in the line of his profession a few months past: as an ingenious workman he is a real loss to the public."

He was buried on the day of his death in the graveyard of St. Philip's church.[5] His tombstone, a slab affixed to the north wall, recently has begun to weather, but only a few years ago the skill shown in the execution of its design, two crossed torches, reversed, with a bowknot above, could still be appreciated. If, as seems reasonable, it was taken from among his store, it testifies to his good workmanship though not to any originality. The inscription runs:

> "Near this Monument lie deposited the remains of John B. Rickets. Architect and Sculptor A Native of Bath in Somerset Shire England. Who after a short illness departed this Life on the 24th day of August 1799 Aged 24 years This small tribute of respect is here placed to his Memory by William Pritchard Jun.
> Fames boastful chisel fortunes silver plume
> Mark but the mouldering Urn or deck the Tomb."

Pritchard, member of a family of shipbuilders, was the administrator of Rickets' estate.[6]

DAVID BURN, and
DEPRESSEVILLE.   Advertised 1785 and 1797, respectively.

Two architects or would-be architects of the Post-Revolutionary period are known by but one advertisement each.

Burn appeared in July, 1785:

> "David Burn, Will begin to teach as soon as a sufficient number of scholars shall offer, the five orders of architecture, planning and shading in the modern taste. Any Gentleman may be attended at his own lodgings; likewise any gentleman may be furnished with plans, elevations, and sections for buildings. Apply at No. 19 Beresford's Alley."[1]

The Beresford's Alley of that day is now known as Chalmers Street.

Depresseville advertised in April, 1797. His French name suggests that he may have been a refugee from Santo Domingo, like Aveilhé, Jahan, de Grasse, and probably Paque. (qqv)

> "Depresseville Gives notice that he continues to keep his Drawing School, in different Parts of Landscapes, with Pencil

or Washed; teaches Architecture, and to draw with method; also the necessary acknowledgments for the Plans. He offers his Services to the Owners and Surveyors, for the most exact Drawings of Plans in Profile, and Elevation of Houses and Buildings; and all sorts of Copies of Plans, either with the Pen or with Colors. He lives in Longitude Lane, in the house belonging to Mr. Righton." [2]

MR. COX.   Working 1799.

The vestry minutes of St. Michael's Church record that on July 27, 1799, "The Church Wardens were directed to have a coach house and Stable built on the Parsonage lot, agreeable to the plan delivered by M[r]. Cox, the amount thereof to be deducted out of the rents of the Parsonage".... [1]

This was probably Joseph D. Cox, house carpenter, who in 1802 was living at 127 Meeting Street. [2]

No such coach house and stable can be found today, although the parsonage, now a private dwelling, 39 Meeting Street, still stands. It was built in 1766-67 by Miller and Fullerton (qqv), and there is no indication that Cox was concerned in it.

DANIEL M'GIVERIN.   Working about 1801 – 1803.

Daniel M'Giverin (or M'Iverin) was termed "carpenter" by the directory of 1802 and "architect" by his Masonic brethren. He built the Masonic Hall in Lodge Alley, as is shown by this notice in the *Times* of December 2, 1801:

> "Ancient York Masons.—By permission of the Grand Lodge of South-Carolina—The officers and members of Lodge No. 11, respectfully invite the officers and members of the several Lodges in this city, under the jurisdiction of the Grand Lodge—and also all transient Brethren, to meet at their Lodge Room,—No.— King-street, To-morrow Afternoon, at 4 o'clock—thence to walk in masonic procession to lay the corner stone of a MASONIC HALL, to be erected in Lodge-Alley, by Brother Elstob, and Mr. Andrews.
>
> Brother D. M'Giverin, *Architect.*
>
> Brethren, O'Kelly, Sweeney, and O'Conner, *Committee of Arrangement.*
>
> By order of the Worshipful Master.
>
> P. E. Prendergast, Sec'ry."

Lodge Alley runs one block from East Bay to State Street and is barely wide enough for one vehicle. Why it should have been selected is beyond conjecture, but Charlestonians are enured to narrow streets.

The Hall took not quite two years to build. An advertisement in the *Courier* of November 1, 1803, states:

"To Let

The Masonic Hall, in Lodge-Alley, second door from the Bay; it is now completely finished, the lower part of which would answer either for a Tavern or Store. Immediate possession will be given. Apply to

Archibald Brebner
No. 11, Tradd-Street."

According to the directory of 1802, which spelled his name *M'Iverin* (perhaps the correct form), Daniel lived in National-Bank-square, that is to say, on a little street which ran at right angles north and east of the Bank of the United States building (now the City Hall), just as Court House square (in reality, a street), still runs north and west of the Court House. M'Giverin's dwelling and street have alike vanished, for in 1818, when the bank became the City Hall, the municipality bought the adjacent land and tore down the houses to form the present City Hall Park, or, as it is officially termed, Washington Square.

FOUR FRENCHMEN

AUGUSTUS DE GRASSE.   Advertising 1800 – 1801.

L IKE MANY OTHERS, AUGUSTUS DE GRASSE ADVER-
tised that he would draw plans and teach architecture.
Whether he actually did so does not appear. Unlike most
similar advertisers, however, of whom nothing is known beyond
their scant notices, de Grasse had a life and background which are
a matter of record.

Alexandre-François Auguste, Marquis de Grasse, to give him his
full name and title, arrived at Charleston, August 14, 1793, in the
brig *Thomas,* seventeen days from Cap François, as Cap Haitien was
then called. He came as a refugee from the negro insurrection in
Santo Domingo. Refugees also were his four sisters, step-mother,
wife and daughters.[1]

He was a member of an old Provençal family, and the son of
Admiral de Grasse (1723-1788), who commanded the French fleet
which so materially helped in causing Cornwallis' surrender at York-
town and the triumph of the Americans. The admiral was known
for his height and courage, his sailors joking that he stood six feet
high ordinarily but six feet, one inch on days of battle. But in the
West Indies, on April 12, 1782, he was soundly defeated by Rodney
and Hood. Carried prisoner to England, he tried to fix the blame
upon his subordinates, and insisted upon an undue deference, which
turned opinion against him, in France as elsewhere, and lost him
the favor of Louis XVI.[2]

The admiral's widow and children were living as colonials in
Santo Domingo when the insurrection forced them to flee to Charles-
ton. According to tradition, they were hospitably received by John
B. Holmes at his dwelling, now 15 Meeting Street.[3]

While in Charleston, two of Augustus de Grasse's daughters were
baptized (one of whom had been born in Santo Domingo), two of
his sisters married, and two other sisters died.[4]

Lack of funds eventually led de Grasse, in June, 1800, to advertise a "School for Designing".[5] In July, the following appeared:

"SCHOOL FOR DESIGNING, ETC.

"AUGUSTUS DE GRASSE

"Has the honour to inform the inhabitants of this city that he proposes to open a school for designing as well as plans of fortifications, architecture & Landscapes . . . He proposes to teach by the most simple theory, the principle of Artillery & Fortifications of the Field and strong places after the modes followed by the Best authors . . .

"N. B. On Mon. Wed. & Fri. he will instruct his pupils in the Art of Fencing.

"His address is in Federal St. in the house belonging to Mr. Peigne."[6]

Federal Street is now part of Society Street.

In August, de Grasse advertised that he would teach the use of the broad sword.[7] In October, he was ready to impart the principles of fortification and artillery as an extra in the school kept by his father-in-law, Jean B. de la Hogue.[8]

The fencing lessons seem to have been most in demand, for de Grasse advertised them again in 1801.[9] The directory of that year listed him simply as "De Grasse Augustus, 9, Federal-street."

He eventually returned to France,[10] heartily glad, no doubt, to leave America.

JEAN BAPTISTE AVEILHE

Jean Baptiste Aveilhé, like Augustus de Grasse, left Santo Domingo as a result of the negro insurrection on that island. He was in Charleston as early as December, 1794, when he gave a release for a house in Port au Prince to one Antoine François Michel La-Jonchere. This document, in poor French (perhaps the fault of an early copyist at the mesne conveyance office), describes them both as "habitants de S[t]. Dominque et resident presentement a Charleston Caroline du Sud".[1]

Aveilhé appeared in the Charleston directories of 1801 and 1802, the first of which did not mention his occupation, while the second termed him architect. His address was given as the east end of Boundary Street (now Calhoun Street).

In September, 1803, he advertised two inventions, a machine "For Boring Holes in Rocks under water, or in any situation, and blasting them", and a patent horizontal windmill, "which for utility has not been exceeded by any piece of mechanism which this or perhaps the last century can boast of." This treasure was said to be "adapted to the grinding of all sorts of grain, and at the same time threshing out wheat and rice, fanning them and pounding the latter, powdering plaster of Paris," (then popular as fertilizer) "cutting tobacco, raise" (sic) "water, &c." The advertisement was signed "John Baptiste Aveilhe, inventor".[2]

No building has been identified as his work.

JOSEPH JAHAN. 1758—January 30, 1833.
    In Charleston c. 1793—1833.

Like de Grasse and Aveilhé, Joseph Jahan fled to Charleston from Santo Domingo. They have another point of resemblance, unfortunately—no building can safely be ascribed to any of them.

Jahan was born at Montargis, France, about September, 1758, but emigrated to Santo Domingo, whence he came to Charleston about 1793.[1] He was called "architect builder" by the directory of 1802, probably a more accurate description than either carpenter or architect, both of which terms were applied to him by later directories.[2] On December 26, 1815, he married (Mrs.) Marie Panpalon.[3] He was a Free Mason,[4] and a member of the Société Française,[5] which is still in existence as the French Society. A Roman Catholic, he became a vestryman of St. Mary's Church [6] and for several years served as churchwarden.[7] He was in the thick of the battle between the vestry of St. Mary's and the diocesan authority, respecting the government of the parish, which resulted in victory for the diocese.[8]

Jahan lived in a house which stood on the west side of Meeting Street, on what is now part of Marion Square.[9] He died on January 30, 1833,[10] survived by his widow. [11] The tombstone on his grave in St. Mary's churchyard bears a laudatory inscription in French.

F. GABRIEL PAQUE.   Working 1806—1807.

F. Gabriel Paque is found in the Charleston directories of 1806 and 1807, listed as "architect builder", at 106 King Street. In the next directory, that of 1809, his address was the same, but his occupation was that of grocer. The change was probably a wise one, since people may build, but must eat.

The Second Presbyterian Church, 342 Meeting Street, built 1809-c. 1816. South side. James and John Gordon, architects.

St. Luke's and St. Paul's Church, Radcliffeboro, 126 Coming Street, built 1811-1816. James and John Gordon, architects.

JAMES AND JOHN GORDON

c. 1783-1814   c. 1787-1835

J
AMES AND JOHN GORDON WERE THE SONS OF AN-
drew Gordon and Mary his wife, who seem to have come to
Charleston from Scotland in 1792.[1] In that year, Andrew, a
builder, submitted an unsuccessful bid for the bricklaying contract
of the Orphan House.[2] In 1800-1801, he was the master bricklayer
for the Bank of the United States building (now the City Hall).[3]
He appeared last in the directory of 1807 and was dead by May,
1813.[4]

In dealing with the Gordons, care is necessary if one is not to
confuse them with contemporaries of the same names, some of
whom were in the building trades. One can feel sure that "Gordon,
John, bricklayer", listed in the directory of 1801, was not Andrew's
son—he was only fourteen then. Neither was John Gordon who in
1802 advertised that he would construct cisterns.[5]

In 1809, the brothers were engaged to build the Second Presbyterian Church in Wraggboro',[6] the building committee showing a
flattering and, as it turned out, misguided confidence in these young
men, still in their twenties. Both architects and builders, they
planned a massive structure with a high steeple, and set about work.[7]

Long before this church was finished, they also designed St.
Paul's, Radcliffeboro' (begun in 1811), and contracted for its brick-
work.[8] The carpenters' work was done by Robert Jackson and Robert
Galbraith.[9] This church, now known as St. Luke's and St. Paul's,
gains added interest from the fact that its erection spared St.
Michael's from being enlarged. Both the Second Presbyterian and
St. Paul's are large, rectangular, brick structures, covered with
stucco. In style, they are like the churches of colonial days. So far
as bulk goes, they bear a closer resemblance to substantial old St.
Philip's (then still standing) than to the lighter St. Michael's, but
show the influence of the latter's portico and (judging from the
unfinished tower of the Presbyterian Church) of its steeple also. St.
Paul's tower shows an unexpected Gothic influence, being crowned
by a parapet with conventional ogival designs on its faces and pin-

nacles at the corners. This "disturbs the critic eye of taste", as Robert Mills phrased it, and was probably clapped on as an afterthought when the plan for a high steeple was abandoned.

The two churches bear distinct resemblances to each other, in size and in feeling. Each has a tetrastyle Tuscan portico at the west, and neither is raised far above the ground. Their dimensions differ, however, the Presbyterian being 125 feet by 70, while St. Paul's measures 164 feet by 70.[10] St. Paul's has an apse which in the Presbyterian Church is absent; while the latter shows a group of four engaged columns on its south side, lending an emphasis to that facade unlike anything at St. Paul's.

Somehow, both churches look better from the back than from the front. Seen from the street, they are not clumsy but they lack grace; from the rear, they have a massive quality which pleases.

Bricks, bricks, and more bricks went into these structures. Their cost mounted. Neither has its intended steeple, and the fault is that of the Gordons. It is evident that they had not grasped the mechanics of their trade, while their estimates fell far short of the required sums. At St. Paul's, the heavy load which was placed on the tower caused it to settle, so that the main walls, to which it was joined by bond timbers, began to split. There was nothing to do but to remove masses of bricks from the tower.[11]

Meanwhile, tragedy came. A boy, climbing adventurously on the unfinished pile, fell and was killed.[12] This certainly could not be blamed on the architects, but it seemed a poor augury.

The congregations found themselves faced by mounting bills. The Second Presbyterian Church cost more than $100,000. "Although great munificence was exercised by the founders of this church, its cost far exceeded both their expectations and their means", as the tablet in the vestibule states. They were forced to resort to a lottery (as the tablet does not state).[13] St. Paul's was even more expensive. Including amounts paid for repairs in later years as flaws came gradually to light, its cost was close to a quarter of a million. [14] It was completed in 1816,[15] and the Presbyterian Church at about the same time.

The interior of the Second Presbyterian Church is not as the Gordons built it, having been remodeled in 1833, when the ceiling was lowered, the floor raised, and space taken from the front to form a vestibule.[16] Less drastic changes have followed.

While the churches were under construction, James Gordon died, on November 5, 1814, "after a long and painful illness which he

St. Luke's and St. Paul's Church, Radcliffeboro, 126 Coming Street, built 1811-1816. James and John Gordon, architects.

bore with manly fortitude".[17] He was thirty-one. It was a sad year for the Gordons, their mother having died in the preceding July.[18]

In an elaborate indenture, made a few months before James' death, the brothers had agreed to "continue their Copartnership and joint trade together", mentioning personal property, implements, "divers Negroe and other Slaves", and lots and buildings.[19] They called themselves bricklayers, by which term they are known in the directories. This indenture was proved after James' death as if it had been a will, with John the heir.

In spite of the difficulties which had attended the erection of the two churches, John Gordon's services were still in demand. In 1820, he did a small job on the military laboratory for the state.[20] He also worked on private houses.[21]

The Episcopal church engaged him to build St. Stephen's Chapel on Guignard Street,[22] and he may well have been its architect. Intended for a poor congregation, it is said to have been the first Episcopal church in the United States in which the pews were free.[23] The cornerstone was laid in 1823,[24] and the building consecrated March 18, 1824.[25] It was burned in 1835 by a fire which destroyed the neighborhood.[26] The present St. Stephen's Chapel, which Gordon did not build, is on Anson Street.

John Gordon became a planter and brickmaker in addition to being an architect and builder. In 1819, he bought Moreland plantation on the Cooper River, and in 1828 an adjoining tract called Pagett's Landing. The latter held a brickmaking establishment which he enlarged until the whole plantation was known as the Brickyard.[27] It produced from 1,200,000 to 1,500,000 bricks a year, and employed more than one hundred slaves.[28] He also owned a neighboring tract called the Grove.[29] In 1831, the directory termed him planter.

Gordon seems to have been a sociable man, a member of the Jockey Club,[30] the Hibernian Society,[31] and the St. Andrew's Society. He was one of the committee which in 1813 selected the plan of Hugh Smith (qv) for the St. Andrew's Hall and supervised the work. [32] By 1819, he was captain of the Irish Volunteers, part of the Twenty-Eighth Regiment of South Carolina militia,[33] and later became a colonel.[34]

In 1819, he was present at a grim interview in the Magazine Street jail, when one John Peoples identified the members of the Fisher gang as the robbers who had attacked him at the Six Mile

House, an inn near the city.[35] The crimes of the gang and the beauty of Lavinia Fisher have made their story one of Charleston's favorite thrillers. Was Gordon among the "number of gentlemen" who had captured the robbers? And when, in 1820, John and Lavinia Fisher met their fate, was he in the huge crowd which saw them hanged? Surmise dons wings and flaps vigorously, but we do not know.

The Gordons' sister, Maria, deserves mention. In April, 1812, she married John Magrath, a merchant [36] who had fought in the Irish rebellion of 1798.[37] She became the mother of Andrew Gordon Magrath (1813-1893), who was governor of South Carolina during the last days of the Confederacy.[38]

John Gordon married Jane M. Burgess. They were the parents of several sons and daughters.[39] Gordon died February 27, 1835, and lies buried beside his mother and brother in the graveyard of the First (Scotch) Presbyterian Church.[40]

His slaves, skilful workmen, were sold at high prices, one bringing $1,425.[41]

Mrs. Gordon married Governor Thomas Bennett on March 5, 1840,[42] and is buried in Magnolia Cemetery.[43]

HUGH SMITH
1782—April 6, 1826

H
UGH SMITH HAS A PLACE AMONG CHARLESTON
architects by virtue of one building, the St. Andrew's Society Hall, which stood for less than half a century, from
1815 to 1861, but gained a place in history.

Like Manigault and Drayton, he was an amateur. His place of
birth is unknown, but he was the son of John Smith, a merchant,
and his wife Agnes, who had been a Scots lassie in Edinburgh before
she sailed to America.[1] Hugh is first heard of in 1802, when at the
age of twenty he entered the competition for the South Carolina
College building, to be erected at Columbia. The elevation, owned
today by the University of South Carolina (the same institution
under another name), is marked "Principal Front/ Of a Design for
S. Carolina College/ Extends 236 feet/ Hugh Smith Archit[ct]". It
shows a longish structure topped by a neat lantern, and has what
appears to be an octagonal wing at one end, the other being plain.
Smith's plan was among those commended but not chosen by the
committee.[2]

Smith became a merchant like his father, and the Charleston
directory of 1822 gave his business address as Smith's wharf, which
seems, however, to have belonged not to him but to Peter Smith, a
factor and former builder.[3] Hugh Smith was a member of the South
Carolina Society and the Charleston Library Society,[4] the latter of
which gave him access to architectural books. He was a private in
the Union Light Infantry, all "sons of the thistle", organized in
1807, one of the many local militia companies.[5] But the pertinent
fact about him is that he belonged to the St. Andrew's Society.[6]

The society had been founded by a group of Scots in 1729, although the story of its hall begins much later. On St. Andrew's day,
November 30, 1813, the building committee was appointed. It included John Gordon (qv), and the entire group is said to have been
zealous in superintending the work. They accepted Smith's design.[7]
The cornerstone was laid July 4, 1814, and on St. Andrew's day,
1815, the society dined in their hall for the first time.[8]

The iron fence across the front of the lot seems to have been added in 1819.[9]

Hugh Smith died in 1826. By the terms of his will, made September 8, 1821, everything was left to his wife, Eliza C., whom he appointed executrix, a friend, Charles Kiddell, being named executor.[10] A slab in the graveyard of the First Presbyterian Church bears these words:

> "Sacred to the Memory of Hugh Smith who departed this life on the 6th of April 1826 aged 44 years & 3 months. To the advantages of a liberal education was added a highly cultivated mind and comprehensive understanding, honor and strict integrity governed all the actions of his short life. This tribute of respect is inscribed by his bereaved Widow & Mother. Also of Eliza C. Smith, his wife who departed this life January 24th 1861 aged 73 years and 6 months. 'She sleeps in Jesus.'"

Close at hand are the tombstones of his mother and of his sons, John M. and Hugh.

In the same year that saw Smith's death, Robert Mills published his *Statistics of South Carolina*, which commended the hall:

> "St. Andrew's Hall presents a neat modern front, in good style. The interior is well arranged, with a large handsome room on the second story, much in use on public occasions." [11]

The hall appears in Hill's birdseye *View of Charleston*, printed in 1851. A better picture is found in *Frank Leslie's Illustrated Newspaper* of May 5, 1860. This shows the hall to have been a two-story building. Four engaged columns with Ionic capitals ornamented the facade, the center of which projected slightly under a pediment. Round- and square-headed windows helped to make a pleasing pattern.

In 1819 the hall sheltered President Monroe, then on his southern tour,[12] and in 1825 it housed Lafayette.[13] Daniel Webster was the guest of the New England Society of Charleston at a dinner there in 1847.[14] For years, the balls of the Jockey Club (mildly brisk), and those of the St. Cecilia Society (decidedly formal) were held there.[15] The story of their delights has often been told; it remained for Mrs. Chesnut to record in her diary the spectator's viewpoint:

"Mr. Hayne said his wife moaned over the hardness of the chaperones' seats at St. Andrew's Hall at a Cecilia Ball. She was hopelessly deposited on one for hours. 'And the walls are harder, my dear. What are your feelings to those of the poor old fellows leaning there, with their beautiful young wives waltzing as if they could never tire and in the arms of every man in the room.' " [16]

But it is not for famous guests or brilliant social life that the hall is remembered. In December, 1860, the tension then existing between the North and the South had reached the breaking-point. South Carolina called a convention to consider seceding from the Union. It met at Columbia, but from fear of smallpox in that city adjourned to Charleston, where it assembled in the St. Andrew's Hall.[17] Here, at 1:15 P.M., December 20, 1860, by a unanimous vote, the ordinance was passed by which the state withdrew from the United States. (It was signed in the South Carolina Institute Hall on Meeting Street.) Soon the bells were ringing as if for fire, and the *Mercury's* newsboys were running with an extra wet from the press, scooping the world with the news: "The Union is Dissolved!" [18]

Twelve months later, the conflagration of December 11-12, 1861, swept diagonally across the city, and the hall was burned to the ground.[19]

The St. Andrew's Society has never rebuilt but meets in the South Carolina Society Hall. Nothing of their building remains behind the spear-headed iron fence except the pavement that once led to the front door, and here the flagstones are being thrust apart by the roots of a tree.

WILLIAM JAY

In Charleston c. 1819-1822

WILLIAM JAY WAS ENGLISH, A NATIVE OF BATH in Somersetshire. He was the oldest son of the Rev. William Jay, a widely known dissenting preacher, and his wife Anne Davies.[1] Lively and witty in the midst of a strictly brought-up household, the child was doubtless happier away from home than in it (after childhood, he was there very little), but it was not an unlucky place for a clever boy to grow in. There he was assured adequate schooling, and what is sometimes more, acquaintance with an unusual man—in this case, his father.

The Rev. William Jay (1769-1853) was a self-made man. The son of a Wiltshire stonecutter and mason, he was apprenticed to his father, and with him worked in the erection of Fonthill Abbey, that extraordinarily fantastic Gothic structure put up by the writer, William Beckford. His studiousness won him the aid of a non-conformist minister, and he broke away from building to obtain remarkable popularity, first as a "boy preacher" of about sixteen, and later as pastor of Argyle Independent Chapel at Bath.[2] His deep convictions were expressed in fervent (and prolonged) oratory. Yet he was far from being forbidding, and one catches glimpses of Saturday afternoon rambles when, conscious that Sunday would prove rigorous, he threw prizes, "apples, books, and pence", to his children as they scampered about the fields.[3]

Bath by the green-flowing Avon was an excellent environment for the future architect. He could not share in its fashion, but the setting was there for him to enjoy. Filled with Palladian buildings designed by John Wood, it was exceptionally well-built. Here young Jay must have caught the feeling for mass which his houses were to show.

The boy's natural bent toward architecture was respected, and he was apprenticed to an architect and surveyor in London.[4] He stayed there a short while after his time was out, and then set sail for America, influenced by the fact that his elder sister Anne had married one of the Bolton family of Savannah, Georgia.[5] Jay arrived at Savannah in December, 1817.[6]

Introduced to the society of the city at a time when prosperity was giving impetus to building, he did not lack clients. Between his arrival and 1822, he designed a quantity of good buildings.[7]

The Savannah Branch of the Bank of the United States no longer stands. With its unpedimented portico and round-headed door and windows, it was an unarchaeological but dignified adaptation of the classic. A copperplate on the cornerstone named Jay as architect, and gave the date 1820, perhaps that of the finished building.[8]

He may have designed the Savannah Theatre, also, another building which has been destroyed.[9]

A few of his dwellings have had a happier fate. Jay handled decoration fearlessly, and these houses, in Regency style, own a wealth of detail, striking staircases, curved rooms, porticoes, and balconies. Perhaps the staircase of the Owens-Thomas house would be more impressive if one did not come so suddenly upon it, if the hall were larger—the eye needs a running start. But the treatment of this shallow hall itself, where deliberately restrained pilasters are used to set off the gilded Corinthian capitals of the columns, is superb.

The Scarborough house, now a negro school, has undergone great alterations. The Telfair house, now the Telfair Academy of Arts and Sciences, has been added to, but with discretion. Here is an octagonal room, and a notable drawing-room with rounded ends, an imposing cornice, and two marble mantelpieces by Frazee on the same wall.

The Bulloch or Habersham house (razed to make way for a municipal auditorium), had a semi-circular portico, through which one entered the hall where a spiral staircase sprang upward, supported by a group of Corinthian columns. This house had a perfectly circular bedroom.

The actor Tyrone Power was certainly referring to Jay's work when he noticed on his visit to Savannah in 1834 that:

"Here are, however, several very ambitious-looking dwellings, built by a European architect for wealthy merchants during the palmy days of trade; these are of stone or some composition, showily designed, and very large, but ill-adapted, I should imagine, for summer residences in this climate. They are mostly deserted, or let for boarding-houses, and have that decayed look which is so melancholy, and which nowhere arrives sooner than in this climate." [10]

The phrase "of stone or some composition" is interesting. Rough-casting may have been meant, or possibly, though not probably, tabby. The basement (though not the rest) of the Owens house is tabby.

Jay belongs to Savannah, rather than to Charleston, but the beginning of 1819 found him in the latter city. He probably went back and forth between them.

The *Courier* of January 5, 1819, held this advertisement:

"TO BE SOLD BY PRIVATE CONTRACT,

A Marine Villa, pleasantly situated on Sullivan's Island, on the east side of the Fort, from which it is well protected on one side, and has a commanding view of the ocean. Great care has been taken in selecting the materials, and it is framed expressly to withstand a gale. It is erected in the Gothic order, and consists of a Saloon 30 by 20 feet, two Chambers 16 by 14 feet, and two Verandas 14 by 13 feet; the principal story is 13 feet, and stands 8 feet out of ground. Further particulars may be known, and the drawings seen at the office of Mr. Wm. Jay, Architect, Tradd-street.

Jan 3"

The villa is gone, and its site became part of the army reservation. Since Jay's known work in Savannah shows no Gothic influence, it seems likely that he found this order already well established in Charleston (where it had long been popular for coach houses and similar buildings) and adapted himself to the fashion.

A year later in 1820, he placed a card in the *Courier:*

"NOTICE

WILLIAM JAY offers his services to the inhabitants of Charleston, and the State generally, in his profession as an ARCHITECT. Any command left at his office in Jones Building, St. *Michael's Alley*, will meet with immediate attention.

January 1." [11]

The end of this month brought news of him from near Columbia, South Carolina, when the Board of Public Works for the state was

organized at a meeting held at General Davie's house on the Catawba River, January 24. The officers without salaries were Joel R.
Poinsett, president of the Board, William Rubinson Davie and
Abram Blanding, commissioners, and William Jay, architect. Sub-
jects considered included inland navigation, the Saluda roads, and
public buildings at Charleston, and it was decided to erect during
the year court houses at Sumter, Chester, Fairfield, and Marlboro,
and jails at Chester, Marlboro, Abbeville, and Pendleton.[12]

The magnitude of this appointment appears when one considers
that the court houses and jails by Robert Mills (qv) which are found
throughout South Carolina were designed by him for the Board of
Public Works. Had Jay remained on the board, the state would
almost certainly be filled with his creations instead of Mills'.

What happened, then, to make Jay leave the board and Mills
join it? The affair is obscure; just as it is unknown whether Jay drew
any plans for the board which came to fruition. Certainly, his designs for the public buildings at Charleston were not carried out.

These are mentioned in the *Courier* of February 11, 1820:

"A beautiful Model of a series of Buildings, designed by MR.
JAY, the Architect, for the East and North sides of the public
Square on Broad and Meeting Streets, and submitted to Council
for their approbation, may now be seen at the City Hall."

Apparently, Council did not approve. Though Jay's plan would
have prevented Mills' beautiful Fireproof Building from being
erected (on its present site, at least), this refusal to follow Jay's
design would seem to have been Charleston's loss.

As it is, nothing in the state has been identified positively as his
work. But he was in Charleston, whether continuously or at inter-
vals, some time longer. The *Courier* of December 19, 1820, printed
a notice from the painter Morse, later famous as inventor of the
telegraph:

"Mr. Morse Has returned to Charleston, and has his Painting
Room in the rear of Jones' Boarding House, in the Room recently
occupied by Mr. Jay, the Architect. Entrance from St. Michael's
Alley."

In this same year of 1820, the miniaturist and amateur architect,
Charles Fraser (qv) painted a miniature of a Mr. Jay, probably the
architect, for which he received fifty dollars.[13]

Ashley Hall School, formerly the Duncan-Nicholson House, 172 Rutledge Avenue.

Ashley Hall School. *(Clarke)*

Ashley Hall School. From a watercolor painted about 1900 by Beatrice Witte Ravenel.

Jay next appears among the original directors of the South Carolina Academy of Fine Arts, organized at Charleston in 1821.[14] The Academy built a wooden structure on Broad Street [15] to house their exhibits, and Jay may have planned it, though this is conjecture. It no longer stands, but is known to have been fairly large.

Finally, he appeared in the directory of 1822:

"Jay William, architect, 59 Church."

Soon after, he returned to England, where he met with disappointments. His failure to succeed may have been partly his own fault—at least, his father wrote that the architect

. . ."Besides professional talent and cleverness, had a large share of wit and humor, qualities always dangerous and commonly injurious to the possessor. So it was, alas! here. His comic powers drew him into company not the most friendly to youthful improvement. He was led into expense by his admirers and flatterers, and for awhile left the path in which he had been taught to go." [16]

We may smile at the Reverend's phrases, and discount his testimony, but this question of expense was serious. Jay by now had a wife, Louisa Coulston from Henley, and a family to support, and he was glad to accept from Lord Glenelg of the Colonial Department the offer of a government appointment at Mauritius in the Indian Ocean.[17]

To this island then, chiefly known as the home of the dodo (extinct even at that date), and the scene of *Paul and Virginia*, Jay emigrated. There, to quote his father again, "his taste and talents met with full encouragement, and his prospects were bright." [18]

Not for long, unfortunately. He was saddened by the death of a son, "little Willy", one of those saintly children of a by-gone day who were made the subject of tracts. (The one written by Louisa Jay about her boy was especially popular.) Soon after, Jay's own death occurred. His widow, with two surviving children, returned to England where she scraped a living by teaching.[19]

Though Jay's influence in Charleston was small, he was not forgotten there. In 1847, "G" (who remains unidentified), reviewing in the *Courier, a History of Architecture* by a Mrs. L. C. Tuthill, declared that "an allusion at least" should have been made to "the private edifices erected by the late Mr. Jay in Savannah." [20]

Vague but persistent tradition says that the dwelling, now 26 Meeting Street, was built by "an English architect", perhaps Jay. A parallel tradition ascribes it to Mills. Tradition holds also that the dwelling at the southeast corner of Meeting and Charlotte Streets, no longer standing, was built by "the same architect" who designed 26 Meeting Street.

The building in Charleston which most resembles Jay's work is No. 172 Rutledge Avenue, now Ashley Hall School for Girls. A Regency villa, it was built when the area still was suburban. It has a riot of curved lines, the curved rooms and curved doors characteristic of his houses, an oval staircase and an apse under the portico. Its exact date has not been determined. The first owner, Patrick Duncan, bought the land in 1798,[21] added a strip to the south in 1807,[22] and was listed in the directory as living on "Pinckney st. cannons' borough" (the present Rutledge Avenue) as early as 1806. Obviously, he was not then in the present structure, (no one has assigned it so early a date) but in an older building. Before 1829, however, he had his villa, for in February of that year, by which time he was residing in Liverpool, he sold it.[23]

Tradition credits this building to "an English architect", and this belief was stated as a fact by an architectural writer, C. R. S. Horton, in 1902.[24] The best argument, however, for this dwelling's being of Jay's design is the dwelling itself.

Another Charleston house should be mentioned, and it too, is a striking one—No. 48 Elizabeth Street, the Robinson-Rhett house, built sometime between 1817 and 1825 [25] and therefore in Jay's American period. The double staircase with iron balusters, just within its entrance, is strongly reminiscent of his work.

Then too, the façade of the Hampton-Preston house at Columbia, South Carolina faintly resembles that of the Owens-Thomas house at Savannah.

ROBERT MILLS

August 12, 1781—March 3, 1855

ROBERT MILLS, KNOWN THROUGHOUT THE NAtion as the architect of the Washington Monument, belongs to South Carolina, first because it was his birthplace, secondly, because examples of his most characteristic work are found throughout the state. These buildings have been comparatively overlooked, as is only natural, since they are scattered and many are off the beaten track of tourists. Moreover, students of his architecture find so much that is his available elsewhere. Mills himself wrote that:

> "The professional labours of the author are distributed in various parts of the Union. The principal part of the designs . . . were executed in Philadelphia, Baltimore, Washington, Richmond, Charleston, Columbia, Camden and other towns of South Carolina, Augusta, Ga., New Orleans, Mobile, etc., etc." [1]

Yet one can hardly know his work well without following it from countyseat to countyseat and observing the felicity with which Mills rang the changes on his austere public buildings. Here may be seen his sweeping and unarchaeological treatment of classic themes, fire-resistant construction, use of high basements and of porticoes, frequently set upon arcades, and the skill with which he tempered the severity of his facades with flights of curving steps. One finds also more superficial but singularly consistent characteristics, the round-headed single windows and flat-headed triple windows, often set in panels, and the courses, niches, blind arches, ventilating skylights, and cupolas in which he delighted.

Mills was born in or near Charleston in 1781 and lived there until c. 1800. In 1804, he returned and practiced briefly in Charleston. Again, in March, 1817, he visited that city. In 1820, he came back to South Carolina, and worked for the state until late in 1829, although his stay was broken in 1824 by a trip to Baltimore. Practically all of his existing work in South Carolina belongs to the 1820-29 period, the Marine Hospital in Charleston being an exception, the plans of which were sent from Washington in 1831. Mills made his home in Washington until his death in 1855.

The architect was one of several children of William Mills, a native of Dundee, Scotland, who spent most of his life in Charleston.[2] He was a well-to-do tailor. In 1790, we find the Orphan House commissioners thanking him for lending a workman to cut out the orphans' clothes gratis.[3] He married, September 24, 1772, Ann Taylor,[4] descendant of a provincial governor and local patriarch, Landgrave Thomas Smith. Ann died in January, 1790, when Robert was eight. The widower married in April, 1795, Rebecca Shrewsberry, a widow.[5]

William Mills gave his clever son an education at the College of Charleston,[6] which, however, was at that time merely a grammar school. The boy is said to have studied also in the architecture class taught by James Hoban (qv).[7] If this is true, Robert Mills' interest in the art began early. Hoban left Charleston about June, 1792, when the boy was not yet eleven.

Others beside Hoban professed to teach architecture in Charleston during Mills' boyhood. The advertisement of the "Charleston Academy" was signed by one Thomas Mills, and while there is nothing to show that he was related to the architect (who, however, had a brother of that name), or that Robert was a pupil, it seems to deserve quoting. After listing the usual courses offered, it stated that:

> . . ."Moreover, a gentleman has been lately engaged to teach the principles of modern architecture, with drawing and designing. The ingenious teacher of these principles will not confine himself to theoretic illustrations alone; they will be practically explained by proportionate models of various buildings, which are now preparing for the purpose. At the commencement of this very useful undertaking, the complete frame of a double three story house, in minature, (sic) will be raised . . . by this method, it will be evident, that a person may soon become a complete architect or master builder, without subjecting himself to that labor and fatigue with which the acquisition of this science is generally attended." [8]

Mills was later to claim that he was the only native-born American who had studied to be an architect, the others having entered the profession from various trades.

When Mills arrived in Washington, apparently about 1800, he found Hoban working on the White House, and through him met

Thomas Jefferson. Mills draughted some plans for the latter's country house, Monticello, which, however, was designed by Jefferson himself. To quote Mills:

"I had . . . been persuing my studies in the office of the Architect of the President's House, etc., and there were no architectural works to be had, Mr. Jefferson kindly offered me the use of his library, where I found several of these works, all of Roman character, principally Palladios, of whom Mr. Jefferson was a great admirer. During this period, I made some plans and elevations for his Mansion at Monticello, according to his views of interior arrangement . . . this was in 1801." [9]

On Jefferson's advice, Mills next studied under Benjamin Henry Latrobe, whom he was later to term "one of the first of Architects in any country".[10] Mills became one of three assistants who aided Latrobe in building the Capitol at Washington.[11] In so doing, he commenced an association with a structure which was to occupy much of his thought in later years.

Mills thus met at the outset of his career both Jefferson, originator of the Classic school of architecture in America, and Latrobe, who brought the Greek Revival from England to this country. He may also have been influenced to a less degree and in a different direction, by the engineer, Christian Senf (qv), whom he was to praise in his *Statistics of South Carolina*. Both Senf and Latrobe built canals, and internal navigation was to prove a very large bee in Mills' bonnet.

In April, 1802, Mills' father died and was buried in the Scotch Presbyterian churchyard at Charleston, where his tombstone may be seen today. He left the architect three houses in Charleston, 273 acres in St. Thomas' Parish, two negro men named Dundee and Jeffrey, a bond and mortgage, the principal of which was worth £637, and "all my unmade up cloathing". Did he feel that, should architecture prove unsuccessful, tailoring might be an anchor to windward? The will also mentions Robert's stepmother, Rebecca; his brothers, Thomas and Henry; his sister, Sarah; and a William Mills, (described only as the "son of the late Mrs. Lewis") whose identity has not been established.[12] Sarah later became Mrs. George Lusher.[13]

In the same year, 1802, Mills submitted a plan in the competition for the first building of the South Carolina College (now the University of South Carolina), to be erected at Columbia. No plan was accepted by the committee, who compiled their own, deciding, however, that "inasmuch as the plan adopted is founded upon some principles taken from the plans offered by Mr. Mills and Mr. Clark, and those artists have taken great pains to prepare an acceptable plan", the reward would be divided between them, $150.00 to each.[14] Clark was Edward Clark, the contractor who built the college.

In 1804, Mills returned to Charleston, where he designed the Circular (Congregational) Church, not without advice from the congregation. This building is said to have afforded the first example in this country of the pantheon-like, auditorium form of church.[15] Mills was to follow this plan again more than once, and it comes as a shock to read that its use was not his own suggestion, but came from a pious lady.

Martha Laurens Ramsay was the sister of Henry Laurens who is said to have been a patron of Hoban's, and the wife of the historian, David Ramsay, M.D. As a very devout person, she became the subject of a memoir written by her husband shortly after her death in 1811. On pages twelve and thirteen of the little volume occurs this astounding footnote:

> "Among her private papers has been found, accurately drawn by her hand, the first plan of the present circular church, but without the western projection afterward added by others. This preceded the elegant plan of the ingenious architect, Mr. Mills, and was introductory to the motion which ultimately terminated in the adoption of the circular plan."

It is noteworthy that the doctor disclaimed for his wife the portico which Mills would not own either, stating in his *Statistics* that it lacked the proportions recommended by the architect. Obviously, more than one or two persons had a hand in planning the Circular Church. Thomas Bennett (qv) may have been among them. But Mrs. Ramsay's contribution must be discounted. No doubt Mills shelved her design promptly, and proceeded to draw his own "elegant plan".

The church was begun in 1804 and finished in 1806.[16] Reichardt (qv) added a spire in 1838; E. C. Jones (qv) remodeled it in 1853; the fire of 1861 destroyed it.

Mills continued to use the auditorium form for churches. One in Philadelphia, built in 1808-1809, was considered a model of acoustics.[17] The case of the Charleston church was different. The 1829 directory wrote that, "The echo created by the lowness of the floor, or the rotundity of the building, produces a disagreeable effect, particularly to one seated in the gallery, and not accustomed to the voice of the officiating minister." Some of the changes made in 1853 were intended to diminish the echo.[18] Mills' Monumental Church in Richmond has echoes also, but they are of a more secret nature, enabling occupants of two particular pews on opposite sides of the building to converse in whispers. There was nothing private about the echo in the Charleston church.

While this building was going up, Mills drew plans for an elongation of the east end of St. Michael's, and explained them, March 11, 1804, to the vestry, who unanimously voted him thanks and a reward of sixty dollars.[19] These drawings are still owned by the church. On June 20, estimates were advertised for.[20] Then, probably for financial reasons, matters halted. St. Paul's, Radcliffeboro', designed by the Gordons (qv), and begun in 1811, absorbed some of the congregation, and the extension of St. Michael's was never carried out. Only a rabid admirer of Mills can fail to feel that the colonial church had a narrow escape.

The high pulpit, rather like a bridge with steps at each end, which he had planned for St. Michael's, was adapted years later in his church at Camden, South Carolina.

In 1807, Mills, then in Philadelphia, sold his South Carolina real estate, which brought him $5,800.00.[21] He was contemplating marriage, but it was only when he secured letters of recommendation from Jefferson and Governor Hamilton of South Carolina that he was able to obtain from General John Smith of Hackwood Park, Frederick County, Virginia, the hand of his daughter, Eliza Barnwell Smith. They were married on October 15, 1808. Four daughters were born of this marriage.[22]

The next few years found Mills practicing in Philadelphia, Baltimore, and Richmond. Two of several buildings in the last city deserve especial notice, the Monumental Church for its fire-resistant construction, typically Millsian, and the Wickham house, now part of the Valentine Museum, for its atypically lavish decoration.

The church (built 1812-14) stands on the site of the Richmond Theatre which had burned in 1811 with the loss of over seventy lives. Mills' persistent attempts at fireproof building are generally thought to have been prompted by this tragedy, but more likely, it merely strengthened earlier opinions. As a boy in Charleston, he must have seen the great fire of 1796, and in March, 1804, when he was in that city, an attempt had been made to burn his brother, Thomas's, store.[23]

The stone Monumental Church, an octagon to which is attached a portico, is exceptional in almost every detail. The Doric columns *in antis* are reminiscent of the unfinished columns of the temple at Cnidus, with flutes indicated only at the top and bottom of the shafts. Instead of triglyphs, the frieze bears bas-reliefs intended either for lachrymatories or burial urns. Acroteria on the pediment are echoed on the window cornices. Handled less masterfully, the church could have been a freak; instead, it has distinction.

Where the church is formal and solemn, the Wickham house is formal and gay. Built in 1812, it resembles in spirit the Regency dwellings which William Jay (qv) was to design later in Savannah. Exact documentary proof of Mills' authorship is said to be lacking, but the house has several of his characteristics, while one small but unusual detail, the continuous riser-end decoration which simulates a vine, is found likewise in the Second Brockenbrough house, now the Confederate Museum, known to be by Mills.

In 1814, the architect was again in Philadelphia, where he held the office of secretary of the Columbian Society of Artists.[24]

July 4, 1815, saw the beginning of his lofty monument to Washington at Baltimore, a column topped by a statue and set on high ground to gain all possible altitude.[25] It derives from the Napoleon column in the Place Vendôme, without aping it.

Mills revisited South Carolina briefly in March, 1817, attending a Race Ball (given by the Jockey Club) at Charleston, and inspecting the Santee Canal, but soon was north again.[26]

In 1820, he returned.[27] By now he had won recognition, and his plans were sought after. The earliest of his works of this period is probably the First Baptist Church in Charleston, the plans of which must have been sent on ahead, since they were in the city by the spring of 1819, although in his unfinished autobiography, Mills included the church among the buildings designed by him while in South Carolina.

The following notice appeared April 20, 1819:

"THE SUBSCRIBERS

Are ready to receive Proposals, for erecting a New Church, in Charleston, the dimensions being 84 by 60 feet in the extreme, the walls to be of brick, the roof covered with slate. Bricklayers,

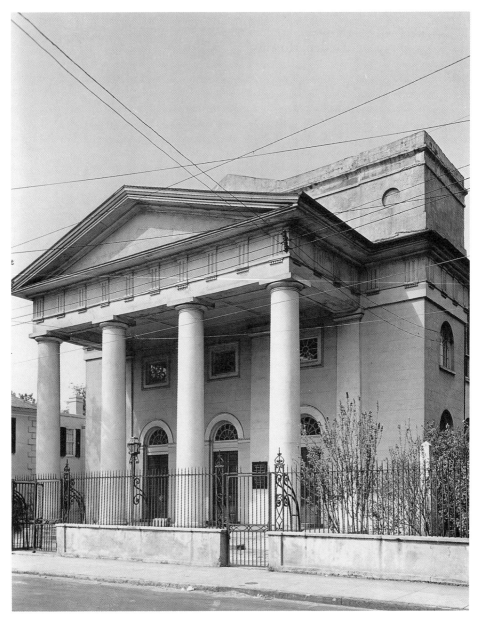

The First Baptist Church, 61 Church Street, built 1819-1822.
Robert Mills, architect.

Carpenters, Plasterers, Painters and Glaziers, who may be desirous of executing the work in their several departments, will, by calling at No. 117 Church street, have an opportunity of inspecting the plans . . . . Undertakers to find all the material in their respective departments" . . . .[28]

The cornerstone was laid September 16, 1819,[29] and the church was dedicated January 17, 1822.[30] It is impressive, even without the cupola it once had, and Mills in his *Statistics* did not hesitate to call it "the best specimen of correct taste in architecture of all the modern buildings in this city".

On December 20, 1820, Mills succeeded William Jay (qv) on the Board of Public Works of South Carolina. He was not listed as architect, however, but as one of the acting commissioners, the other board members being Joel R. Poinsett, president, Abram Blanding, acting commissioner, John Couty, engineer, and William H. Gibbes, Jr., secretary.[31] Mills was to spend much of his time on inland navigation plans, some of which were carried out. But as member of the committee on public buildings,[32] he turned out designs like a machine, with this difference, that there was no rubber stamp about them.

However, he was soon removed from a post in which he was most useful, that of superintendent of public buildings. The *Courier* of February 27, 1824 wrote in this connection that

. . . "Architecture . . . can accurately be known by those only, who have studied it professionally.—Such men are invaluable citizens of a state, contributing where they are successfully employed to its character for refinement, as well as its facilities for convenience. We have such a man, a native of South-Carolina. We invited him from Baltimore, where he was profitably employed and remunerated, into the service of this State. As superintendent of public buildings, Mr. Mills, the gentleman alluded to, saved the State upwards of $30,000, and yet erected very superior edifices. Upwards of a year since, the Legislature thought proper to substitute another gentleman in his place, without the shadow of any imputation against him; and at the last Session, they abolished the office altogether—leaving the design and superintendence of the public buildings to gentlemen not professional men, but chosen because they enjoy the good opinion of the Legislature.

"We regret this for many reasons. It was ungrateful treatment towards Mr. Mills—it will injure the tasteful character of our public buildings; and we know from facts communicated to us, that it will increase their cost at least 20 per cent. So much for false economy."

Early in 1824, the legislature appointed Mills one of the commissioners of public buildings for the district of Charleston. Frederick Wesner (qv) was a colleague.[33] Moreover, Mills continued to work for the state on inland navigation, the compilation of his splendid atlas (a remarkably accurate and useful work recently republished), and of a book to accompany it, his *Statistics of South Carolina*, which appeared in 1826. It derives much from Ramsay's history of the state, and abounds with errors in regard to history and natural history, but is valuable in giving descriptions of buildings, and in displaying Mills' character. In writing of his home, he revealed himself. He showed his opinion of war ("the school of every vice"), his belief in education for girls (though he did not say of what it should consist), his delight in the gushing streams and giddy heights of the Up Country, and his limited appreciation of any architectural style other than his own.

Notwithstanding the love of his state which glows between the lines of the *Statistics*, Mills did his best to leave her, writing numerous letters in an effort to wrest employment from the Federal government. Ironically, when he did receive such an appointment, it was in the administration of a self-confessed South Carolinian, Andrew Jackson.[34] The architect went to Washington, D.C., by the end of 1829,[35] leaving South Carolina architecture incomparably richer than it had been at his arrival.

Mills' buildings in the South suffer from the fact that they are generally seen by visitors in winter or spring, whereas they look their best in blazing August. Under a sun like that of Provence, the architect need not emphasize ornament; the unsubtle light does it for him, throwing the least raised surface into high relief, and giving unwonted values to color.

Court houses and jails lead the list. Today it is hard to determine how many he designed, and what percentage of his plans were executed. A few buildings of this kind are ascribed to him without documentary proof, and while internal evidence points to Mills, they may have been the work of imitative contemporaries, the "gentlemen not professional men" alluded to by the *Courier*. Others, however, are undoubtedly by Mills.

In February, 1822, he had advertised for estimates on work and materials for court houses in Williamsburg, Newberry, Greenville, and York counties, and jails in York, Lancaster, Union, and Spartanburg.[36] He is known to have designed the court house at Camden, also.[37] In addition, he is said to have done those at Winnsboro and Marlboro,[38] while the appearance of the court houses at Walterboro, Conway, and Georgetown indicates that they were his designs.

Economy foreordained that these buildings should be un-adorned, a state of affairs agreeable to the architect. Having proved in the Wickham house that he could handle decoration, he had chosen austerity, preferring a simplified Greek Doric to the Corinthian, and the Greek key to the anthemion. In their formality, his public buildings have a mathematical quality like that found in music, and it would hardly be too much to compare them, with their variations and repetitions, to a fugue. This figure would scarcely have displeased Mills who delighted in organ music and even in the long drawn-out sound of the stagecoach horn in the woods.[39]

Some of these buildings, Greenville's court house, for instance, are gone. But much remains. In the Williamsburg county court house at Kingstree, Mills' fire-resistant construction was put to the test in 1883 when the second story caught fire. Boddie's *History of Williamsburg* tells the outcome:

> "When the fire was discovered, the county officials who had their records in their offices on the ground floor very quickly removed their books and papers from these offices. The second story was burning for three days, during which time the officials learned that their offices were fire proof and began using them before the embers above had ceased to burn. It was then re-membered that Architect Robert Mills, the same out of whose mind had come plans for the Treasury Building and the Washington Monument, in the District of Columbia, had erected this old Court House in his younger days and that he builded well."

The court house at Camden shows a colossal portico rising from the ground floor, without the customary Millsian basement. Porticoes on basement arcades are found on the court house at Walterboro, now dwarfed by two modern wings, and on the court house at Conway, a charming little building, unstuccoed, with bricks laid in running bond (an early example for coastal South Carolina). The court house at Georgetown with its six lofty columns was remodeled in 1854 by George E. Walker (qv).

In March, 1822, came Mills' advertisement for estimates for re-modeling the Charleston jail,[40] on Magazine Street, a Newgate-like pile of unknown authorship dating from about 1803. He wrote in 1826 that:

"There has lately been added to it a four story wing building, devoted exclusively to the confinement of criminals. It is divided into solitary cells, one for each criminal, and the whole made fireproof." [41]

Today Mills' annex stands only three stories high. The bricks are laid in running bond, but with only three rows of stretchers between the headers. The crenellation and dripstones on both old jail and annex may have been added by Mills, but there is a chance that the responsibility for them rests on Barbot & Seyle (qv), who re-modelled the institution c. 1855.

In spite of Mills' solitary cells, solitary confinement does not seem to have been carried out strictly in the Charleston jail,[42] though it amounted almost to a mania with penologists of the time. Mills used a cellular plan for the Louisiana penitentiary also, which he designed while in South Carolina.[43]

In April, 1822, he advertised for estimates for building the "Fire Proof Offices" (the County Record Building, popularly called the Fireproof Building) at Charleston.[44] It was finished by 1827.[45] Sternly beautiful, perhaps the most beautiful of his buildings, it contains an oval hall, lit by a skylight, and marked by a curving stair of some steepness. (Mills liked mountaineering and it shows in his staircases.) The exterior relies almost altogether on proportion for effect, even the wrought iron being severely patterned.

In 1822, also, the Lunatic Asylum at Columbia was begun, and in the summer, we find Mills toasting the governor at a dinner which celebrated the laying of the cornerstone.[46]

For display, the asylum boasts a colossal Tuscan hexastyle portico. In plan, it consists of a central block from which long symmetrical wings extend obliquely. Its roof garden has been hailed as the first in America, but Mills' ingenuity and humanitarianism were shown in more than one feature progressive for that date. To quote the *Courier:*

. . . "Not the smallest appearance of a prison is manifest in the building. *Security* is agreeably disguised under appearances familiar to the eye in every private house. The iron bars take the

The wing added to the old County Jail, 21 Magazine Street, between 1822 and 1826.
Robert Mills, architect.

The Fireproof Building, 100 Meeting Street, built between 1822 and 1827, now the
headquarters of the South Carolina Historical Society. Robert Mills, architect.
The steps, originally curved, were changed after the earthquake of 1886.

Staircase, Fireproof Building.

similitude of sashes; the hinges and locks of the doors are all secret; so that every temptation is put out of the way to make an escape. The means, in the winter, of heating the number of rooms which we have noticed are as simple as they are effectual —consisting of two furnaces, which are built in the basement story, contiguous to the kitchens. The medium used for conveying to the rooms the heat generated in these furnaces, is atmospheric air. This is made to pass, through tubes, over heated surfaces in the midst of the stove or furnace, which afterwards is collected into reservoirs, and from these distributed by flues to the different stories. The principle laid down by Mr. Mills, (the architect of this building) to effect the object in question, with economy, is this: to make the corridors into which the cells open, the great reservoirs of heat—the temperature of the air of these cells would be soon changed and partake of that of the corridors. Mr. M. adopted this mode of heating the cells and infirmaries of the Baltimore Hospital, with complete success. The *degree* of heat can be varied at pleasure." (Another advantage was found in) "the constant influx of a current of fresh air, thus rectifying the contaminated atmosphere of the rooms".[47]

The asylum cost more than had been expected,[48] and was long in building.

During part of 1823, Mills' time was appallingly wasted in arranging minor changes at the South Carolina College, such as "repairing the fences of the President and Professors' gardens".[49] This institution now treasures a tracing of a sketch which he made there in July of that year during the presence of a "double rainbow of a perfect segment". The monument to President Jonathan Maxcy, a shaft unveiled on the campus in 1827, was designed by Mills.[50]

In 1824, he began his powder magazines on Charleston Neck,[51] which he described in the *Statistics* as "nine in number, all of circular form, with conical roofs, and disposed in three ranges 130 feet apart." One roof was supported by a brick, mushroom-shaped column, which has been compared to the modernistic columns in the Chrysler building at the New York World's Fair of 1939.[52] Long abandoned to hoboes and criminals who sometimes sheltered in them, seven of the magazines remained into the 1940s, when their demolition was begun.

Mills visited Baltimore in 1824 in connection with his Washington Monument there, and in October presented an invitation from the town authorities of Columbia, to Lafayette, then on his Ameri-

Powder Magazines on Charleston Neck, begun in 1824. Robert Mills, architect.

Center column in the largest powder magazine on the Neck.
Robert Mills, architect.

can tour, to visit South Carolina. In the following summer, he met Lafayette again, when the latter dedicated the DeKalb Monument, designed by Mills, at Camden.[53]

Besides his public work, Mills had a private practice in South Carolina. He designed at least three houses of worship in addition to the First Baptist Church, already mentioned. St. Peter's Roman Catholic Church in Columbia he described as a "handsome brick church in the form of a cross; with a tower and spire in front; in the Gothic style of architecture."[54] It no longer stands. St. John's Church, Colleton, on John's Island, a Classic Revival structure, has also vanished except for one brick pier. Its specifications, published in 1923 by Samuel Lapham in the *Architectural Record*, make interesting reading, and show Mills' belief in roughcast, both for appearance and for preventing dampness. Another Classic Revival church, Bethesda Presbyterian in Camden,[55] fortunately still exists.

All over the state stand dwellings attributed to Mills without documentary evidence, which as a rule is scant in regard to private houses. The Second Ainsley Hall dwelling, however, in Columbia, is known to be his work.[56] Fiske Kimball interprets a Mills manuscript as saying that he designed the First Ainsley Hall dwelling, also,[57] though other authorities are less sure. The DeBruhl-Marshall house in Columbia, and the William Mason Smith house in Charleston, are sometimes credited to Mills.

After leaving South Carolina for Washington, Mills sent the plans for a Federal building, the Marine Hospital at Charleston, in 1831. He had previously designed like hospitals for New Orleans and other cities. It opened in 1834.[58] Here he used pointed arches and clustered columns on a lofty piazza to produce a crisp, unmediaeval Gothic, which owed little to the Strawberry Hill school, and certainly did not forecast that of the Victorian Gothic Revival. In this beautiful structure, doctors once poured incredible draughts of calomel and quinine down men already ill enough with yellow fever, while the dead wagon stood at the door, and the city prayed for frost.

One more building in South Carolina must be considered. This is the library at the University of South Carolina, built c. 1840, long thought to have been designed by the professors under the influence of Mills, as a tablet attests. Recently, the statement has been published that Mills designed it in imitation of Bulfinch's Old Library of Congress, since burned.[59] Unless documents can be produced to prove that Mills actually made the plan, it seems more likely that

The Old Marine Hospital, 20 Franklin Street, built between 1831 and 1834. Robert Mills, architect.

the professors designed the library, influenced both by Mills and Bulfinch. Imitation was hardly a weakness of Mills'—he preferred his own work to that of almost anybody. A dogged worker, sustained by large pinches of snuff, he considered every structure an exploit, and was generally right. This homely, blunt-featured, and reddish-haired man knew his own worth, which should not diminish it for others.

Mills' buildings outside of South Carolina are legion. In 1836, he was appointed architect of public buildings at Washington, serving until 1851. He planned the E Street front of the old Post Office there, the F Street front of the Patent Office, the long colonnade of the Treasury Building, and the Washington Monument, that trans-cendant obelisk, which, as executed, is somewhat lower than he in-tended, and lacks the pantheon planned to stand at its foot, but rears in the Washington sky with a dignity comparable to that of a snow-capped mountain. It was the tragedy of Mills' life that he died March 3, 1855, at his home on Capitol Hill, in Washington, while the monument was unfinished.[60]

Mills is remembered as an architect, but he was equally con-cerned with engineering, his interests embracing canals, swamp reclamation, waterworks, bridges, railroads, and to some degree, lighthouses. In 1821, he published *Inland Navigation, Plan for a great Canal between Charleston and Columbia, and for Connecting our Waters with Those of the Western Country,* and in 1822, *Inter-nal Improvement of South Carolina, Particularly Adapted to the Low Country.* His ideas were not carried out. In 1825, the city of Charleston gave a company headed by Mills the right to supply the city with water.[61] The scheme failed, but in 1850, long after he had left the state, the *Mercury* of Charleston printed four letters signed by "Robert Mills, of South Carolina, Engineer and Architect", urg-ing the construction of a water system, and suggesting the use of Edisto River water,[62] which Charleston employs today. His bridges included one over the Schuylkill near Philadelphia, regarded as a model of engineering. His book on lighthouses, *The American Pharos, or Light-House Guide,* was meant as an aid to navigators, but is interesting when one recalls that Mills had studied under Latrobe, himself a pupil of Smeaton who had won fame with the Eddystone Light.

As for railroads, Mills wrote in his unfinished autobiography that, having "induced" the introduction of railroads at Baltimore, he "returned to South Carolina and there presented the subject of the *Railroad System*, first to the Legislature, where it was treated as a *visionary* scheme, and secondly to the commercial interests of Charleston, where it met with a favorable response, and a charter was soon after obtained from the Legislature to form a company to construct such a road between Charleston and Hamburg on the Savannah River" ... The road was built, though Mills seems to have had no more to do with it. When completed in 1833, it was the world's longest passenger steam railroad.

Mills remained interested in railroads all his life, and even dreamed of a single-rail line, on which the cars were to hang on either side of a support, "saddlebags fashion", as one unsympathetic newspaper put it.[63]

A minor activity, that of writing guide books of Washington, D. C., proved unusually successful.

Mills has escaped the oblivion which has fallen over most of the architects of his native state. Not only was his merit greater, but he practiced in a wider field. His home has not forgotten him—a housing project in Charleston is named Mills Manor, and the certificate of registration of the South Carolina Board of Architectural Examiners is dedicated to him. His work in Washington won him a national reputation, and he is thought of, not as South Carolinian, or even as Southern, but as American.

Detail, gates of St. John's Lutheran Church.

FREDERICK WESNER
January 14, 1788—March 11, 1848

REDERICK WESNER'S CAREER FALLS INTO TWO parts. Before 1831, as architect and master builder, he set up well-proportioned buildings and serene Greek porticoes, and gave the courtyard of even his most massive structure a look of not ungraceful strength. In 1831 and after, first as captain of the night watch and then as head of the negro prison, he was grimly employed.

He was of German blood, but a Charlestonian. His father, Henry Philip Wesner, senior, is first heard of in 1775 when he became one of the original members of the German Fuseliers, a company raised in Charlestown on the eve of the American Revolution to oppose the British.[1] After the war, the elder Wesner kept an inn on King street,[2] and was fairly well-to-do. The Census of 1790 shows that he owned ten slaves. He died in March, 1795, leaving a widow, Barbara (born Legg), two sons and two daughters. They are listed in his will, made March 4, which contains the earliest known mention of Frederick, then aged seven.[3] Frederick's sister, Mary Susannah, was to become the mother of John H. Seyle (qv) of the firm of Barbot & Seyle, architects.

The boy was ten when Barbara Wesner died, on October 1, 1798, "after a very painful illness, which she bore with Christian fortitude."[4] From the terms of her will, which devised nothing to the Wesner children, it seems likely that she was merely their stepmother.[5]

Frederick was probably apprenticed to a carpenter, for as one he reappears, in the Directory of 1809. In 1813, he was in business with a Mr. Johnson,[6] but the partnership was of short duration, for by 1815 he was again working alone.

This year saw him engaged on what may have been his first important contract. The congregation of St. John's Lutheran Church, to which he belonged, had determined to replace their wooden building by a brick church. As was customary, the contracts for the brickwork and woodwork were divided, the former going to John,

Jr., and Henry Horlbeck (qv), while Wesner received that for the wood.[7] The church, which was dedicated January 8, 1818,[8] is an attractive building, with rich woodwork bordering the ceilings of the nave and apse. The *Mercury* of June 20, 1859, stated that Wesner "designed as well as built it", and while this evidence is much later than the building, it may well be correct.

In 1822, Wesner was elected warden, an official corresponding to the present-day alderman. The date was to make the post important, for in June a contemplated negro insurrection was discovered and barely averted. This plot, led by Denmark Vesey, a freed man, and Gullah Jack, a conjurer, planned the slaughter of every white male in Charleston. Measures were taken in haste. On the evening in question, June 16, the conspirators found a fore-armed city, with troops stationed at every important point.

Meanwhile, a "Committee of Vigilance and Safety" was chosen from the members of City Council. Wesner was one of those selected.[9] The official report of the trials of the ringleaders records the capture of Denmark Vesey:

> "As early as Monday, the 17th, he had concealed himself. It was not until the night of the 22d of June, during a perfect tempest, that he was found secreted in the house of one of his wives. It is to the uncommon efforts of Mr. Wesner, and Capt. Dove, of the City Guard, (the latter of whom seized him) that public justice received its necessary tribute in the execution of this man. If the party had been one moment later, he would, in all probability, have effected his escape the next day in some outward bound vessel." [10]

As Dove made the actual arrest, Wesner's part is not clear, but may have consisted of detective work.

Nevertheless, when Saby Gaillard, a free negro, went on trial for implication in the plot, "Mr. Wesner attending on his behalf as his friend" succeeded in saving his life. Saby was found guilty, but his sentence was transportation, not death.[11]

Alarmed at what might have occurred, the authorities, among other precautions, reorganized the old City Guard into a more efficient unit called the Municipal Guard (of which more later), and ordered the building of a "State Arsenal", a stronghold which might serve, moreover, as a place of security in case of need. This is the structure now known as the Old Citadel. The architect chosen was Wesner.[12]

Gates, St. John's Lutheran Church, designed by Abraham P. Reeves and executed in 1822 by Roh.

But before the State Arsenal was built. Wesner was to do other work. He was a member of several organizations, the German Friendly Society,[13] the Carpenters' Society (he was president in 1821),[14] and the South Carolina Society.[15] This last, then as now, met in their hall on Meeting Street. For them, Wesner designed the portico which was added to the building in 1825 at a cost of $3,500.[16] This addition is so much in harmony with the original structure as to appear an integral part—no mean accomplishment, for the hall was planned by Gabriel Manigault (qv). One may criticize the lack of entasis in the columns of the lower story, but the effect of the whole is successful. Samuel Gaillard Stoney has pointed out that it was suggested by the Agora at Pergamum.

In his history of the South Carolina Society, Professor Easterby praises the portico as "an excellent example of the sincerity with which ancient Greek designs could be applied in early nineteenth century America." [17]

Only the year before, Wesner's abilities had been questioned by an anonymous critic, whose letter, in the *City Gazette and Commercial Daily Advertiser*, was signed only "Trigliph." The iron fence which still protects the City Hall Square was about to be erected, and the letter-writer objected to the line it follows, which leaves undefended the street sides of the public buildings there. He wrote, in part:

> . . . "It is said that Mr. Wesner is the father of the present plan, if so I regret it, as it shows in him both a want of taste and judgment. Mr. Wesner may be a very good carpenter, but his abilities as an architect or civil engineer, I very much doubt, he has never been out of his native city, to my knowledge, and, therefore, can have no conception of what can be either useful or ornamental to a city" . . .[18]

This blast apparently had no effect, for officialdom continued to patronize Wesner.

In 1827, he designed, in the Adam style, the Medical College which stood at the northeast corner of Queen and Back (now Franklin) Streets.[19] It was of brick, and cost $15,000.[20] As built, it stood two stories high, with a tetrastyle portico, and urns on the parapet. The Ionic style was used throughout, in the columns and pilasters and in the doorway, and was repeated by the woodwork of the ground floor auditorium. The portico crashed to the ground in the earthquake of 1886,[21] and was never replaced. Badly neglected, the

Gates of Washington Square, commonly called City Hall Park, at
Meeting and Broad Streets, c. 1824.

building retained a vestige of dignity until torn down in 1938 to make room for part of a government housing project.

Meanwhile, the State Arsenal was begun. Mills described it in his *Statistics,* published in 1826:

"An extensive citadel, or fortified arsenal and barracks, is now erecting at the upper end of the city, on the site of the old tobacco inspection, where the principal stand of arms, &c. will be kept. The works will be guarded by bastions at the four angles, on which cannon will be mounted—the whole surrounded by a high wall." [22]

The directory of 1829 (published, however, in 1828) spoke of it as "nearly finished," and " a splendid building of its kind."

Not until the Arsenal was well on its way to completion was the last of the Tobacco Inspection removed. On June 27, 1828, a contractor, Thomas A. Vardell, was killed when a wall fell on him as he was pulling it down. [23]

By February, 1830, the Arsenal was up and ready for roughcasting. [24] As first constructed, it was a plain, two-story, brick affair with a wooden parapet. [25] The bricks, smallish and of various colors, were laid in English bond, the strongest bond of all, and the place was planned for stern utility rather than for appearance. Nonetheless, the arches enclosing the rectangular courtyard gave the interior a picturesque quality.

Albert Simons finds that the use of semi-circular arches of great thickness, unembellished by any architrave moldings around the face, and supported on massive Doric columns, is exceptional, but occurs in the background of David's painting, *The Oath of the Horatii,* and suggests that Wesner may have seen an engraving of this picture and associated its architectural forms with the ideas of military virtue and patriotism.

This arsenal in 1843 became the home of the South Carolina Military Academy, and remained so until 1922 when the college was removed to the Greater Citadel by the Ashley River. [26] During this time, the original building was twice made higher, and wings were added. These changes heightened the effect of the courtyard by superimposing two tiers of small arches above Wesner's large spans; but the exterior lost its original character when it was Gothicized by Edward B. White (qv). The place is now the Charleston County Center.

The South Carolina Society Hall, 72 Meeting Street. Designed about 1800 by Gabriel Manigault, it acquired this portico, by Frederick Wesner, in 1825.

The Old Citadel, Marion Square, completed about 1830. Frederick Wesner, architect. Originally it had only two stories.

The Quadrangle, the Old Citadel.

Wesner submitted a plan for the Marine Hospital, but that of Robert Mills was chosen.[27]

Ever since 1822, Wesner had held minor civic positions, but they had not been onerous enough to keep him from building. He was warden from Ward Four in 1822, '23, '25, and '26,[28] and at various times was commissioner of the poor house,[29] and of the water works (then merely experimental),[30] and on the committees on retrenchments,[31] and contracts.[32] He was a fire master in 1825,[33] and by 1826 had become president of the newly organized Phoenix Fire Engine Company,[34] one of the fancifully uniformed volunteer groups which were our ancestors' defense against conflagrations.

More to the point is the fact that Wesner was one of the Commissioners of Public Buildings in 1824, and thus came into close contact with Mills, also a member of the committee.[35]

But with the building of the State Arsenal, the first part of Wesner's life closed. It is true that he was among the contractors who rebuilt the market in 1833,[36] and that he was listed as one of the Commissioners of Public Buildings in the Directory of 1837-38. He also designed the Church of St. Thaddeus, at Aiken, South Carolina, built 1842-43.[37] But beginning with 1831, his chief employment was no longer architecture. In that year, he became captain of the Municipal Guard,[38] which has been mentioned as having been formed after the attempted insurrection. It was organized as a military unit rather than as a police force, and patrolled the city and the Neck nightly after nine o'clock in winter and ten in summer, arresting negroes who were out after curfew and having no few fights with seamen.

In the following year, Wesner was made master of the Work House, the negro prison.[39] The building, since destroyed, stood at the southwest corner of Magazine and Mazÿck (now Logan) Streets, and had once been the prison for whites, but had been superseded by a later structure—the present "Old Jail," now a part of the government housing project.[40] In the Work House, prisoners were punished by flogging or the treadmill, and order was maintained by negro overseers armed with cowhide whips.[41] Discipline was not entirely inhumane, and every autumn at the approach of cold weather, a newspaper notice warned the masters of imprisoned slaves to send them blankets, or these would be furnished by the city at the owners' expense.[42] The Work House had impressed the sightseeing Duke of Saxe-Weimar Eisenach in 1826 as better kept than the prison for whites.[43] Nevertheless, Wesner's connection with the institution proves that he was not thin-skinned. He held the position from 1832 through 1840.[44]

Besides having other interests, he was a plantation owner. The *Courier* of January 25, 1839, said:

> "FIRE—We regret to learn that the fine mansion of Frederick Wesner, Esq., on his plantation, in St. James, Goose Creek, was accidentally destroyed by fire a few nights since."

Wesner died on March 11, 1848,[45] at Aiken, South Carolina.[46] He left a widow, the former Elizabeth Abigail Reeves, sister of Abraham Paycom Reeves (qv), and a son and daughter.[47] He was buried in Charleston, back of St. John's Lutheran Church which, as a young man, he had helped to build.[48]

JOHN HORLBECK, JR., AND HENRY HORLBECK

September 24, 1771—February 26, 1846

October 27, 1776—December 18, 1837

L IKE THEIR FATHER, JOHN HORLBECK, AND LIKE their uncle, Peter, John Horlbeck, Jr., and his brother Henry were builders who sometimes drew their own plans. Their partnership was formed at least as early as 1801, and dissolved only on October 13, 1836.[1]

They built the German Friendly Society Hall, which stood on the west side of Archdale Street almost opposite Beresford (now Fulton) Street. The brothers were prominent in the society. John, Jr. had been president in 1800, and was to hold that office again, while Henry was likewise to head the organization more than once.[2]

The story of the hall has been told in the history of the society which the Reverend Dr. George J. Gongaware has written, based on the old minutes. The contract price was 1219 pounds sterling,[3] Charlestonians of that day still preferring to reckon in English money, despite the years which had elapsed since the Revolution. On March 11, 1801, the cornerstone was laid.[4] The society opened the building on December 16, 1801, with a "sumptuous and elegant dinner," while later in the day, "all the workmen who had been employed at the building were convened in the lower part of the house and there were liberally treated." [5]

In this hall, the society maintained a school, remarkable for its supply of scientific apparatus and the fact that girls as well as boys were taught its use, and here also they held meetings and festivities. In December, 1825, they entertained a royal guest, the Duke of Saxe-Weimar Eisenach, who wrote of the occasion:

> . . . "The party met at half past three o'clock . . . Two brothers, Messrs. Horlbeck, presided at the dinner, which was very well arranged. They had the politeness to nominate me an honorary member of the society" . . .[6]

The hall burned on September 17, 1864,[7] and not in the great fire of 1861, as is sometimes asserted.

[147]

In July, 1815, the Horlbecks contracted for the brickwork for St. John's Lutheran Church on Archdale Street, the woodwork being done by Frederick Wesner (qv), who may have furnished the plan. The church was dedicated January 8, 1818.[8]

Henry Horlbeck and another member of the family, E. Horlbeck, together built St. Stephen's Chapel, still standing on Anson Street, and may have been its architects. This building should not be confused with the earlier St. Stephen's, on Guignard Street, built by John Gordon (qv), which burned in 1835. Henry and E. Horlbeck, personally laid the cornerstone of the new chapel on St. Stephen's Day, December 26, 1835, and the consecration took place October 24, 1836.[9]

The Horlbecks built mainly, if not entirely in brick, and John, Jr., and Henry maintained an extensive brickyard at Boone Hall, a plantation in Christ Church parish, across the Cooper River from Charleston.

A large brick house at the southwest corner of Meeting and Calhoun Streets was said to have been the work as well as the property of the Horlbecks. As early as 1822, it was the home of John, Jr., and it remained in the family until 1884.[10] Three stories high on a lofty basement, it stood with its gable-end to the street in the single house manner, entrance being obtained through the downstairs piazza. The lavish woodwork was graceful rather than forceful; the windows had folding inside shutters, and the delicately carved piazzas, with columns supporting shallow arches, were among the most beautiful in Charleston. Staunchly mortared, this dwelling proved a tough nut for the wreckers who destroyed it in 1939.[11]

John, Jr.'s houses received a compliment from an unexpected quarter in 1812, when, having entered local politics, he was assailed by a member of the opposite camp who wrote in the long since defunct *Investigator* that—"Mr. Horlbeck is a good architect and mechanic and . . . he has contributed in a considerable degree to beautify our city, by erecting a number of fine brick buildings, but it is generally believed there was a *quid pro quo*" . . . .[12] This was a mild assertion for an old-fashioned campaign. Horlbeck's tombstone states that he "fulfilled faithfully and honorably the duties of many municipal offices and of the legislature." [13]

John, Jr., married in 1795, Elizabeth Lindauer, a girl of sixteen,[14] with whom he probably acquired the Lindauer tract near the Ashley River which he sold in 1800 to Dr. Edward Jones, since when it has been known as Jones.[15] Elizabeth died in 1803.[16]

St. Stephen's Church, 67 Anson Street, completed in 1836. Henry and E. Horlbeck built it and probably designed it.

John, Jr., died suddenly of apoplexy, February 26, 1846,[17] survived by his second wife, Maria.[18]

Henry Horlbeck, the younger member of the partnership, had attended the grammar school of the College of Charleston, leaving in 1792.[19] In 1808, he became president of the Charleston Mechanic Society, and served four terms.[20] He was a member of the board of firemasters, and a commissioner of the poor house and of markets.[21] In 1824, he was one of the "Commissioners for opening Streets, Lanes, Alleys, &c. Appointed by the Legislature,"[22] whose path, literal and figurative, was not made easy by the property owners who fought to hold every inch.

He had married in 1798 Margaret Buckingham,[23] who died in 1835.[24] They had eleven children.[25]

Henry Horlbeck died December 17, 1837, after some five weeks of illness.[26] His family for some time continued to build, and to conduct the brickyard at Boone Hall, which left their hands only in the present century. His miniature, owned today by a descendant, and painted by Geslain, shows a large nose, dark eyes and brows, graying hair, and humorous mouth.[27]

RUSSELL WARREN

August 5, 1783—November 16, 1860

R USSELL WARREN WAS A NEW ENGLANDER, BORN in Tiverton, Rhode Island, the son of Gamaliel and Ruth (Jenckes) Warren, and a descendant of Richard Warren who came over on the *Mayflower*. One of several brothers who were builders, he became a successful architect, working first in a continuation of the Adam tradition, before turning to the style of the Classic Revival.

It is questionable that he bridged the Great Pedee River in South Carolina, as is sometimes stated. However, the Warren truss, used in steel bridge construction, generally is attributed to him.[1]

He had a fondness for columns, porticoes, quoins, cupolas, for flankers attached to the main building by arcades, for fairly simple but effective interiors, and for dramatic spiral staircases. Warren's work in New England is well known. He built some of the most gracious dwellings in Bristol, and worked also at Providence, New Bedford, and Fall River.[2] He is much less well known in South Carolina, though he is said to have built extensively at Charleston.

He appeared in one Charleston directory, that of 1822, which termed him simply "carpenter." He called himself "housewright." [3] At that date, he lived at 4 Ellery Street,[4] probably in one of the wooden houses which he built there.

Two records of him are in the Mesne Conveyance Office at Charleston:

"Russel (sic) Warren to James Hamilton, Mortgage .... As it is out of my power to take up with Convenience the note for $130 Which I Gave to Jas. Hamilton Jur" [Junior] "agent for the Vesuvius Steam Mill for the Purchase of Lumber on the 12 July 1824 I have therefore requested the said J. H. to receive a new note for the am^t. which note he is to discount in the Bank U. S. until the last of next November by such renewals as may be necessary when I engage to take up the same in full & in order to Secure the same Jas. Hamilton In fully for his said endorsement I do hereby by these presents transfer and sell in plain &

The Nathaniel Russell House, 51 Meeting Street, built by 1809.

The Nathaniel Russell House.

open Market all my right title & Interest in a Lease hold with the improvements thereon of a Certain lot in Ellery Street belonging to the Estate of Nath[l]. Russell the possession of the same Secured to myself until the last November & then in the event of my paying said note in full this Memorandum of Sale to be null & Void. Charleston S° C[a] June 24 1824 Russel Warren." [5]

In the next year he sold the property:

"Russel Warren to Arthur Middleton, Conveyance . . . . Know all men by these presents that I Russel Warren of Bristol in the State of Rhode Island Housewright in consideration of the Sum of two thousand & six hundred Dollars to me in hand paid by Arthur Middleton of the City of Charleston in the State of S° Carolina Gentleman" . . . [hereby transfer] "all those two dwelling houses erected by me on Ellery Street in the City of Charleston aforesaid and on the land of Mrs. Sarah Russell together with all the fixtures placed by me erected as aforesaid to him the said Middleton his heirs and assigns . . . . 6 September 1825 . . . Signed Sealed, Delivered in the Presence of Nath[l]. Bullock State of Rhode Island." [6]

These houses no longer exist, all that neighborhood having been swept by fire in the 1830's.[7] The street itself, which ran between East Bay and Anson Street, was closed in 1840.[8]

From the similarity of names, one might suppose a relationship or connection to have existed between Russell Warren and Nathaniel Russell, mentioned above, who was likewise a Rhode Islander by birth, though he made Charleston his home.[9] The next step would be to wonder whether Warren designed the Nathaniel Russell house, 51 Meeting Street, built by 1809,[10] one of the loveliest dwellings in the city. No evidence, written or even traditional, exists to show that he did, but the house resembles the buildings of his early style, and the splendid staircase, set in a well at the side of the hall, is strikingly like that which he placed in The Mount, James De Wolf's magnificent house at Bristol, designed by Warren in 1808, and destroyed by fire in 1904.[11]

On the other hand, similarities of Russell's house to other Charleston buildings, particularly the Blacklock house and Vanderhorst Row, both dating from 1800, make it doubtful that Russell Warren was its architect.

One Charleston building may possibly be a product of his Classic Revival period. This is the brick Miller house, now 138 Went-

The Nathaniel Russell House.

The Miller House, 138 Wentworth Street, new in 1842. Perhaps by Russell Warren. (*Tom Peck*)

worth Street, new in 1842.[12] In its Temple of the Winds type of columns, (which here somehow have a faint Egyptian feeling, with the foliage seeming as much lotus as acanthus), in the heavy row of dentils under the roof, and in the shape, size, and disposition of panes in the second story windows, it resembles the wooden Shepard house, 19 Charles Field Street, in Providence, Rhode Island, designed by Warren about 1840.[13] The Miller house had a "very large Cistern, and well of water, the waters of which are conducted by means of pipes into the various buildings, where use and comfort may require them." (*Courier*, March 7, 1842.) This was an early mention of plumbing for Charleston although it was usual there by the 1850's.

CYRUS L. WARNER
Working 1839

BETH ELOHIM SYNAGOGUE, AT 90 HASELL STREET, is a beautiful and stately example of the Classic Revival, with an imposing portico and a domed ceiling. Built 1840-41, it replaces a Post-Revolutionary building which burned in the fire of 1838.

The building contract, still in existence, was signed in 1839 by the trustees and David Lopez, the contractor, a Charlestonian. It specifies that the structure be "of the plan and construction set forth in the design furnished to the Trustees by Cyrus L. Warner, architect, New York."

It is uncertain whether Warner visited Charleston or merely sent his plan. No other work of his is known locally, which is to be regretted, for his synagogue ranks high among the buildings of the city.

Beth Elohim Synagogue, 90 Hasell Street, built 1840-1841. By Cyrus Warner.

CHARLES FRASER

August 20, 1782—October 5, 1860

C HARLES FRASER'S NAME AWAKENS MEMORIES IN the world of American miniature painters, not in that of architects, into whose field he ventured seldom and then, somewhat anachronistically, as an amateur in an age when these had become scarce. It is his work as a painter which has kept him from neglect; his life has been written, his technique studied, and the better part of his sketchbook, begun when he was fourteen, has been reproduced in color.*

The small watercolors of that book show that Fraser was even then interested in buildings. With the direct literalness of youth, he set them down as he saw them in the late eighteenth and early nineteenth centuries, drawing barn and "big house," Fort Mechanic and peaceful dwellings, brick church and wooden chapel. In recording these buildings, most of which no longer stand, Fraser unwittingly made a real contribution to the study of American architecture.

Fraser was born during the American Revolution on August 20, 1782 in Charleston which was then held by the British.[1] He was of Scotch and German descent, the youngest of fourteen children of Alexander Fraser and his wife Mary Grimké.[2] His grandfather was the adventurous John Fraser who had gone among the Indians as a trader and with his wife had escaped massacre only through the friendship of a Yemassee brave, Sanute.[3]

Sandwiched between the Indian trader and the painter, Alexander Fraser appears an obscure figure, but it may be from him that Charles Fraser derived his love of art, for Alexander was interested both in music and in architecture. He was one of the original members of the St. Cecilia Society,[4] which began in 1766[5] as a musical organization, maintaining an excellent orchestra.[6] In 1791, the year

---

* *Charles Fraser.* By Alice R. Huger Smith and D. E. Huger Smith. (New York, Frederic Fairchild Sherman, 1924). *The Technique of Charles Fraser, Miniaturist,* by Ruel P. Tolman. (*Antiques* magazine for January and February, 1935.) *A Charleston Sketchbook.* With introduction and notes by Alice R. Huger Smith. (Carolina Art Association, 1940).

St. John's Lutheran Church, 10 Archdale Street, built in 1815-1818, perhaps designed by Frederick Wesner. This steeple, added in 1859, was designed by Charles Fraser.

of his death,[7] he submitted a design for the Orphan House.[8] His plans were rejected, those by Thomas Bennett (qv) being chosen. If Alexander and his family felt disappointment, it does not appear in the enthusiastic account of the laying of the cornerstone, written years after by Charles Fraser who as a schoolboy witnessed the ceremony.[9]

In boyhood, Fraser lived on Tradd Street.[10] Later, his dwelling was the old brick house, now 55 King Street.[11] Although he sketched from his youth up, he practiced as a lawyer before becoming a professional painter.[12] It was the lawyer, not the painter, who in 1814 ran unsuccessfully, for the state legislature on the Federalist ticket.[13] From youth to age, he painted close to 500 miniatures, many of which survive.[14] His most famous sitter was Lafayette, whom he painted in 1825.[15]

Pictures of Fraser witness to a Roman nose and a kindly expression. He spoke politely of women and never married one. His means assured him economic freedom, and his life was fairly serene, varied by visits to the North, and made pleasant by friendships with other painters and the very real esteem of his fellow citizens.[16] One good friend was John B. White,[17] father of the architect, Edward B. White (qv). Another was a beloved dog, Julia.[18]

The regard in which Fraser was held was not confined to his own race. A free person of color, Isaac Bateman, made a will on March 4, 1843, appointing the painter his executor and leaving him a bequest:

> "To Mr. Charles Frazer I bequeath my Servant Nancy in trust, for her own use and benefit, believing he will protect her, and take care of her, and act as her guardian." [19]

In 1854, Fraser published a book, *My Reminiscences of Charleston*, which grew out of papers read before the Conversation Club, of which he was a founder.[20] Written in easy, loose-jointed sentences, without particular attention to syntax, it is eminently readable and contains valuable information on Charleston buildings, including the statement that William Drayton (qv) designed the Court House.

Fraser is numbered among the architects by reason of two cupolas. The older and better is no longer in existence. It stood on the Old Exchange, replacing the original cupola which had been destroyed, and was put up by the builders J. H. Seyle (qv) and Albert Elfe.[21] The *Courier* of November 9, 1833 said:

"We are gratified to observe, that in compliance with the wishes of our merchants, a cupola is now being erected on our Custom House, to which fine old building it will no doubt prove a striking ornament. When finished, it will serve as an excellent observatory, to note the approach of vessels, and will doubtless be a place of frequent resort to view the city and survey the beauties of our capacious harbour, and the adjacent country."

The cupola is no longer in existence, but pictures show it to have been a pleasing if conventional ring of arches supporting a domed roof. Simms, the novelist, called it a "sort of pepper-box on a terrapin's back," [22] but Simms admired little that was not built in the 1850's.

Fraser's other cupola may be seen on St. John's Lutheran Church on Archdale Street. The church was built in 1815-18, but at first had only a short square tower.[23] Fraser is said to have designed the cupola in 1843, but it was not erected until 1859.[24]

Fraser died in Charleston, October 5, 1860. After funeral services next day at the Huguenot Church, he was buried in St. Michael's graveyard.[25]

HYDE, REEVES
AND SOME LESSER LIGHTS

JOSEPH HYDE.   In Charleston, c. 1835—c. 1838

JOSEPH HYDE APPEARED IN CHARLESTON, DE-
signed the present church of St. Philip's (though not its
steeple), and the Masonic Temple on Market Street, no
longer standing, and advertised that he taught architecture. Specu-
lation has connected him with the Hyde family of New England,
several of whom have been named Joseph, but history does not tell
us whence he came or whither he went.

Old St. Philip's, which dated from the first half of the eighteenth
century, had burned one windy night in February, 1835. The cornerstone of the present building was laid on November 12. At first, the
intention of the bereaved congregation was to replace their old
church exactly as it had been.[1]

Had this determination been carried out, Hyde would have been
merely a supervising architect. As it is, the present church stands
several feet higher than did the older one, the floor of which had
been almost level with the ground, and it is approached by stone
steps; a chancel has been added; the pews are arranged differently;
most important of all, instead of the massive Tuscan pillars of the
old interior, fluted columns support elaborate capitals and rosette-
studded arches. This change was authorized at a meeting of the
congregation, held June 27, 1836, when it was resolved, "That the
heavy pillars of the interior of the church be dispensed with, and
that in lieu thereof Corinthian columns (as far as practicable) after
the style of St. Martin's in the Fields, London, be adopted."[2]

Who suggested these changes, architect or building committee?
The former would seem the more probable. In any case, Hyde's
church is a very different building from its predecessor, at once
lighter and airier though less magnificent, since it lacks the marble
monuments which clung to the pillars of the older structure.

The exterior of Hyde's building has since been changed by the
addition in 1848-50 of a steeple designed by Edward B. White (qv).

St. Philip's Church, 146 Church Street, built 1835-1838. Joseph Hyde, architect.

This is fortunately in keeping with the church, both being Palladian in spirit.

While the church was being built, Hyde advertised in the *Courier* of October 24, 1836:

> "Joseph Hyde.—Architect, respectfully informs the public that his evening instruction in Architectural Drawing and Mechanics, commences this evening the 24th at 7 o'clock and will continue Mondays, Wednesday, and Fridays, the Winter months. Office Church street."

The Masonic Temple designed by Hyde stood briefly at Market and Meeting Streets. It had pilasters and was coated with roughcast. The walls of the ground floor, which was part of the city market, were pierced by arches,[3] while the second and third floors held a ballroom and a Masons' Hall.[4] Sutton & Fogartie were the builders.[5] The cornerstone was laid August 23, 1837.[6] The building was not quite finished when the fire of April, 1838, destroyed it.[7] Today the site is occupied by the Market Hall, designed by E. B. White.

Hyde appeared in one Charleston directory, that of 1837-38:

> "Hyde, Joseph, architect, 115 Church St."

ABRAHAM P. REEVES. Born 1791—Died September, 1832.

Abraham P. Reeves, architect and builder, was termed carpenter by the directory of 1822, and architect by those of 1829 and 1831. He was baptized at the Circular (Congregational) Church, May 9, 1791, the son of Enos Reeves,[1] a silversmith from Pennsylvania who settled in Charleston.

Alston Deas, authority on Charleston ironwork, has discovered that Reeves designed the elaborate gates and fence of St. John's Lutheran Church, which were made in 1822 by the ironworker Roh.[2] Reeves' brother-in-law, Frederick Wesner (qv), was one of the contractors for the church, and may have been its architect.

In 1819, Reeves advertised an architectural night school.[3] The following year, in a like notice, he added that he drew "Architectural Designs of every description, according to the Grecian, Roman, Gothic, Chinese, or Modern Style."[4] In 1828, the emphasis was on staircasing.[5] He stated in 1829 that, "if a sufficient number will apply, he will also teach Naval Architecture, in which he will be assisted by several practical Mechanics in the Ship Building line, with the advantage of Models, &c. to illustrate the application of theory to practice." [6]

His granddaughter, Marian Calhoun Legaré Reeves, using the pen-name of Fadette, was a popular novelist of the 1860's and '70's.

THE CURTIS FAMILY OF MASTER BUILDERS

Two churches on Edisto Island, near Charleston, were seemingly designed by members of the Curtis family of builders. One of these structures has burned, but the other still stands, and its unpretentious but successful use of a Greek theme makes one wish that more were known of its maker.

In 1819, one C. Curtis, who may have been of this family, advertised sign, ornamental, and fancy painting.[1]

In 1827, a letter in the *Courier* concerning a dispute over curb stone and a cistern mentioned "Mr. C. the Master Architect," which may refer to a Curtis.[2]

Four years later, the Presbyterian Church on Edisto Island, the temple-form building which still stands, was erected. It is attributed to James M. Curtis. The church was somewhat changed in 1833, Greek Doric columns being substituted for the first, more slimly proportioned, supports.[3] James M. Curtis in 1857 was the builder of a house designed by Francis D. Lee. (qv)

In 1840, the authorities of the Protestant Episcopal Church on Edisto decided to replace their old house of worship, built about 1774, with a new one, because the old building lacked "proper sittings for the coloured people." The building committee reported that "Mr. E. Curtis had submitted several plans," one of which they selected. They were thereupon authorized to contract with him, "according to the plan approved of." The estimated cost was $7,000. This church was consecrated November 14, 1841.[4] It burned in or soon before 1875.[5]

This was almost certainly Ephraim Curtis, who in 1840 was employed by the city of Charleston to erect a slave mart in the Work House yard.[6] Before this, slaves had been sold in a street by the Old Exchange, but unfavorable publicity from Northern and English visitors who attended the sales and printed their impressions, caused a removal to a more secluded place.

A member of the Curtis family had been one of the builders of the theatre designed by Reichardt (qv), in 1837.[7]

The Joseph Aiken House, 20 Charlotte Street, built 1848-1849. James M. Curtis, architect.

The George Edwards House, 14 Legare Street. A large single house, typically well built, typically anonymous, which acquired an elaborate fence and gate soon after 1816.

The George Edwards House.

The hurricane of August 24, 1851, demolished a newly finished carpenter's workshop in Rutledge Street, owned by E. M. Curtis,[8] who may have been Ephraim, or a relation.

There was also a William Curtis, who died September 13, 1858.[9] The following spring, a building on Sullivan's Island, advertised for sale, was described as "that delightful House built by the late W. Curtis." Whether this meant that he was its builder, or simply that it was built for him, is uncertain. The notice was signed by "Curtis' Paint and Oil Depot, 137 East Bay." [10]

The Joseph Aiken house, built 1848-49, at the northeast corner of Charlotte and Alexander Streets, a notable brick dwelling which combines a Classic Revival portico on the front with an Italian Villa loggia on the side, is reminiscent of the work of Edward C. Jones. Discovery of a photograph of this house marked "James M. Curtis Architect" has caused its design to be attributed to him. This house gains added interest as the birthplace of William Martin Aiken, supervising architect of the Treasury, 1895-96, and designer of the second Roper Hospital,[11] at Calhoun and Lucas Streets.

JAMES DUPRE.   Working about 1807-1816.

James Dupre is included here because of one reference which terms him architect. He is first found in the directory of 1807, listed as a house carpenter at 4 Wall Street. He appeared also in the directories of 1809 and of 1816, both of which called him carpenter. Most likely he was a builder.

However, he is mentioned in J. L. E. W. Shecut's wordy *Topographical, Historical, and other Sketches of the City of Charleston*, published in 1819, which gives an account of a house, said by tradition to have been built by Captain (later Lord) Anson, the navigator. (If this was true, it was probably the same "Anson's house" near which Peter Henry Bruce (qv) placed a battery in 1745.) To quote Shecut:

> "The house of Captain Anson was originally built of the best black cypress, but was afterwards considerably enlarged by Gen. Gadsden, and has lately been further altered and improved. A block of the main sill of the first house has been deposited in the museum of the *Literary and Philosophical Society of South-Carolina,* by Mr. James Du Pre, the Architect, and is as sound, as

the day on which it was laid on the foundation, although seventy-eight years have elapsed since that period." [1]

This house no longer stands.[2]

MR. READY OR REEDY. Working 1822

In the south aisle of St. Paul's, Radcliffeboro,' now St. Luke's and St. Paul's, may yet be seen a marble wall monument, surmounted by a relief of a cosily curled lamb, resembling a house cat, and a lamentable young woman, resembling nothing, products of the year of grace, 1822. A letter from "A Friend to Arts & Sciences," in the *Courier* of August 15, 1822, commended the affair as a "specimen of native genius," and stated that "The design is from the pencil of Mr. Ready, an architect in this city."

No Ready is in the directories of the period. There is, however, a James Reedy, carpenter, in the directories of 1837-38, and 1840-41, who may be the man intended. He was probably not an architect.

JAMES DICK. Advertised 1839. Died 1840.

James Dick's tragic story is found in two newspaper items.

The first was an advertisement in the *Courier* of October 24, 1839.

> "Architecture.—A class, three evenings a week, is proposed to to opened at 25 King-street, by the subscriber, on or about first November. For instructions in the elements of Architecture, embracing, besides the Orders, the Section of Solids, and particularly of the Cylinders so extensively useful in the construction of Stairing, Bridges, and other Arches, &c. illustrated by models. Terms made known by applying as above.
>
> James Dick."

The second item, in the *Courier* of June 2, 1840, dealt with a coroner's report which stated that "James Dick, a native of Scotland, late of New York, stone cutter, aged about 50 years" killed himself by leaping from a window of the poor house.

TWO GREEK REVIVAL GIANTS

WILLIAM STRICKLAND. c. 1787—April 6, 1854

WILLIAM STRICKLAND OF PHILADELPHIA, painter, engraver, and architect, may or may not have come to Charleston, but he designed the building of the College of Charleston, erected in 1828-29 which still remains, disguised by additions, as the core of the present main building.

Of Strickland's importance and achievements, there is no need to speak in detail here. Like Robert Mills (qv), he studied under Latrobe, for whom John Strickland, his father, had worked as a carpenter. Like Mills, also, he was enthralled by railroads and canals, but foresaw that the former would supersede the latter.

An early building of his, the Masonic Temple in Philadelphia (1810) was an attempt at Gothic. Turning to the Greek Revival, he avoided decoration more and more as he grew older. Well-known among his works are the austere Custom House at Philadelphia (1824) and the more graceful Merchants' Exchange there (1834). By placing upon the Exchange a copy of the Choragic Monument of Lysicrates to take the place of a dome (unknown to Greek architecture), he set a fashion.[1]

A marble bust shows Strickland with strong features and luxuriant side whiskers.[2]

He died in 1854, while superintending the building of the capitol at Nashville, Tennessee, and is buried beneath it.[3]

His college building was unspectacular but gave satisfaction. The *Courier* of July 7, 1828, wrote:

> "The new College edifice, erecting by the voluntary subscriptions of the citizens of Charleston, is nearly completed. The design was given by Mr. Strickland, Architect, of Philadelphia. So far as we are capable of estimating its merits, we think it reflects much credit on Mr. S.'s talents, as an architect, and we would congratulate him on having workmen, to execute the plan, so well skilled in their business, as Messrs. Bell and Schnierle.
>
> "We remark with great pleasure, the large size of the windows; which, in our climate, is a point of great importance, and

too much neglected by our mechanics. Those in the College building, are well calculated to insure a free circulation of air, and will conduce to more vigorous mental exercises, as well as to a more healthy action of the bodily powers" . . . .

In March, 1829, the *Courier* stated again that the building was nearly completed.[4] In December, it remarked that discipline at the college had improved, since it had entered its new home.[5]

This building, as it was originally, figures on the college seal. It was a simple, rectangular, brick affair, two stories high on a basement, with a pedimented projection in the center of the southern facade, and gable ends on the east and west.

In 1840, a coating of roughcast or of Roman cement was recommended for the building.[6] It wears such a covering today, which for long years has been colored pink, but whether this shade was given it with the first coating is not known.

In 1850, a grandiose colossal portico and wings were added by Edward B. White (qv), who also designed the porter's lodge and replaced the campus wall by the present iron fence. The library building was added by George E. Walker (qv) in 1855-56. White's wings were badly hurt by the earthquake of 1886 and were rebuilt, the east one according to a design by E. R. Rutledge, modified by Dr. Gabriel E. Manigault.[7] In 1930, the west wing was extended to College Street by Simons & Lapham.[8]

THOMAS USTICK WALTER.   September 4, 1804—
    October 30, 1887

Thomas U. Walter of Philadelphia is another nationally known figure of the Classic Revival. Like his teacher, Strickland, before him, he is represented in Charleston by only one building. This is the once beautiful and still imposing Hibernian Hall.

Walter was of German descent, the son of a bricklayer and stone mason, Joseph Saunders Walter and his wife, Deborah Wood. The boy was apprenticed to his father, but studied at the Franklin Institute, where Strickland was among his teachers. Walter grew up to have two fervors, the Baptist religion and architecture. Among other works, he completed the Treasury at Washington which Mills had begun, and added wings to Mills' Patent Office.[1]

Walter traveled in Europe in 1838, and later visited South America, where between 1843 and '45, while building a breakwater at La Guaira, Venezuela, he was saddened by the death from fever of his eldest son and assistant Joseph.[2]

Together with J. Jay Smith, Walter contributed to and compiled *Two Hundred Designs for Cottages and Villas,* published in 1846.[3]

The story of the Hibernian Hall dates from about 1835, when, answering an advertisement of the Hibernian Society, a social and charitable organization which still flourishes, Walter sent plans which were preferred to those of the other competitors.[4] He let his imagination soar with his double staircase, but on the exterior, he kept his building correctly classical, where six Ionic columns upheld a simple pediment.

His design was somewhat altered in the interests of economy by the building committee, Thomas Bennett, John Hunter, Alexander Black, William Aiken, and John Robinson, whose names appear on the cornerstone, as do those of the builders, John White, Andrew Cunningham, and George Thompson, respectively stone cutter, carpenter, and bricklayer, while that of the architect is not mentioned.[5]

The cornerstone was laid on March 18, 1839, as the seventeenth, St. Patrick's Day, came that year on a Sunday.[6] While the building was under way, a part of the portico fell, injuring a boy,[7] and not until January 20, 1840, was the hall opened for the first time. The ceremonies included an address by the Roman Catholic bishop, a supper, and a dance. The last was unscheduled, but, as the committee reported, "if, under such enlivening circumstances and such happy feelings youth, beauty and loveliness were to petition with beseeching looks, from all subduing eyes to indulge in a little mirth and innocent festivity, your committee would not believe the society would have the heart to forbid it, they, therefore, yielded." [8]

The hall has since seen dignified balls, and lively debutante dances, as well as jovial dinners of the Hibernian Society. Thackeray lectured there. In 1861, two church services were held at the same time, Roman Catholics upstairs, Congregationalists downstairs, bereaved alike of their churches by the great fire. In recent years, militia with fixed bayonets have entered to seize ballot boxes.

The pediment collapsed in the earthquake of 1886, and for no conceivable reason was replaced by one with modillions of the Corinthian order, at variance with the Ionic columns, and a center window of no order at all.

The Hibernian Society Hall, 105 Meeting Street, completed in 1840.
Thomas U. Walter, architect.

The Sword Gates, 32 Legare Street, made about 1838 by Christopher Werner.
Perhaps designed by Charles F. Reichardt.

CHARLES F. REICHARDT

In Charleston, December, 1836—c. 1840

C HARLES F. REICHARDT ARRIVED IN CHARLES-
ton on Christmas Eve, 1836, aboard the packet ship *Bur-
gundy*, from New York.[1] He was said to be, and may well
have been, a pupil of Karl Friedrich Schinkel (1781-1841), celebrated German exponent of the Greek Revival. Certainly, he aped
Schinkel more than once.

The Greek Revival had come to Charleston in the 1820's, borne
south by Robert Mills, who as a young man had studied with Latrobe, after spending more than a year with Jefferson, watching
Monticello rise on an enchanted spur of the Blue Ridge. Now it had
come again, heavier, more ornate, but still with elements of beauty.
It is Charleston's loss that none of Reichardt's buildings is known to
survive.

Reichardt was a member of the American Institution of Architects, a group which included Isaiah Rogers[2] The design of the
Charleston Hotel, which stood on Meeting Street until a few years
ago, often is attributed to Rogers, but records of the time name
Reichardt as author of the plans.

The *Mercury*, of January 12, 1837, said: "We understand that
the plan for the New Hotel by Mr. Reichardt having been chosen,
a contract was made with that energetic and skilful Architect, Col.
Jacob Small, of Baltimore, for its immediate execution. The more
bulky materials are now on their way . . .

"The proposed plan embraces a Collonade one hundred and fifty
feet on Meeting-street front, which for taste and elegance will be
unsurpassed by any edifice of the same character in the United
States.—Patriot."

This first structure was destroyed by the fire of 1838, but its
foundations and cisterns survived, and were embodied in the second
building.[3] In June, 1838, N. F. Potter, James A. Potter and James E.
Kelsey contracted to clear the ruins "and to rebuild and completely
finish in all respects a New hotel according to the Specification &
Plans Made out by M^r. Reichardt architect" . . .[4]

Possibly Reichardt altered his first design, since the directory of 1840-41 stated that "The Charleston Hotel has been rebuilt, in a style even more magnificent than before." The hotel was reported finished in July, 1839, but a shipment of furniture sank in the brig *Star*, and it did not open until November.[5]

The colossal colonnade (echo of Schinkel), had fourteen Corinthian columns, standing upon a crypto-portico. Acroteria were almost the only other ornament.

Daniel Webster, Jenny Lind, and Thackeray all stayed at the hotel, as well as royalty in the shape of Queen Victoria's daughter, Louise.

Reichardt's "Grand Stand, and other buildings for the accommodation of ladies, and the invited guests of the Club," at the Washington race course, where Hampton Park is now, were free of architectural pretension, but gained him the liking of the rich and influential "turfites." [6]

His New Theatre, an ambitious structure, showed the influence of Schinkel's Royal Theatre at Berlin, much boiled down, with wings and superstructure omitted, and four instead of six Ionic columns on the portico, which was approached by wide steps between abutments.[7] Two stories high, it was of brick, stuccoed to resemble freestone. The builders were Curtis, and Fogartie & Sutton.[8] It first opened in December, 1837.[9] References to it are frequent, and it won a niche in theatrical history as the scene of the great Rachel's last performance. Like a host of other buildings, it was swept away by the fire of 1861.

In 1837, also, Reichardt designed a Mariner's Church for the Port Society.[10] It was meant to be a second-story affair, to stand above the east end of the market, but was never built.[11]

An ecclesiastical work which reached completion was that of extending the steeple of the Circular Church "about seventy feet." [12] The building committee first advertised for bids in September, 1837, but matters halted until November, when the plans were completed, "which have been unavoidably delayed in consequence of the absence of the Architect." [13]

The steeple was built in 1838, and the *Southern Rose* of September 1 of that year said:

> "Mr. Reichardt, the present architect, labored under the disadvantage of having to complete another's design; but the

The Charleston Hotel, 200 Meeting Street, Charles F. Reichardt, architect. From a lithograph by B. W. Thayer, c. 1839. No longer standing.

manner in which he executed his task, gave, we believe, universal satisfaction. . . . It has been surmised by some persons that the spire of the circular church is a few feet higher than that of St. Michael's; but this is erroneous" . . . (The building committee) "were not actuated by the poor ambition of a certain gentleman in our country, who, when about to build him a house, sent over one night and had the dwelling of his neighbour secretly measured, in order that he might make his own *six inches longer* than the other!"

The steeple was later remodeled by Edward C. Jones, and eventually was destroyed by the fire of 1861.

In 1838, also, Reichardt's Guard House was built at the southwest corner of Broad and Meeting Streets.[14] A beautiful structure, austere and solid as befitted its purpose, it had a portico of six Doric columns in front on Broad Street, and a colonnade along the east side. The latter columns were removed in 1856 to widen Meeting Street.[15] The "sword gates," beloved of tourists and now at a Legaré Street dwelling, were made for the Guard House by the ironworker Christopher Werner. Alston Deas, author of *The Early Ironwork of Charleston*, believes that Reichardt may well have designed them.[16]

The Guard House was injured by the earthquake of 1886 and subsequently removed. Its site is occupied by a post office in Renaissance style.

While the Guard House was being built, the fire of 1838, which destroyed Reichardt's first hotel building, swept away the not quite finished Masonic Hall by Joseph Hyde (qv). Reichardt designed a hall to replace it, the *Courier* of June 9, 1839, containing an advertisement for estimates for building a "new Market and Masonic Hall," the plans and specifications of which were "at Mr. Reichardt's office." Like the Mariner's Church which was to have been at the other end of the market, this project came to naught. The Masons decided to build elsewhere; and the present Market Hall on the site is by Edward B. White (qv).

In 1839, Reichardt drew the plans for flooring over the second story of the City Hall,[17] thereby destroying the interest of the interior of that charming building. One can only say for him, that if he had not done it, someone else would have; in fact, the interior has been completely remodeled since.

The proceedings of City Council of February 27, 1840, record a petition from George W. Logan, who had been prominent in both the hotel and theatre companies, and was therefore well acquainted with the architect, "praying the consideration of Council to the account of Charles F. Reichardt, for additional work and drawing executed to suit deviation from the original plans of the New Guard House, by the direction of the Committee, and also preparing plans &c. of the alterations of City Hall, amounting to ($235) two hundred and thirty five dollars." [18] The petition seems to have had no effect.[19]

Reichardt had a share, how much is uncertain, in the Apprentices' Library Society Hall, a large building on Meeting Street with columns in front. It was built in 1840 and opened in January, 1841.[20] The report of the board of trustees of the society stated that the hall had been "originally designed by Mr. Bennett and drafted by Mr. Richardt" (sic).[21] Mr. Bennett was probably Governor Thomas Bennett, or perhaps his son, W. Jefferson Bennett, both of whom were interested in architecture. This hall, too, burned in 1861.

After leaving Charleston, Reichardt seems to have visited the West Indies and Central America. One C. F. Reichardt, probably our architect, wrote two books in German, *Centro-Amerika* and *Nicaragua*, brought out by a Brunswick publisher in 1850 and 1854, respectively. These volumes give the author's impressions and his ideas for the development of the region by German immigrants, but their chief interest lies in a discussion of an isthmus canal.

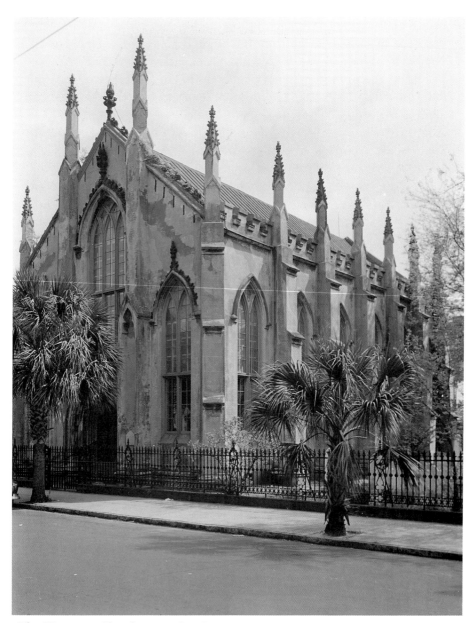

The Huguenot Church, 136 Church Street, built 1844-1845. E. B. White, architect. This is the earliest Gothic Revival example in Charleston.

EDWARD BRICKELL WHITE

January 29, 1806—May 10, 1882

EDWARD BRICKELL WHITE WAS BORN AT MID-
night, January 29, 1806, at Chapel Hill plantation, St.
John's parish, South Carolina, the residence of his aunt's
husband and his own namesake, Doctor James Brickell.

He was the eldest son of John Blake White and his first wife,
Elizabeth Allston.[1] The tracing of inherited characteristics is often
a delusive process, but it is at least interesting that his grandfather,
Blake Leay White, had been a builder as well as a plantation
owner.[2] On his mother's side of the family, there was artistic ability,
exemplified by the painter, Washington Allston.[3] From his father,
who conscientiously dissipated his talents among painting, sculp-
ture, writing, and the law,[4] he received a versatile strain, useful in an
eclectic age, which was to show in the variety of styles he used—the
classic and Gothic revivals, and the tradition of Wren.

White entered architecture obliquely from engineering, and
engineering from his training as an army officer at West Point. Graduating from the United States Military Academy in 1826, he became an artillery officer. In 1832, he served on the Black Hawk expedition, on the staff of General Abraham Eustis.

He assisted in the construction of Forts Pulaski and Adams and
a bridge over the Potomac at Georgetown, and in the survey of the
projected Charleston, Louisville and Cincinnati railroad, on which
duty he continued after resigning from the army in 1836.[5]

On the survey which sought a pass where this line might cross
the Blue Ridge, White was closely associated with some of the leading engineers of the state and a number of lesser men. Among his
subordinates was an exuberant youth, Savannah-born, Charleston-
reared John Charles Frémont, soon to become known as California's
"Pathfinder". Frémont described the survey as a picnic,[6] but for
White, it was a hard, responsible task, perhaps no less so that Frémont was in his group.

Work for projected railroads, the Louisville & Cincinnati, the
Cheraw & Waccamaw, the Wilmington Seaboard, occupied White

The Huguenot Church.

The Huguenot Church. White liked pierced wooden screens.

for the next three years. In 1839, he published a report of the reconnaissance for the last (there termed the Charleston, Georgetown, and All Saints), a careful piece of planning which came to nothing.[7]

Then came architecture. He received important commissions early, and a letter published in the *Courier* of August 1, 1842, in which he endorsed Duval's patent tin roofing, a local product, gives evidence of extensive practice.

> . . . "At your request, I state below some of the buildings on which I have known your patent to be used in this city, viz: the Market Hall, the High School, the German Lutheran Church, and the Second Baptist Church, (for all of which I made the plans and specifications) and on Mr. Faber's new stores, on East-Bay, the construction of which I am now superintending. I have specified it in my designs for the Hall of the I.O.O.F., which is to be built in this city. Have recommended it for a villa, which I designed lately for Judge David Johnson, and for the U. S. Arsenal (to be built in Charleston) the plans for which I made a short time since."

Of these buildings, the most important is the Market Hall, which seems obvious at first glance, but repays study, with its temple form, rustic lower story, and double flight of stone steps which ascend to a pedimented portico supported by four Roman Doric columns, so spaced as to leave a greater span in the center. It has lavish ironwork and a Doric frieze with bucrania and rams' heads.

The Market Hall occupies the site of the Masonic Hall, by Joseph Hyde (qv), which burned in 1838. White received $300 for his plan, and petitioned for, but was refused, an additional hundred.[8] In July, 1840, the contract was given to Andrew Cunningham and John White,[9] who were at odds by the following April, the latter claiming that "the whole of the money I have received on account of the Market Hall job, don't more than pay the freight of the Stone from New York." [10]

The plan for the High School was adopted by City Council, September 2, 1840, after a previous plan by White had been rejected as entailing too great an expense.[11] The school was built on Society Street about 1842,[12] without the portico, which White was to add in 1850.[13]

The German Lutheran Church (1841-42), outwardly Tuscan, has galleries with balustered fronts, like piazza railings, which give

Grace Church, 100 Wentworth Street, built 1847-1848. E. B. White, architect.

The Old Citadel, Marion Square. One of two wings added by E. B. White about 1850.
The corner crenellations mask chimneys.

the interior a Charlestonian touch. It is now St. Johannes Evangelical Lutheran Church.

The Wentworth Street or Second Baptist Church (now the Centenary Methodist Episcopal Church, colored) is a Doric temple with a hexastyle portico. White's attitude to his work at this period is shown in a letter published in the *Courier* of February 3, 1842, about this church:

> "Messrs. Editors: In your paper of the 2d instant, a writer, under the signature of "Calvin", makes certain remarks on the New Baptist Church now erecting in Wentworth-street. His criticisms are entirely correct. He objects to the location of certain doors in the building. That it is a violation of architectural propriety and good taste to place doors or any other apertures, *behind* columns, is most true.
>
> "'Calvin' in the course of his remarks, blames the architects for these faults. Being the individual who designed the building, it is my duty to inform him, and all other liberal critics, that the points to which he objects, do not enter into my design. By reference to my plans and specifications, it will be seen, that none of the *small* doors in question are introduced. The building committee desired to have them. I objected, especially to those in the front of the Church. But when overruled by the Committee, I advised them (if they were determined to have the doors) where they should be placed; namely *between* the columns. So far from approving of or even countenancing their present improper location, I declined altogether to superintend the construction of the building, unless the committee would consent to place the doors where they should be.
>
> Edw. B. White,
> Civil Engineer, Architect and Surveyor."

The building committee stood pat (as they have a way of doing), and the small doors flanking the main portal still skulk behind columns.

The United States Arsenal (now Porter Military Academy), a big, brick affair, was built in 1844.[14] It has suffered additions.

The same *Courier* which published White's endorsement of Duval's roofing, that of August 1, 1842, also contained proof that the architect's career extended beyond the state.

The railroad gates on Ann Street. Probably by E. B. White.

The Market Hall, 188 Meeting Street, completed in 1841. Edward B. White, architect. *(Henry W. Mitchell)*

"Notice—The subscriber intending to visit the Northern Cities, on professional calls, which will engage his attention until the first of November next, will receive and execute at the North any orders in the Architectural branch of his profession with which he may be charged . . .

> EDW. B. WHITE,
> Civil Engineer, Architect and Surveyor."

The *Courier* of November 24, contained a notice that he was home again.

Abreast of his times, White next adventured into the Gothic, first of the Charleston architects, and among the first of the Americans, to join in the revival of this style, then emanating from Oxford. The Huguenot Church, built for a group of Episcopalians who decided to return to the faith of their French Protestant forefathers, was begun in 1844 and finished in 1845.[15] A brick and stucco structure, it shows a quantity of pinnacle-topped buttresses, a battlemented parapet, and dripstones. As the first "solemn" Gothic building in Charleston, it has its interest.

A gun shed for the Washington Artillery,[16] and a secular Gothic building, the Military Hall on Wentworth Street, followed. Neither remains. The cornerstone of the Hall was laid September 30, 1845, and the building was completed in 1847, for the Board of Field Officers of the Fourth Brigade of Militia. As in the case of the Huguenot Church, Ephraim Curtis was the builder.[17] The Hall measured 117 by 84 feet and, according to the *Courier,* was "in the style of an English castellated building of the 16th century". Turreted and parapeted, with an "embattled Bartizan" on each of six salient angles, it was thought "quite sufficient to afford a shelter against a sudden enemy, not provided with artillery." The upper story was given over to a drill room with wall arranged to imitate blocks of stone (as in the Huguenot Church), and the ceiling was open timbered, "in imitation of the beautiful oaken roofs of the 16th century." [18]

In reckoning the forces which have influenced Charleston's architecture, one must not forget the novels of Sir Walter Scott!

In 1849, White added cupolas to the Hall, in one of which hung an alarm bell, thought to be of enormous volume, but, according to one listener, indistinguishable "unless they had ear trumpets".[19] It was later removed to the Orphan House.

Still in Gothic style, White designed two churches, Trinity in Columbia, South Carolina, built in 1847, and Grace in Charleston,

Porter Military Academy, formerly United States Arsenal, 167 Ashley Avenue. Main building built in 1844. E. B. White, architect.

United States Arsenal. Building on north side, near gate. Probably by E. B. White.

United States Arsenal. Flanker. Probably by E. B. White.

Porter Gaud School, formerly United States Arsenal. Powder Magazine.
Probably by E. B. White.

The Centenary Methodist Episcopal Church, formerly the Second Baptist Church, 60 Wentworth Street, built 1842. E. B. White, architect.

built 1847-48. E. W. Brown was contractor for both.[20] They still stand.

In 1847, also, White reverted to the tradition of Wren, with a singularly felicitous result. St. Philip's Church, burned in 1835, had been rebuilt, with considerable changes, by Joseph Hyde (qv) in 1835-38. But it lacked a steeple. White now designed one, 200 feet tall. The work did not begin till January, 1848, and continued into 1850. Brown was the builder.[21] White's engineering skill stood him in good stead, and his artistic sense as well. The steeple is a thing of beauty; considering when it was erected, it is a thing of wonder also, in that its architect rose so triumphantly superior to the spirit of his time.

The law office for the celebrated James L. Petigru, now 8 St. Michael's Alley, a substantial building with consoles on the street façade, dates from 1848-49.[22]

The disarming little wooden Gothic church of the Episcopal congregation at Walterboro, South Carolina, was begun in 1850.[23] St. Michael's Sunday school building, of brick and stucco, since much enlarged, dates from this time also.[24] The year was a busy one, in which White did a variety of work for the city of Charleston. An extravagant municipal government had determined on improvements, and the architect, who since 1847 had been concerned with the Battery sea wall,[25] received his share of patronage.

He designed the wings and colossal portico now added to Strickland's simple building at the College of Charleston, the porter's lodge, and apparently even the railing (executed by the ironworker, Werner), which encloses the campus.[26] Simultaneously, he added a colossal portico to his High School on Society Street, built some years before.[27] Clay capitals were shipped from Boston, in Roman Ionic style for the college, and Corinthian for the school, which latter received clay modillions also.[28] The school has lost these decorations, and its columns, with bare blocks where capitals should be, have a bleak look.

White's plans for a marble temple to house Powers' statue of Calhoun were accepted by the city, but this edifice, intended for the center of City Hall Park, was never built.[29]

Till now, except for an occasional tiff with a building committee, White's path seems to have been smooth. Late in 1850, however, doubts were expressed as to the permanency of that part of his sea wall at White Point Gardens (the Battery) which was made of concrete. In a dignified letter, he asked that a committee of "scientific

St. Johannes Lutheran Church, 48 Hasell Street, built 1841-1842.
E. B. White, architect

The College of Charleston. The core of the building is by Strickland, but
portico and wings were added in 1850 by E. B. White.

St. Philip's Church steeple, built 1848-1850. E. B. White, architect.

gentlemen" be appointed to examine the work.[30] Meanwhile, work at the college had been delayed because the contractor, William Jones (qv), was insolvent. The workmen left; the roof was open; rain hurt the interior, and White was blamed and dismissed. In the opinion of Professor Easterby, historian of the college, this action by the city fathers was unjust.[31]

The dismissal had small effect on White's popularity, and orders continued to come. In 1851, he designed the Odd Fellows Hall at King and Liberty Streets, a semi-Gothic affair, perhaps intended for Jacobean, never so elaborately decorated inside as was contemplated.[32] The front with its curving gable and its Gothic dripstones trimmed with Greek egg-and-dart molding was one of the strangest in the city. This building was pulled down in 1946.

About this time, White enlarged the Citadel,[33] built some twenty years before by Frederick Wesner (qv), and outwardly Gothicized it. But news that he was about to add a powder magazine brought protests that this might endanger the lives of the Citadel cadets. At this point, a magazine in Hungary opportunely blew up. The scheme was dropped.[34]

White would probably have designed even more buildings than he did, had he not become superintending architect for the Custom House, which occupied him from 1853 [35] to the outbreak of the Confederate War. He has often been credited with the design of the building, but this, it seems, belongs rightfully to "Mr. Young of Boston" (qv), probably Ammi Burnham Young. For years, with the aid of various young architects, White was chiefly concerned in raising the great stone structure, costing thousands, and invested with Federal majesty and red tape.

He did, however, find time to plan the Chapel of the Cross at Bluffton, South Carolina, begun in 1854, an ambitious though wooden Gothic structure with an impressive open-timbered roof;[36] and the semi-classic Winyah Indigo Society Hall at Georgetown, South Carolina, built 1856-57.[37] He served as architect for the Episcopal church home society, though in what way is obscure,[38] and designed a diploma for the Washington Light Infantry.[39] He was responsible for the eagle-topped shaft at Cowpens battlefield, erected 1856,[40] and for the William Washington monument with its marble rattlesnake, unveiled at Magnolia Cemetery in 1858.[41] By 1856, he had succumbed to the mania for brownstone fronts, designing two buildings on Broad Street which have them, one of which,

The former High School, 55 Society Street. White designed both the hall, built c. 1842, and the portico, added in 1850. The columns have lost their capitals.

opposite State Street, still bears the name of the New York stone-cutter, W. G. Chave, on its facade.[42]

Bishop Albert S. Thomas in his history of the Protestant Episcopal church in South Carolina mentions two buildings by White, dating from 1858, St. Andrew's Chapel, Mount Pleasant, and Christ Church, Charleston. The latter was torn down in 1930.

White was not to finish the Custom House. The Confederacy interrupted the work, and he was busy with military matters. After leaving the army in 1836, he had been active in the militia.[43] Now he helped organize the Palmetto Battalion and was made major, and later, lieutenant-colonel. He saw service near Charleston on James Island, and in North Carolina, where he surrendered at the end of

The James L. Petigru law office, 8 St. Michael's Alley, built in 1848-1849.
E. B. White, architect.

The South Carolina Power Company building, 141 Meeting Street, built in 1876.
E. B. White, architect.

the war.[44] From Albert Simons comes an illuminating sidelight on White's wartime experience:

> "My father, Dr. Thomas Grange Simons, who entered the Confederate Army as a college boy, recalled Colonel White years later as a small and rather pompous officer in very large boots, who was known to the rank and file as "Puss in Boots'. As he rode a very large horse, the sentries never lost an opportunity to require the little Colonel to dismount and advance on foot to be recognized, causing him great inconvenience both in descending from and regaining his equestrian eminence."

When peace came, White returned to his practice, but Charlestonians, weary and penniless, were building scarcely at all. His wife came to the rescue. He had married at New London, Connecticut, April 18, 1832, Delia Adams, daughter of Eli Adams of that place.[45] They had four children.[46] Now, in reduced circumstances, Mrs. White opened a school for young ladies.[47]

In 1866, the architect repaired the interior of St. Michael's (built 1752-61), where the bombardment of 1863-64 had completely wrecked the inside of the chancel and damaged much else. Expressing thanks, the vestry commended his "assiduity and success in restoring the interior of the Church with pleasing effect and in keeping with the original design."[48]

White planned the Palladian building, now the South Carolina Power Company's office, 141 Meeting Street, built in 1876.[49]

By 1879, he had moved to New York, whence he sent the plan for the granite pedestal of the bust of William Gilmore Simms on the Battery.[50] It deserves mention only as one of his last works.

White died in New York, May 10, 1882,[51] and is buried with his wife in St. Michael's graveyard in Charleston.

Should one seek to attribute buildings tentatively, on the basis of style or mannerism, the railway gates on Ann Street, and the Gothic building on John Street, both of which resemble his work at the Citadel, would seem plausible choices. Old Calvary Church on Beaufain Street, finished in 1849 at a time when White was busy with work for the Protestant Episcopal church, may have been his design.

EDWARD C. JONES

Working c. 1848—1861

E DWARD C. JONES WAS ONE OF SEVERAL CHARLES-
ton architects who gained a statewide reputation in the
Ante-Bellum era without becoming known nationally. The
Church of the Holy Cross at Stateburg and the Richard Furman
Hall at Furman University prove that he could design satisfying
buildings.

From 1852 to 1857, he was associated with his former pupil,
Francis D. Lee, in the firm of Jones & Lee. Both men showed the
eclecticism and exoticism characteristic of the period, so that in
many cases it is impossible to say which partner contributed the
whole or the preponderant share of the design. Buildings of "Italian
villa" type are generally attributed to Jones, however, who seems to
have employed the style more often than did any other local
architect.

Besides planning buildings, Jones remodeled so many that one is
tempted to think that only the cessation of work caused by the War
between the States saved all Charleston from being done over to
suit Victorian taste.

Evidently he found his bent early. The *Courier* of May 5, 1840,
mentioned him among the youths who were reading at the Apprentices' Library Society, which had the largest collection of architectural books in the state.

In 1845, Jones joined Marion Lodge, International Order of Odd
Fellows.[1]

In 1848, he inserted a card in the *Courier:*

"EDWARD C. JONES,
ARCHITECT,
63 Broad-Street; Office Hours 9 to 3 o'clock." [2]

He won popularity with the Westminster Presbyterian Church,
often called the Central Church (now Trinity Methodist) on Meeting Street, built 1848-50. After this time references to him are frequent. The design, a product of the Classic Revival, met with en-

[203]

Trinity Methodist Church, formerly the Westminster Presbyterian Church, 273 Meeting Street, built 1848-1850. E. C. Jones, architect.

The Colonel Ashe House.

thusiasm. An article in the *Crumb Basket,* copied in the *Courier* of August 26, 1848 (by which time work had begun), said in part:

"We were much gratified yesterday, by an examination of the working plans for the Presbyterian Church, proposed to be erected for the Rev. W. C. Dana's congregation . . . . It will be in "Temple" form, with Portico of six Corinthian columns, fronting on Meeting street, and one on each return in addition to the Ante. The ascent to the portico will be by eleven steps—five to the first platform, and six to the "Portico" proper. The exterior dimensions will be ninety-six feet in length, fifty-four feet in width, and fifty-six feet (including basement) in height . . . .

"The plans and drawings are by a very promising young Artist, Edward C. Jones, a native of our city. They indicate decided talent, and if faithfully carried out in the completion of the building must establish at once the reputation of Mr. Jones, in Charleston, as an architect, entitled to patronage and respect . . . . the edifice we are now contemplating has no *false ornament* about it."

The church was dedicated February 3, 1850.[3] It is less austere than the quotation would indicate, the interior having florid but effective plasterwork.

Jones was one of the founders of the South Carolina Institute, established in November, 1848,[4] and became its secretary.[5] Jones & Lee were later to build Institute Hall for this association, formed to encourage local arts and industries.

By 1849, Jones had at least two students in his office, Lee and Louis J. Barbot.[6] He was busy with plans for a variety of buildings, including a church at Combahee (pronounced Cumbee), South Carolina,[7] the Vigilant Fire Engine House on State Street, the plans and superintendance of which brought him $160.00,[8] and the Moultrie House, a large, rambling hotel entirely surrounded by a two-story piazza on Sullivan's Island.[9] It opened in 1850, and we find him attending a costume ball there as a "junior manager",[10] the same ball which Simms described in his *Flirtation at the Moultrie House.*

In January, 1850, Jones' plans were chosen for the Roper Hospital on Queen Street.[11] James Curtis was the builder.[12] Much of it was destroyed by the earthquake of 1886, and the vestige is now an apartment house. It is in Italian villa style, showing the characteristic square towers, brackets under wide eaves, large, high-ceiled

The Colonel John Algernon Sydney Ashe House, 26 South Battery, built in or or by 1853. E. C. Jones, architect.

rooms, and arcaded piazzas. The airy rooms and piazzas seem suited to local conditions, but the present-day observer balks at brackets which are almost always non-functional, clinging to the eaves rather than supporting them.

To this style belongs the one dwelling identified as Jones' work, the Colonel John Algernon Sydney Ashe house, 26 South Battery, built in or by 1853.[13] It shows the typical brackets and arcades, with an atypically lavish use of curved lines.

In the same month that his hospital plans were accepted, Jones became the surveyor and architect of Magnolia Cemetery,[14] two facts which seem, however, to be unrelated. The work was rapid, and by July the *Courier* could say:

> "The grounds are already enclosed; the main avenues, embracing an extensive ride, are graded and constructed; the chapel, which is of the gothic style, is in rapid progress of erection; and a large portion of the ground has been laid out and surveyed into burial lots. The lake or lakes, which intersect the grounds, are to be supplied with water from Cooper river, under control of a floodgate, and, when bridged over, according to the design, will give variety, as well as a picturesque beauty to the prospect." [15]

The Gothic chapel has disappeared, but the buttressed receiving vault, which still exists, is probably by Jones.

A large Gothic work by the same architect, the New Work House or colored prison, was begun in 1850 at the southwest corner of Magazine and Mazÿck (now Logan) Streets.[16] It replaced an older prison on the same site. C. C. Trumbo was the builder.[17] An old photograph shows that it had castellated turrets.[18] It no longer stands.

In 1854, City Council gave a contract to place both plumbing and steam heat in this negro prison,[19] a proof that these conveniences were much more widespread in Ante-Bellum Charleston than is generally realized.

The cornerstone of Jones' most unusual building, the cruciform Church of the Holy Cross at Stateburg, South Carolina, was laid September 11, 1850.[20] It is made of *terre pisé* (packed earth).

To 1850 belong also a Court House for Bennettsville, South Carolina;[21] and the small hall of the Palmetto Fire Company on Anson Street between Pinckney and Hasell,[22] recently converted into apartments.

Meanwhile, Jones had entered the competition for the design of the Charleston Custom House, and in March his plan had been selected by the commissioners in the city, subject, however, to the approval of the secretary of the treasury.[23] Subsequently, his plan was to be thrown out in Washington, and the decision given to "Mr. Young" (qv), apparently Ammi Burnham Young, while Jones' chief rival, Edward B. White (qv), became superintending architect. So little was the upset expected, that in Hill's birdseye *View of Charleston*, printed in 1851, a frowning Gothic castle, evidently Jones' design, is shown as a fact—and a strange contrast it is to the classic Custom House which actually stands on the spot. Jones' disappointment must have been enormous, but perhaps was tempered by the quantity of business which flowed in on him.

In 1851, Jones drew the plans of two hotels, the Aiken House at Aiken, South Carolina,[24] and Shell Hall Hotel at Mount Pleasant, South Carolina.[25]

By February, 1852, he had designed the Bank of Augusta at Augusta, Georgia.[26] This was in Italian style, with pediments decorated by Mercury's caduceus and Neptune's trident.[27]

The year was an important one for the architect, for on July 1, a notice appeared in the *Courier:*

"THE SUBSCRIBERS

Have this day associated themselves in business, under the firm of Jones & Lee, Architects.

Edward C. Jones.
Francis D. Lee."

They were to remain partners for four and a half busy years

Jones was by now recognized throughout South Carolina. W. J. McGlothlin, historian of Furman University at Greenville, tells how Jones was chosen by the building committee of the college, who termed him "the most skillful architect which our state could afford." He designed for them a preparatory building in Italian style, which was not built but fixed the style of the university buildings. Before August, 1852, however, work commenced on the main building now known as Richard Furman Hall, apparently completed in 1854.[28] Mr. McGlothlin states that "Lee and Jones" were the architects; but since they had entered into partnership only in July, while the building was underway before August, and since Jones had designed another building for the college in the same style, it would seem that most, if not all, of the credit should go to him. The hall

The Charleston Orphan House, 160 Calhoun Street. Designed by Thomas Bennett and built 1792-1794, it received its cupola from Jones and Lee in 1853-1855.
No longer standing.

Zion Presbyterian Church, 123 Calhoun Street, completed in 1859.
E. C. Jones, architect. No longer standing.

is a striking building, with the graceful loggia and characteristic square tower of the "Italian villa" type, but substantially built, and lacking the disagreeable brackets. Bullseye windows add the unexpected, with pleasing effect.

About 1852, Jones designed a department store in Charleston which evoked extravagant praise from a Baltimore paper:

> . . ."The store of Messrs. Browning & Leman is probably the most beautiful as well as the most extensive establishment in the world . . . .
>
> "The external style of the edifice is quite imposing; but the effect and arrangement of the interior surpass anything in New-York or London. Extensive rows of lofty columns lead the eye along the lower floor, from which it ranges upward around the graceful galleries of three stories until it reaches the dome-like roof, whence a flood of mellow light displays at a glance the gorgeous contents of the bazaar. At the end of the lower floor a stairway leads to the carpeting department, where the long lines of brilliant tapestry are hung through the three stories, and afford a dazzling background for the pure white of other portions of the edifice. The effect of the grand staircase, with the arched entrance to the saloon beyond, is described as extremely noble" . . . .[29]

The press had discovered that buildings were news. The *Courier* of August 27, 1853 devoted columns to "improvements" then underway or contemplated, and named various architects. This one issue credited the firm of Jones & Lee with a long list of buildings. Three of these, Furman, the Combahee church, and the Augusta bank, were by Jones, as has been seen. Evidence from other sources indicates that several others were by Lee (the Farmers' and Exchange Bank, the Unitarian Church, the Citadel Square Baptist Church, and probably the Fish Market). The rest, which may have been by either partner or both, were as follows:

> Wofford College at Spartanburg. (This is in Italian villa style, somewhat like Furman, with two towers instead of one, and is probably the work of Jones.)
> A church at Sheldon.
> A church at Ashepoo.
> The Church of St. Mark's, Clarendon, with a bell gable and open-timbered roof. (This is St. Mark's, Pinewood.)

"A villa of no inconsiderable extent and elegance at Cheraw".

A villa near Columbia.

Several dwellings in South Carolina "and the adjoining States".

The Planters' Bank of Fairfield at Winnsboro, "with three lofty arched openings on the front, supported by rustic piers."

A Court House in Gothic style for Greenville (? Although the *Courier* does not state so, in so many words, the impression is given that this was designed by the firm.)

A store in Gothic style, adjoining the Bank of Augusta.

Several dwellings at Augusta.

Mrs. E. F. Evans' boarding house, and Col. Blum's building, both large affairs on King Street near Horlbeck's Alley, in Charleston.

The remodeling of the Planters' and Mechanics' Bank, an ornate Roman Doric building, on East Bay.

The South Carolina Institute Hall. "The style is Venetian." (This building held an exhibition hall, room for machinery, engine room, and directors' room,[30] and was ornamented outwardly with arches, leopard-head keystones, and lion-head brackets.[31] It was begun by March, 1854, and publicly opened December 27 of the same year.[32] The Ordinance of Secession was signed here in December, 1860. The hall burned in the fire of December 11-12, 1861.)

The Church of the Holy Communion. (But Jones & Lee's plan appearing too small, the church was built according to another design, the authorship of which is now unknown.)

This long list by no means includes all of the firm's activities in or around 1853. They designed the Italianate building, faced with Connecticut brownstone, of the State Bank at 1 Broad Street,[33] and the adjoining Sebring building on Broad Street, now Walker, Evans, & Cogwell's.[34] Jones, aided by Lee, remodeled and enlarged the Orphan House (designed by Thomas Bennett (qv), giving it an Italianate flavor, with a variety of window cornices and a high, rusticated belltower in place of the modest cupola.[35] Lewis Rebb contracted for the work, with estimates of $57,340 for the body of the building, and $3,370 for the belfry.[36] The remodeling began June 24, 1853, and on October 14, 1855, the children again occupied the building.[37] It no longer stands.

Jones & Lee (or probably Jones alone) remodeled the Circular Church,[38] (designed by Mills, the steeple added by Reichardt),

The Palmetto Fire Company Hall, 27 Anson Street, built in 1850.

1 Broad Street, built 1853. Jones & Lee, architects.

The Planters' and Mechanics' Bank, 139 East Bay. Remodeled in 1853 by
Jones & Lee. No longer standing.

The Directors' Room, the South Carolina National Bank, 16 Broad Street.

The Directors' Room, the South Carolina National Bank.

making considerable changes within and without. It was reopened August 7, 1853.[69] It no longer stands.

On August 1, 1854, the Calhoun Monument Convention chose "one of the plans submitted by Messrs. Jones & Lee—the one embracing the Corinthian shaft".[40] This was a different design, however, from the monument which was erected.

On January 5, 1857, the partnership was dissolved.[41]

A jail for Williamsburg District, South Carolina, was planned by Jones in 1859.[42]

April 3 of the same year saw the dedication of Zion Presbyterian Church on Calhoun Street. Jones was the architect and David Lopez the contractor of this barnlike structure, with its twin high-arched porticoes.

> "Every door opens outwardly, so that in case of alarm, the room, which is capable, when crowded, of containing and seating 2500 persons, may be emptied with great facility—a consideration that those who construct large halls so frequently lose sight of." [43]

Jones became an elder of this church, which was largely devoted to missionary work among the colored people. Most of the congregation were colored, and are said to have sung magnificently.[44]

Three buildings in Henderson County, North Carolina, designed by Jones in the 1850's, are recorded by Sadie Smathers Patton in *The Story of Henderson County*. These are the Flat Rock (Farmers') Hotel, later known as Woodfields, and two churches, St. John in the Wilderness, at Flat Rock, and Calvary, at Fletcher.

Like George E. Walker, Jones was responsible for several educational buildings. Furman and Wofford have already been mentioned. For Charleston, he designed the domed Normal School (later Memminger), built by Benjamin Lucas, and the Friend Street Public School, built by Walter Cade.[45] Miss Mary Taylor, historian of Memminger, believes that Jones was influenced by the plan of Bennett School, designed by W. J. Bennett, which had opened shortly before.[46] The Normal School no longer stands, and the present Memminger School is a modern building.

The Friend Street School, which opened May 20, 1859,[47] burned in the fire of 1861. According to Henry P. Archer, Crafts School (built 1882), which occupies the site, is made on the same model.[48] Crafts shows a weak Gothic note.

Jones had a brother, James C. Jones (died 1861) and a half-brother, John Russell (1813-1871), and is said at one time to have been associated with them in the bookselling business.[49] Russell and James C. Jones, as the firm of Russell & Jones, published *Russell's Magazine*, a brief-lived but well considered periodical, and the book-shop was a meeting place for the literary men of the state.

Jones was married by the Rev. Arthur M. Small to Miss Martha J. Small, second daughter of Robert Small, February 17, 1857.[50]

In May, 1854, Jones had been among the signers of a petition from the merchants of Charleston, requesting a quarantine against the West Indies to avoid the introduction of yellow fever.[51]

With the coming of the Confederacy, he was attached to the commissary of the Regiment of Reserves, in 1861.[52]

After the war, he went to Memphis, Tennessee, and is known to have been there in 1867.[53]

He (or another of the same name) bought a lot in Charleston in 1879, and added to it in 1884.[54]

The gate of a burial lot at Magnolia Cemetery is labeled "E. C. Jones"; however, the small obelisk within bears the names of others of his family, but not his.

Two arcaded buildings in Italian villa style, 30 and 32-34 Montagu Street, may perhaps be attributable to Jones. So too, perhaps, may be the ornate building, now part of the South Carolina National Bank, with its loggia and directors' room decorated with marbleized pilasters under a coved ceiling.

The Unitarian Church.

FRANCIS D. LEE

1826—August, 1885

FRANCIS D. LEE PRACTICED IN CHARLESTON DURing a little more than a decade, 1850-1861, for almost half of which time he was a partner of Edward C. Jones (qv). The eclecticism of the period shows strongly in his work. One may regret the juxtaposition of dissimilar forms which resulted, but considered individually, his structures are so successful that Samuel Lapham has written that "Lee was a master of any style".[1]

He was born in 1826,[2] one of several children of William and Elizabeth (Markley) Lee of Charleston.[3] Through his father, he was descended from the colonial portrait painter. Jeremiah Theus.[4] His sister, Mary Elizabeth Lee (1813-1849), wrote a quantity of magazine verse which was collected in book form after her death.

At the College of Charleston, where the records give his middle name as Dee,[5] he won a gold medal with a speech on "Imagination" in 1845,[6] and was graduated in 1846.[7]

In the following year, he joined the short-lived South Carolina Lyceum, a group which heard lectures on scientific discoveries, his name coming last on the list of curators.[8] He was later to join Union Kilwinning Lodge No. 4, Scottish Rite Masons,[9] and the South Carolina Society,[10] and to be recording secretary of the Carolina Art Association,[11] all of which organizations still exist.

Lee taught in Mr. Sachtleben's school in 1848 and '49,[12] but by the end of the latter year, was again a pupil, studying architecture in Edward C. Jones' office. Louis J. Barbot (qv) was a fellow student. Lee's architectural drawings won him a silver medal, the highest award in this class, at the South Carolina Institute's 1849 fair.[13] He is said to have aided Jones in laying out Magnolia Cemetery in 1850.[14]

By November, 1850, he was on his own, a practicing architect with an office on Broad Street.[15]

Lee's early work includes two examples of the Gothic Revival. One is the pinnacled Elbert P. Jones marble monument near the great oak at Magnolia Cemetery, made at Philadelphia in 1852-53 at

The Unitarian Church, 6 Archdale Street. Gothicized in 1852-1854 by F. D. Lee.

a cost exceeding $6,000.[16] Lee thought well enough of it to sign it, but its interest lies in its parallelism to a larger work in the same style, the remodeling of the Unitarian Church in 1852-54.[17]

Here he drew his inspiration for the interior from the fan-tracery vaulting and pendants of the chapel of Henry VII at Westminster. Lee's vaulting is not structural, however, but superficial, and made of laths and plaster. His real problem was to fit it in. To quote the *Courier*:

> "A certain degree of reverence for the old walls, induced the congregation to retain, and if possible, to adapt them to a more pleasing and graceful structure. Indeed the cost of re-construction could hardly have exceeded the expense of perforating the faithful old masonry to admit of the new and lofty windows, or of compassing the ancient massive tower to build up one more lofty and imposing.
>
> "The difficulties which presented themselves in carrying out the design, seemed almost insurmountable, inasmuch as the shape of the old structure being almost square in plan, was ill adapted to the Gothic style, that species of architecture being decided on by the committee . . . .[18]

This church, especially the decoration of the tower, suffered in the earthquake of 1886, which should be remembered when judging Lee's design.

Almost contemporary with the remodeling of the church was a very different work, completed early in 1853, the grocery store of S. S. Farrar & Brothers, at the southwest corner of East Bay and Cumberland Street, running through to State Street, and containing some 42,184 cubic feet of storage space. Here Lee used cast-iron pillars.[19] He was to employ iron in quantity again in the Fish Market, and near the end of his life he was to design extensive department stores at St. Louis, Missouri, so that this large commercial building may be considered somewhat prophetic. It may be, however, that he won his knowledge of stores from Jones, who had drawn the plans of a notable example in Charleston.

On July 1, 1852, Lee became Jones' partner in the firm of Jones & Lee.[20] The time was auspicious. Cotton was high, and railroads were to enrich everyone, or so many believed. Building boomed. The partners received orders from all over South Carolina and even from adjoining states. Several of the works of the firm which have

St. Luke's Church, 22 Elizabeth Street at Charlotte, begun in 1859. F. D. Lee, architect. The steeple, planned for the northwest corner (left) was not built.

been considered in the chapter on Jones may have belonged by right to Lee. Others, in this chapter, seem almost certainly his.

He was the architect of the Farmers' & Exchange Bank on East Bay,[21] built 1853-54,[22] an admirable little structure in Moorish style. Lopez and Trumbo were the contractors.[23] Lee used the unpointed horseshoe arch, reminiscent of the Alcazar at Seville, on a facade made up of pale Jersey and somber Connecticut brownstone,[24] producing the striped effect dear to Moorish builders.

William Gilmore Simms wrote that, beside its neighbor, the Roman Doric Planters' & Mechanics' Bank, it looked "as a toy-box under the eaves of the tower of Babel." [25] The location was unfortunate, but "toy-box" is misleading. Perhaps the subtropical sun is responsible, and the fact that the thirty-second parallel of latitude skirts Charleston and Morocco alike, but the bank wears an air of sincerity, and does not look as if it had escaped from a fairground.

As Lee is credited with the design of the bank, he may, by analogy, be thought to have planned the Moorish Fish Market, which newspapers of the time ascribe to the firm. This astounding affair was made of iron and concrete, It was 44 feet square by 21 high, and stood at the foot of Market Street, beside a boat basin 42 feet by 90, which was fitted with granite steps.[26] One regrets the absence of a picture.

The ironwork was made by Cameron, Mustard & Co., one of nine Charleston foundries of the time.[27] Due to the bursting of a coffer dam, change of contractors, etc., the Fish Market approached completion only late in 1856.[28]

Another Oriental design, the Vanderhorst tomb at Magnolia Cemetery, made of brownstone in Egyptian style, may, perhaps be a product of Lee's eclecticism. The narrowing of the upper part of the doorway is not unlike that at the Farmers' & Exchange Bank, and though this is a small detail by which to judge, the skillful handling of the unfamiliar order brings Lee to mind.

In the busy year of 1853, Lee took time from weightier matters to design the silver trumpet which the Phoenix Fire Engine Company gave their president.[29]

Lee aided Jones in the large task of remodeling the Orphan House in 1853-54.[30] The contractor was Lewis Rebb, who also built the Citadel Square Baptist Church in 1855-56. Papers of the day name Jones & Lee as the architects. If Lee drew the plans, the church is one of his most important works in point of size, but less spirited than most of his designs. The *Courier* described it as "Norman, with all the details and ornaments of that picturesque style,

The former Farmers' and Exchange Bank, 141 East Bay,
built 1853–1854. Lee used the Moorish style throughout this building.

but without the extreme massive and heavy proportions." [31] It has suffered from the diminution of its steeple, the spire of which blew down in 1885, toppling outward in an arc with a roar heard above the hurricane.

The partnership with Jones ended January 5, 1857,[32] and Lee moved his office from the corner of Broad and Church Streets (now the Chamber of Commerce building) to the State Bank building, No. 1 Broad Street.[33]

From this year dated a two-story, clapboard dwelling on the northwest corner of Rutledge Avenue and Doughty Street. His imagination did not display itself here. It is as if his client had said, "No nonsense, Mr. Lee." Neither did it owe much to local architectural tradition, although he gave it ample piazzas. This house showed that by the late fifties, even relatively unimportant buildings in Charleston were sometimes designed by architects. The builder, James M. Curtis, contracted to build the house with its appurtenances, to furnish the material and to perform the whole under Lee's direction for $5,200.00.[34] This dwelling was pulled down in 1963.

In 1860, a hotel planned by Lee was opened at Florence, South Carolina, which had just become a railroad junction.[35]

In the preceding year, he had designed St. Luke's Church, at the northeast corner of Charlotte and Elizabeth Streets. Patrick O'Donnell was the contractor.[36] The cornerstone was laid May 12, 1859. It is amusing to learn from the *Courier* that the style, "perpendicular Gothic, of the Tudor period," is "from the extreme lightness when compared with the other styles of Gothic . . . . peculiarly adapted to our Southern climate." The church forms a Greek cross. A steeple, 210 feet high, was to have stood in the angle of the north and west arms,[37] but guns boomed at Fort Sumter, and it was not built.

Its lack is not felt. The exterior of this church is the only Gothic Revival work in Charleston which has about it the flavor of the style it imitates. (Inside, the story is different—here is merely another creditable interior.) Lee gave it honest lines, but something is due to the accident which left revealed the texture and hearty deep red of its walls. Like other churches of the day, it was to have been slicked over with stucco, but patriotism intervened, and the lime was given to the Confederacy.

Entering the Southern army, Lee served with distinction as an officer of engineers, reaching the rank of major. Coastal fortifications planned by him included Fort Walker at Hilton Head,[38] in the defense of which he saw active service,[39] and Battery Wagner on

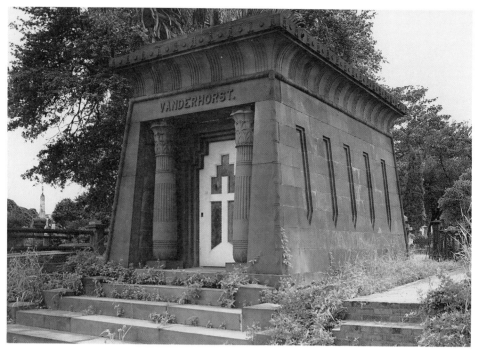

The Vanderhorst tomb, Magnolia Cemetery.

Dwelling at Rutledge Avenue and Doughty Street, built 1857. F. D. Lee, architect. Destroyed, 1963.

Morris Island.[40] He invented a spar-torpedo which attached to the semi-submersible, *Little David,* damaged the armored steam-frigate, *New Ironsides,* flagship of the Federal fleet.[41] Soon every Confederate iron-clad ram carried such a weapon. South Carolina appropriated $50,000 toward the purchase and refitting of a heavy boat to carry the torpedo, but as the sum proved insufficient and neither the army nor navy departments at Richmond would further the plan, the vessel remained incomplete at the end of the war.[42]

When peace came, Lee went to France in an endeavor to interest Napoleon III in his weapon.[43]

He returned to Charleston, as is shown by a plat of Magnolia Cemetery, preserved at the office there, which is signed and dated "Enlarged from a Lithograph/By/Francis D. Lee/May 1866". The architect appeared in the *Charleston Directory of 1867-68* also. But his Post-Bellum career belongs not to South Carolina but to Missouri. He went to St. Louis in 1868.[44]

There, a member of the firm of Lee and Annan, he designed the Merchants' Exchange, completed in 1875.[45] Other works by him there include the Jesuits' College,[46] the red brick and sandstone Roe Building, built about 1883 in Gothic Revival style, and the recently demolished "Gay's Central Building," completed in 1880-81.[47]

Lee died on a fishing trip in Minnesota, August, 1885, and lies buried in Bellefontaine Cemetery at St. Louis.[48]

An editorial in the *News and Courier* (Charleston) of August 29, 1885, deserves to be quoted in full though it is incorrect on several points, notably as concerns the place of Lee's death, and the attribution to him of St. James' Methodist Church (the Spring Street Methodist Church, by Barbot & Seyle), the Westminster Presbyterian Church (by Jones), and the Glebe Street Church, the early date of which (1847-48) makes a connection with Lee improbable.

"Major Francis D. Lee.

"The news has been received in Charleston of the death of Major Francis D. Lee, which occurred at St-Louis, Mo, on Wednesday last, from apoplexy. Major Lee was a Charlestonian by birth, and passed his early youth in this city. He was born in the year 1827, and was the son of Mr. William Lee and the nephew of Judge Thomas Lee. He was graduated from the College of Charleston, and immediately afterwards entered upon the study of architecture, which he adopted as his profession. He was taken into the office of Mr. Edward Jones, where his studies were completed, and he was made junior partner of the firm of Jones & Lee. He remained here until the breaking out of the war, and in that time had assisted to construct and plan a number of the best known public edifices and grounds in and around the city. He assisted in planning the laying out of Magnolia Cemetery and the remodeling of the Orphan-House. He was the architect of the Unitarian Church, St. Luke's Church, the Glebe Street Church, St. James' Methodist Church in Spring street, the Westminster Church, and the first Holy Communion Church built in this city. At the beginning of the war he was given a commission in the engineer corps of the Confederate army, and in that position rendered valuable service to the Confederacy. He was always Gen. Beauregard's right-hand man, and in the siege of Charleston filled an important part in the defence. It was during this period that he invented a valuable submarine torpedo, which caused Gen. Beauregard to exclaim, upon witnessing its first test, which was made in this harbor just in front of the Battery: "Charleston is now safe." Major Lee was engaged in the first battle at Fort Walker, at Port Royal, and subsequently planned Battery Wagner on Morris Island. He served throughout the war with considerable distinction, and at its close went over to France upon the invitation of Napoleon the Third, who had become interested in his torpedo. He remained in France long enough to have four or five interviews with the Emperor, and then returned to this country, settling at St. Louis. He made that city his home and soon rose to the foremost rank of his profession at that place. He became thoroughly identified with the interests of the city and planned two of its largest and best known buildings, the Merchants' Exchange and the Jesuits' College.

"Major Lee was a magnificent draftsman and a man of unusual intellect, and was as skilled in the use of the pen as of the sword. He was of fine physical appearance, and his handsome, genial face was always to be seen at the social gatherings of the day. He was married to Miss Ancrum, of Camden, South Carolina, and upon settling in St. Louis his house became the headquarters for all South Carolinians who passed through that city, and those who have once been entertained by him can never forget his grand hospitality. A man of genial spirits, the possessor of a kind heart and cultivated mind, his death will be long and sadly felt by the hosts of friends whom he has made, both in St. Louis and Charleston."

LOUIS J. BARBOT AND JOHN H. SEYLE

L OUIS J. BARBOT AND JOHN H. SEYLE FORMED
the firm of Barbot & Seyle on August 2, 1852,[1] and were
partners as late as 1856.

Barbot was descended from a French family who had come to
Charleston from Santo Domingo. He studied architecture in the
office of Edward C. Jones (qv) in 1849, and at the South Carolina
Institute Fair of that year received a diploma for the second best
architectural drawing exhibited, Francis D. Lee (qv), a fellow stu-
dent, winning first place.[2] Barbot joined the South Carolina Society,
October 12, 1852.[3] By 1853, he was secretary of the Charleston
Mechanic Society.[4]

Seyle was the son of Samuel Seyle and his wife Mary Susanna
Wesner, a sister of Frederick Wesner (qv).[5] He was primarily a contractor, and was termed carpenter in the directories of 1840-41 and
1849, and builder in that of 1867-68. In 1833, he and Albert Elfe
placed a cupola designed by Charles Fraser (qv) on the old Exchange building.[6] In 1849, he exhibited India ink drawings and a
clock case at the South Carolina Institute Fair.[7] He was a member
of the Fellowship Society.[8] In July, 1855, with his wife and six children, he returned on the steamer *Carolina* from a visit to the south-
ward.[9] His wife died on October 16, 1860.[10] Not infrequently his
name was written Seyles.

In August, 1853, the *Courier* reported that:

"The Charleston 'Club House' is now in process of erection
by Mr. Albert Elfe, after plans furnished by Messrs. Barbot &
Seyle . . . . In front of the building will be a space of 100 feet in
depth, which will be laid out into flower beds, meandering walks,
&c . . . . Five elegant fountains will be introduced, to be supplied
from reservoirs in the upper portion of the building. The Club
House itself, will be furnished throughout richly and consistently,
according to the highest style of the Corinthian order . . . . three
stories, or a base and two stories—the distance from floor to
ceiling being, respectively, 9, 15 and 18 feet. The front view will
present a rusticated base with arched windows, with all orna-

The Spring Street Methodist Church, 68 Spring Street at Coming, begun in 1856.
Barbot and Seyle, architects.

mental appendages allowed or admitted by the order. Above, will be enriched pilasters, entablatures, and balustrades. The windows are of the largest size consistent with good effect and proportions, and are so arranged that the sashes may be run entirely within cases in the walls, so as to allow the fullest and freest admission of air . . . . The entrance" (will be) "surmounted by a Corinthian pediment . . . . The front will be finished externally, with the imitation brown stone mastic (the building being of brick), with terra cotta ornaments and projections somewhat in the style of the *Mills House*, so far as finished externally. The other portions of the exterior will be cemented—the roof will be of the best slate" . . .[11]

The club house was occupied by June 1854.[12] It was a better looking building than this somewhat overpowering description would convey, to judge from a photograph taken when it stood in ruins. Its career which began with so much fashion had been short and chequered. In Reconstruction times, it held the constitutional convention of 1868,[13] the "ring-streakéd and stripéd" assembly which discarded the time-honored state constitution in favor of the present one, based on that of Ohio. The building became the Federal Court House,[14] and later belonged to the German Artillery.[15] In 1886, the earth shook, and the club house was shattered beyond repair. The lot now houses the post office annex.

Barbot & Seyle designed a church for the village of Pocotaligo, South Carolina. The *Courier* of February 19, 1853, announced:

"Contract wanted, for Building a Church, 64 by 32, Doric order, plainly but neatly finished. The location is within a half mile of a landing for schooners, 60 miles from the city. It is desired that proposals be submitted for building of either brick or wood. Bricks can be had one mile from the spot at $8 per M. The plans and working drawings will be shown and explained by Messrs. Barbot & Seyle, 59 Broad-st., Charleston, S. C.

        W. F. Hutson
        A. F. Gregorie   } Committee
        W. D. Gregorie

Pocotaligo, Feb. 18, 1853".

In the same year, the firm designed an "Italian villa" for General W. E. Martin on Sullivan's Island. The materials were prepared for joining and framing by J. H. Long (qv) at Columbia, floated down on rafts, and set up under Long's supervision.[16] This house burned in 1858.[17]

During 1853, also, the firm remodeled two buildings, the Protestant Episcopal Library on Chalmers Street,[18] and the defunct cotton mill, designed by Charles Tillinghast James (qv) in Hampstead, which they made over into an Alms House.[19] They also drew plans for fitting up two shops on King Street,[20] and served as agents for "Telegraphic Lightning Conductors".[21]

In 1854, they entered unsuccessfully the competition for the design of the Calhoun Monument.[22]

They planned the three-story brick store, built in 1855, which stood until 1963 at the southeast corner of King and George Streets.[23] By the end of the year, they had drawn plans for improvements to the Old Jail on Magazine Street.[24]

In 1856, they designed a variety of buildings, the Branch Bank of the State of South Carolina in Camden,[25] two outbuildings for Thomas O'Brien's lot on Rutledge Street near Beaufain,[26] and the Charleston Fire Engine Company house, later the German Fuselier Hall, an attractive brick structure, which was ruthlessly pulled down in 1937.[27] Also designed in 1856 was their largest existing work, the Spring Street Methodist Church.[28]

This brick and stucco temple, which is reminiscent of Jones' Westminster Presbyterian Church, has a portico with Corinthian columns. It is set on a high basement, but its most striking features are the unusual pilasters along its sides and back, which are stepped, diminishing as they ascend. Those on the west are best preserved. Though occupied in 1858, the church was not completed until after the War between the States.[29]

Bishop Albert S. Thomas, in his history of the Protestant Episcopal Church in South Carolina, mentions Barbot & Seyle as architects of the Church of the Holy Apostles, at Barnwell, consecrated 1857.

The firm had dissolved by 1859, in which year Barbot was busy with two large buildings. He designed a Catholic Orphan School for Boys, intended for the south side of Queen Street, nearly opposite Archdale, two and a half stories high, with a dormitory, piazza, lofty ceilings, a heating system composed of both fire places and hot air, and a 10,000 gallon cistern. James Kenney (qv) was to be the general contractor.[30] If this building was ever completed, it has disappeared, probably in the fire of 1861.

In March, 1859, Barbot advertised for estimates for building "a

The Alms House, formerly the Cotton Factory, Columbus Street, built in 1847-1848. Charles T. James, architect. Remodeled in 1853 by Barbot and Seyle. No longer standing.

Church at Prince Frederick, Pee Dee." [31] Generally known as Prince Frederick's Winyah, this is a brick and stucco Romanesque structure with a pinnacled tower.

It is sometimes called Gunn's Church, from the name of a contractor who died, it is said from falling from the tower while it was being built, delaying the work, which was further interrupted by the war.

In the directory of 1867-68, Barbot was listed as civil engineer of the city of Charleston. In this capacity, he furnished statistics on storm tides to the Year Book of 1893. [32]

For many years, his home was the old Horry house on the northwest corner of Meeting and Tradd Streets. [33]

MR. YOUNG

I N DESCRIBING WORK THEN UNDER WAY IN CHARLES-
ton, the *Courier* of August 27, 1853, said of the Custom House:
"Mr. Young, of Boston, is the Architect, and Col. Edwd B.
White, is the Superintending Architect."

Years later, *Charleston, South Carolina in 1883*, a volume of excellent heliotype views with accompanying text, said of the structure: "Among the plans submitted, that of Mr. Young of Washington, was adopted."

It seems certain that Mr. Young was Ammi Burnham Young,
architect with Rogers •of the Custom House at Boston, completed
about 1846.[1] The Boston building has since been altered drastically
by the erection of a tower, until it has been described as all tower;
the Charleston structure was never completed to the extent contemplated in the plans. But as designed, they bore decided resemblances to each other. Both were cruciform, with pedimented porticoes approached by wide steps. The Boston structure was Doric,
with a flattish dome above a rotunda. For Charleston, the Roman
Corinthian style was substituted, and a tall dome planned above a
rectangular hall.

The erection of the Custom House caused a flutter among architects and builders. As early as 1848, Congress appropriated the
funds.[2] In 1849, Fitzsimons' Wharf was bought for a site.[3] An advertisement for plans and specifications, offering $300 for those adopted,
appeared in February, 1850.[4] Among the architects who competed
were E. B. White, P. H. Hammarskold, Edward C. Jones, all of
Charleston and J. S. Norris of Savannah.[5] The commissioners
awarded the decision to Jones,[6] but were overruled by the authorities at Washington.

The *Courier* of October 12, 1850, stated that "the Scientific Committee, to whom the plans were submitted, have come to a decision,
and selected positions" (portions?) "from several of those placed before them." But it appears improbable that the results of this min-
gling entered into Young's plan, which—as drawn—bore so close a
resemblance to that of the building at Boston.

By 1853, as we have seen, Young's plan had been chosen, White was superintending architect, and construction had begun.[7]

The *Courier* of July 15, 1854, wrote:

> "The style selected is *Roman Corinthian,* which gives an elevation of the two upper stories decorated with attached columns and porticos, supported by a rusticated basement story, and surmounted by a dome, the highest point of which will be 160 feet from the pavement. The general plan is a cross, the longest arm from East to West being 259 feet, while the shorter arm extending North and South, will measure 152 feet . . . .

> "The entire foundation has now been completed . . . these foundations are laid just outside of the line of fortifications which enclosed 'Charlestown', previous to our revolutionary war—the west end slightly intersecting the face of 'Craven's Bastion'. The remains of this old work were discovered in the excavations made for the Custom House foundations, and the direction thereof was traced by lines of cedar pickets, some of which are now to be seen at the office of Col. E. B. White . . . . more than seven thousand piles have been driven down to a depth of forty feet, so that they rest securely in a bed of firm sand, which in that locality immediately overlies the marl formation. On these piles is rested a massive *grillage* of the best timber which supports a compact stratum of concrete, and on the latter the mason work foundation begins.

> "The basement walls, which are of granite, have reached the height of six feet on a greater portion of the foundation. The two upper stories will be of the finest building marble. The structure will be strictly fire proof throughout, the materials employed being granite, marble, and iron" . . . .

Interrupted by the War Between the States, the Custom House was finished afterward, but on a reduced scale. It lacks the dome, it lacks the north and south porticoes, and in consequence, its intended proportions. It is nonetheless impressive.

The United States Custom House, 200 East Bay, begun in 1853. Ammi B. Young, architect.

The John Rutledge House, 116 Broad Street. Altered and modernized by
P. H. Hammerskold in 1853. *(Tom Peck)*

P. H. HAMMARSKOLD
Working c. 1849-1856

P. H. HAMMARSKOLD WAS, FOR A FEW YEARS, A popular architect in South Carolina. References to him are frequent. The *Mercury* of March 3, 1849, stated:

"Mr. Hammarskold, civil engineer and draughtsman, exhibited to us yesterday a drawing of Lucas' West Point Rice Mill, intended as a copy for a similar establishment to be erected on the Baltic, about one hundred and fifty miles from Stockholm, the capital of Sweden.

"The drawing is beautifully executed, and exhibits with great minuteness and accuracy the interior arrangements and machinery of the establishment."

Again, in speaking of the plans which he entered, unsuccessfully as it turned out, in the competition for the Custom House, the *Courier* of March 2, 1850, said:

. . . "They are most elegantly executed. The delicateness of the touch given to the finer ornamental parts, is exquisite, and the several fronts present a magnificent appearance" . . . .

Here is shown Hammarskold's strength, the draughtsmanship which made him an attractive architect—on paper. It won for him the silver medal at the South Carolina Institute Fair of 1852, when he entered two architectural drawings.[1] With practical problems, he was to prove less fortunate.

In 1850, he worked for the city of Charleston under Edward B. White (qv) on the High School and the additions to the College of Charleston.[2]

In a letter from Charleston dated March 22 of the same year, Fredrika Bremer, the Swedish feminist, wrote of a member of Hammarskold's family in a way which indicates a previous acquaintanceship:

. . . "I have likewise seen today Mrs. Hammarsköld (Emilie Holmberg) and her mother. Tears of longing for Sweden filled the eyes of the old lady. The younger lady is a much esteemed teacher of music here." [3]

The following year, Hammarskold had what then appeared a tremendous stroke of luck—his plans were chosen for the new State House at Columbia, South Carolina,[4] which was to replace the old wooden building designed by James Hoban (qv). In the new structure, iron was extensively used. Hammarskold was born of a family from Sweden where a relation had been in the iron business, and in 1850 had himself become a director in the Nesbit Iron Works of Spartanburg, South Carolina.[5] This knowledge of the metal may have had its effect with the committee.

The *Courier* of January 15, 1852, grew fulsome:

"THE STATE CAPITOL

"We noticed at the time of the ceremony, the laying of the cornerstone of the new fire-proof building at Columbia, which is designed to furnish not only suitable and indestructible depositories for the archives of the State, but also halls for the two branches of the Legislature, and also rooms for all the public officers. The plans for this building by Mr. P. H. Hammarskold, the architect, were approved by the last Legislature, and a liberal appropriation was made for carrying them out. A beautiful drawing by the architect, exhibiting the principal front of the building, has been left at our office for public inspection. We do not think that any thing more grand in the general effect, or more chaste in the details, can be found in any public building in the United States. In the admirable finish of his design, Mr. Hammarskold has shown how completely he is master of his profession, and the plan, as it comes from his hand, is happily touched with the exactness of science, and the mellow and graceful tints of art."

The following year, 1853, was a busy one. In March, a careless servant allowed his office to catch fire, and nearly all his drawings and plans were destroyed.[6] He drew more. He designed a church for the Independent or Congregational sect at Mount Pleasant, South Carolina.[7] He altered and modernized (as modernization was then understood) the John Rutledge house, now 116 Broad Street, placing terra-cotta cornices over the windows, similar to those used by Earle (qv) on the Mills House, and adding the iron balconies and fence. The two-story kitchen building with pointed windows also is due to Hammarskold.[8] For William Izard Bull, chairman of the commissioners of the new State House, he designed a dwelling.[9] This stood near the west end of Tradd Street and was the last house to burn in the great fire of 1861.[10]

At the beginning of 1854, Hammarskold was at the top of his career. The State House was proceeding slowly, but apparently satisfactorily. In February, he advertised for builders' estimates for altering and adding to the court house in Williamsburg District,[11] which Mills (qv) had designed. Recommended by Christopher Gustavus Memminger, later secretary of the treasury for the Confederacy, and even then prominent, Hammarskold drew the plans of a professors' house at the University of South Carolina, which was built and admired.[12]

Then came the blow. The commissioners inspected the State House and found the work defective. On June 22, 1854, they advertised that they would elect on August 2, "a competent ARCHITECT," who must reside in Columbia.[13] They received twenty-nine offers, mostly from Northern men.[14] John R. Niernsee of Baltimore was employed as consulting architect, and George E. Walker (qv) of Charleston became superintending architect.[15] Their difficulties are told in the following chapter.

Hammarskold sued the commissioners, but the proceedings were quashed in the court of appeals in 1856.[16]

Hammarskold married Miss A. J. Hancock, January 15, 1856, in Columbia.[17]

By 1859, he was in Memphis, Tennessee, where the old Robertson Topp house with its Corinthian portico is said to be of his design.[18]

GEORGE EDWARD WALKER

Worked c. 1850-1861, Died September 19, 1863

GEORGE E. WALKER DID MUCH OF HIS WORK FOR schools and colleges. He made his reputation with Free School No. 6, begun in 1851 [1] and dedicated June 29, 1852,[2] which stood on the east side of Meeting Street between Mary and Wragg, near the site of the present Courtenay Public School.[3]

As the first of a series of improved free schools, it attracted attention. "H." (who remains unidentified), in a letter to the *Courier* of June 30, 1853, waxed enthusiastic.

> "But how beautifully *taste and utility* can work together, is best illustrated in the new Free School in Meeting-street. It is a pretty Tuscan temple, and is *the most remarkable building in Charleston*—being the first monumental evidence of the new-born interest in Popular Education."

In fact, "H." found nothing to criticize except the lack of "Italian jalousies" to keep out the glare. Again, in the July 2 issue of the same paper, he stated:

> "The architect of our beautiful Free School Edifice was our young fellow-townsman, Mr. George E. Walker—to his taste and skill are we indebted for a School edifice, at once commodious to pupil and teacher, and ornamental to the city."

Unfortunately, the value of this praise is diminished by the lack of critical faculty which "H". betrayed, when he deprecated the Hibernian Hall, comparing it unfavorably to "the new Cathedral, Grace Church, Roper's Hospital, the new Work House, the Unitarian Church, the Engine Houses, the Private Dwellings on the Battery." [4] To a present-day observer, the Hall, by Thomas U. Walter, is by no means outshone by any of these buildings, the work of several architects of the fifties, which apparently impressed "H". by reason of their newness. While the encomium he bestowed must therefore be discounted, as coming from someone who was no judge, an indisputable testimony to Walker's ability is furnished by the library building, still standing, which he designed for the College of Charleston.

Before he planned this, however, he was employed in his capacity as surveyor and civil engineer,[5] to straighten and widen the streets of Moultrieville on Sullivan's Island, in 1853, at a salary of ten dollars a day.[6] The changes were fairly drastic, and included the removal of a windmill.[7] No prophet, he allowed his roads to retain curves unsuited to modern traffic conditions.

At this time, he had his office at the New Custom House,[8] then in the early stages of being built, under the supervision of E. B. White (qv). Walker was assistant constructing architect.[9]

In 1854, he remodeled the stately court house at Georgetown, South Carolina.[10] It is unlikely that Walker improved it, but one can say to his credit that he did not spoil it.

In 1854, also, he drew the plans of the library building of the College of Charleston.[11] The contract was given to William F. Patterson in January, 1855, and the building was opened in July, 1856.[12] In his floor plan, Walker was undoubtedly influenced by the library building of the University of South Carolina. Walker omitted two of its salient features, however, the portico and the stairway encased in a semi-circular projection. He simply adapted the plan of the main room, which rises two stories surrounded by a gallery, under which the bookshelves are arranged in alcoves leading to the windows, leaving the center of the room for reading tables. Walker set it upon a half-story basement, ran up a flight of stone steps to the door, and had his building. It is an admirable structure, which depends for exterior effect upon quoins and round-headed windows, and inside, gains grace through the use of arches under the galleries. It remains much as it was built, except that the basement has been deepened to serve as an additional floor.

In the summer of 1854, Walker was appointed constructing architect for the State House at Columbia [13] in place of P. H. Hammarskold (qv), and became a resident of that city. His first duty was to see that the defective walls already built were removed, and that materials were prepared for the new construction.[14] But his connection with the State House was short and acrimonious.

In an undated pamphlet, *Exposition of the Proceedings of Commissioners of the New State Capitol, Columbia, S. C.* "By G. E. Walker, Late Architect," he claimed that he had been unjustly treated by the commissioners. Walker stated that he had been led to expect that he would be allowed to make the new plans, and that he therefore submitted a design which the committee pronounced excellent, but that they also allowed John R. Niernsee of Baltimore, the consulting architect, to submit several sets of plans. Niernsee's plans, Walker alleged, did not conform to the desired dimensions, and contained absurdities, such as making a pathway of the library, which mistake (according to Walker), Niernsee tried to explain as a draughtsman's error. At a meeting. Walker called Niernsee a "humbug." For this show of temper, he was blamed by the commissioners, who termed Niernsee "affable and obliging". Walker was dismissed from his post on April 14, 1855, and resolutions censuring him were passed by the commission. His pamphlet, which has been largely ignored, contains valuable information on the building of the State House, including correspondence between him and Niernsee, and the statement that Werner, the well-known Charleston ironworker and founder, did not execute the ironwork used in the defective building, but in large measure transferred his contract to a Baltimore firm.[15]

By January, 1856, Walker had designed the Columbia Female College [16] at Columbia, known also as the Methodist Female College and more recently as the Methodist College. This building was to serve for a time as a Confederate hospital. It was spared at the burning of Columbia in 1865 because some nuns took refuge there.[17] A colorful account of life in this college in Post-Bellum days is found in John Andrew Rice's *I Came Out of the Eighteenth Century*. The institution still exists, but Walker's building was torn down in fairly recent times.

Walker drew the plans for Newberry College at Newberry, South Carolina, built by the Lutheran synod at a cost of approximately $18,000. The contractors were Osborne Wells and Wallace A. Cline. The cornerstone was laid July 15, 1856, and the building was opened October, 1858. It was damaged by Federal soldiers in 1865, and two years later was reported as "crumbling".[18] It was an ambitious building with Gothic buttresses. Smeltzer Hall stands on its foundations.[19]

Walker was also the architect of the State Agricultural Society fair buildings at Columbia.[20]

The treasurer's report of the South Carolina College (now the University of South Carolina) dated November 1, 1859, shows that in May, Walker was paid for professional services to that institution.

Undoubtedly, some of his best work was in church design. Bishop Albert S. Thomas, in his history of the Protestant Episcopal Church

The College of Charleston Library, completed in 1856. George E. Walker, architect.

in South Carolina, names Walker as architect of beautiful Trinity Church, Abbeville, built 1859-60; and of Christ Church, Columbia, built at the same time and burned by Sherman's army in 1865. Bishop Thomas also states that St. Luke's, Newberry, built 1854-55, followed a drawing by "Architect G. M. Walker of Columbia", probably a misreading of G. E. Walker.

With the coming of the War Between the States, he entered the Confederate service, and built Battery Bee at the west end of Sullivan's Island in 1862. This was an important unit in the defenses of Charleston Harbor. Brigadier-General R. S. Ripley, C.S.A., termed Captain Walker an accomplished engineer, who was "careful to build his works with especial reference to the effect of modern artillery." [21]

In 1838, Walker had shared in the partition of the estate of Robbert Walker,[22] a cabinet maker,[23] who owned several pieces of real estate. This was probably his father.

The architect was married, December 27, 1850, by the Rev. Dr. Bachman of St. John's Lutheran Church to Agnes M. Frost, eldest daughter of John D. Frost of Fairfield District.[24]

Walker died September 19, 1863.[25]

His name was generally written George E. Walker, but is found in full on the record of a mortgage in 1845.[26]

MID-CENTURY MODERNS

CHARLES TILLINGHAST JAMES.   September 15, 1805—
October 17, 1862

CHARLES TILLINGHAST JAMES HAS BEEN CALLED
the "great prophet of steam-driven cotton factories." During the forties, his efforts resulted in starting twenty-three
steam mills, sixteen of which were in his native New England.[1]

He was born at West Greenwich, Rhode Island, son of Silas
James and his wife Phebe Tillinghast. Although his father was a
local judge, the boy received little schooling, before learning the
carpenter's trade. His great interest was in mechanics, especially in
relation to the construction of textile machinery.[2]

James was the architect of the cotton factory in Hampstead (now
part of Charleston), the cornerstone of which was laid October 2,
1847.[3] Sanders and H. D. Walker were the contractors.[4] On April
12, 1848, the first loom was set to work and homespun made.[5]

Hopes were bright. But the factory lost money. The first company
sold out to a second group, and in 1852, the second company sold out
not much better than the first.[6] The city bought the main buildings
and engaged Barbot & Seyle (qv) to remodel the place into an Alms
House.

James, a Democrat, went to Washington in 1851 as senator from
Rhode Island. He was a major-general in the Rhode Island militia
and is remembered as a tall, fine-looking man. While he was experi-
menting with a shell in 1862, it exploded, wounding him fatally.[7]

JOHN E. EARLE.   Working 1853

JOHN E. Earle designed the Mills House, now the St. John
Hotel, at the corner of Meeting and Queen Streets. William Gilmore
Simms, in *Harper's New Monthly Magazine,* June 1857, erroneously
ascribed the Mills House to Hammarskold, whom he mistakenly
called a German; but Earle was cited as the architect by the *Courier*
of August 13, 1853.

The Mills House Hotel, formerly the St. John Hotel. Originally the Mills House,
115 Meeting Street, completed in 1853. John E. Earle, architect. The balcony came from
Philidelphia; the terracotta window cornices from New England.

Architecturally unimpressive, the building none the less has its interest, since it was the first structure in Charleston in which both running water and steam heat were supplied on a large scale.

It opened November 3, 1853,[1] though the "Opening Banquet" was not held until November 5.[2] There is no lack of information about the five-storied building—columns in the press of the time described it and named everyone concerned, from the architect to the purveyor of crockery. J. P. & R. Earle, the general contractors.[3] were almost certainly relations of the architect. We find them working for Jones & Lee on Sebring's building on Broad Street (now the Walker, Evans & Cogwell building) during the same year.[4] That James P. Earle had pride in his work is shown by his behavior eight years later, when the Mills House was threatened by the great fire of 1861. He was one of a handful of friends who assisted the proprietors and their servants in fighting the flames from the windows for more than five hours, and succeded in saving the building.[5]

Working under the Earles on this hotel, Rebb & Cownover contracted for the carpentry and woodwork.[6] More important, however, was "Mr. Hathaway of Worcester, Mass.", who furnished the terra-cotta window cornices and pediments.[7] These were considered fireproof and created a furor, so that similar ones were placed on houses all over the city.

The hotel relies for effect on these cornices, a long balcony of Philadelphia ironwork, and an entrance with rusticated columns. Externally, at least, it has changed little, except that the walls no longer are colored in imitation of brownstone.

Safety and comfort were considered to a surprising degree. Enormous cisterns supplied water.

. . . "For all household purposes there will thus be a convenient supply at hand—for the sake of protection and security against fire, there will be introduced, also, an abundant supply of hose so arranged and connected with the system of supplying pipes, that any portion of the House could be flooded in an instant.

"Comfort and luxury, as well as mere necessities, are also consulted here, for on each floor are eight bathing rooms for ladies exclusively, which are furnished with every requisite for warm, cold or shower baths. On the first floor are rooms similarly furnished for the use of gentlemen." [8]

The heating arrangements compromised between the old and the new, public rooms and halls having steam heat, while bedrooms relied upon coal grates.[9]

Running water and even steam heat had been seen before in Charleston,[10] but never on such a scale. The cost of the Mills House, including the ground but exclusive of furnishings, was about $200,000.[11]

Earle was responsible also for an office building, described in 1853 as follows:

"R. Douglass & Co., the enterprising proprietors of our omnibus lines, have put up a bijou of an office on *King*-street, near *Line*. It is a tasteful and unique affair, rather on the cottage order, and was erected by Mr. Cownover, after plans of Mr. Jno. E. Earle." [12]

This building stood at the corner of King and Shepard Streets.[13] One searches in vain for an architectural "bijou" on or near that corner now.

JAMES A. LONGLEY, Working 1840 AND JOSEPH H. LONG, Working 1840—c. 1856

"Architects & Carpenters" were the terms James A. Longley and Joseph H. Long applied to themselves when they advertised in the *Charleston Directory of 1840-41* that they had entered into partnership under the firm name of Longley & Long, at 43 Queen Street, and were ready to furnish designs and contract for erecting all types of buildings.

This is the only mention which has been found of Longley. More is known of Long, who advertised carpentry as late as 1856.[1] In 1840, one hears of a John H. Long, who seems to have contracted to build the Apprentice's Library Society Hall.[2] (He was not its architect). This is probably a mistake for Joseph H. Long.

No building of Long's design is known, but one example of his work as a contractor deserves notice—a pre-fabricated house, set up in 1853 on Sullivan's Island. Barbot & Seyle (qv) were the architects.

. . . "The materials having all been prepared for joining and framing, by Mr. J. H. Long, at Columbia, were floated down in rafts. Mr. Long is now superintending the erection, and the work, when completed, will present a finished specimen of the Italian *villa*, or summer architecture, at once appropriate and ornamental." [3]

Although this one dwelling only was mentioned as made in this way, the method foreshadowed that used in modern mass-production.

Long was a Northerner who settled in South Carolina. Late in 1839, the *Courier* had published his marriage notice:

"Married on Wednesday evening, last, by the Rev. Dr. Capers, Mr. Joseph H. Long, of Northboro', (Mass.) to Miss Mary White, of this city.

"(We return our acknowledgments for a specimen of the wedding cake, which accompanied the above notice, and tender to the happy couple our best wishes for their future prosperity.) Eds. Courier." [4]

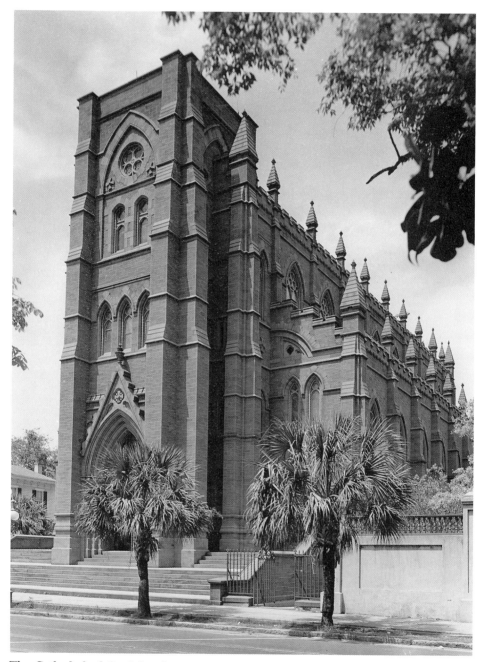

The Cathedral of St. John the Baptist, 122 Broad Street at Legare, built 1890-1907
on the same plan and site as the Cathedral of St. John and St. Finbar, built
1850-1854. Patrick C. Keely, architect of both. The steeple of the present
building is incomplete.

CHURCHES AND CHURCH SCHOOLS

PATRICK CHARLES KEELY.   August 9, 1816—August 11, 1896

P ATRICK C. KEELY OF KILKENNY AND BROOKLYN, is represented in Charleston today by two Roman Catholic churches of the Post-Bellum era, St. Patrick's, built in 1886-87, and the Cathedral of St. John the Baptist, built 1890-1907.[1] While these are too recent to be considered here, the cathedral stands on the foundations, and in most points follows the plan, of an Ante-Bellum edifice by Keely, the Cathedral of St. John and St. Finbar, begun in 1850 and dedicated April 6, 1854.[2]

The *Mercury* of August 1, 1850, made an interesting assertion:

> . . . "The Architect, Mr. Keely, is a pupil (the only one in the United States) of the celebrated Pugin, and this is the twenty-third Church in this country on which he has been engaged."

Two Young men, L. O'Connor, of Beaufort, South Carolina (later, by 1854, of New York), and James Farmer, of Brooklyn, were successively employed as superintending architects and assistants.[3]

The cathedral was said to be in early English style. Made of brownish freestone from Middlesex, Connecticut, it could seat 1,200 persons comfortably, and was 153 feet long at its greatest extent, by seventy-three feet wide, with a steeple 121 feet high, topped by a wrought-iron cross from Werner's foundry.[4] The cost, including that of the fence, was over $103,000.[5]

The *Courier* of May 28, 1853, wrote:

> "St. Finbar's Cathedral.—This stately edifice, so highly ornamental to the street in which it is located, is now steadily progressing to completion. For a week or ten days past, the workmen have been busily engaged in covering in the skeleton of the steeple, which had some time previously secured upon its massive stone tower, and yesterday the large ball and the cross which surmounts it, were hoisted up and placed upon its pinnacle. The men engaged in this apparently perilous employment, when viewed from the street, looked little larger than pigmies."

[255]

The Cathedral of St. John the Baptist.

The cathedral burned in the fire of December 11-12, 1861. In October, 1888, Keely inspected the ruins. The cornerstone of his present cathedral was laid in 1890. The builder of the first cathedral, Henry L. Cade, began this structure also, but died when it was well under way and was succeeded by Henry Oliver.[6] The steeple has never been erected, so that the exterior does not give a true impression of the former building.

Keely, Irish-born and trained, came to this country about 1841 or '42, settling in Brooklyn, where he died at the age of eighty. No matter how we today may consider his buildings, they undoubtedly were popular with many of his contemporaries. The University of Notre Dame gave him its Laetare Medal. He built the extraordinary number of 700 churches, including that of Saints Peter and Paul, at Williamsburg, New York, his first large job, and cathedrals at Albany and Buffalo.[7]

JAMES KENNEY

James Kenney (or Kenny) was engaged in 1859 as general contractor to build the Catholic Orphan School for Boys, of which the architect was Louis J. Barbot (qv).

However, in 1867, Kenney himself drew the plans for the Academy of Our Lady of Mercy at Sumter, South Carolina, a long, piazzaed, frame building later known as old St. Joseph's Academy. The *Sumter Watchman* (quoted in the *Daily News* of Charleston, March 8, 1867) said that "The architect and builder is Mr. James Kenney, an old and accomplished mechanic contractor of Charleston."

The Roper House, 9 East Battery. An outstanding example of a
mid-nineteenth century dwelling.

MINOR ANTE-BELLUM ARCHITECTS

EDWARD BENJAMIN BRYAN. 1827—April 28, 1861

EDWARD BENJAMIN BRYAN OF JOHN'S ISLAND, architect, cotton grower, and secessionist, belonged to the plantation caste which produced Manigault and White.

He was educated at West Point, graduating July 1, 1848, and was commissioned a second lieutenant in the artillery, but resigned the day on which he was to have reported for duty.[1]

From the end of 1848 until 1853, he practiced as civil engineer, architect, and surveyor at Charleston.[2]

In 1853, Bryan abandoned architecture for reading and study, and, incidentally, the planting of long staple, the aristocrat of cottondom, on John's Island near Charleston.[3] He wrote prolifically in favor of secession, some of his work appearing in the *Charleston Mercury*.[4] From 1854 until his death, he was in the state legislature, first as representative and then as senator.[5]

Bryan entered the Confederate service,[6] but died of illness at his plantation, April 28, 1861.[7] His widow and a son survived.[8]

A miniature by Bounetheau shows Bryan as a straight-featured young man in uniform with a mustache and short beard, his dark hair worn long as was then the custom.[9]

CHRISTOPHER C. TRUMBO. c. 1817—September 17, 1892

Christopher C. Trumbo of Baltimore was in Charleston as early as February 24, 1840, on which date he married Mary Ann Parker, a local girl.[1] The 1855 directory called him "Trumbo, Columbus C.", which leads to the surmise that his given names may have been Christopher Columbus. His last name survives in Trumbo Street.

He was generally, and correctly, referred to as mason, bricklayer, or contractor,[2] and references to his work as a builder occur from the forties into the late sixties. Only one directory, that of 1859, termed him architect. One mention of plans dates from 1853:

"On the west side of *King* and above *George*-street, two large brick stores, three stories each, have just been completed . . .

The Roper House.

fronts being of the best Baltimore pressed brick. The work was done and the plans furnished by Messrs. Cownover & Trumbro". (sic) [3]

In the same year, while Trumbo was erecting a bank designed by F. D. Lee (qv), he went to the aid of workmen of another builder who were involved in a serious accident while pulling down a house on the site of the State Bank, now No. 1 Broad Street. The *Courier* wrote:

> "We cannot conclude our mention of this sad occurrence without honorably mentioning the conduct of C. C. Trumbo, who on hearing of the accident immediately sent for the hands employed by him in erecting the new building for the Farmer's and Exchange Bank, and, with their assistance, removed the unfortunate men from the ruins." [4]

Trumbo died on September 17, 1892, aged seventy-five.[5]

WILLIAM BELL

William Bell, a contractor, occasionally furnished plans. A short description of Greenville, South Carolina, published in a Charleston newspaper in 1847, mentioned the "Mansion House, a spacious and handsome brick building, of three stories and an attick, built by Col. Toney (according to a plan furnished him by Wm. Bell, Esq., of Charleston), and successively kept by him, Dr. J. Crittenden, and Col. Jno. F. Coleman, the present worthy host." [1]

WILLIAM JONES

William Jones, who should not be confused with his contemporary, Edward C. Jones of the firm of Jones & Lee, was a contractor who sometimes designed the buildings he constructed. The type of dwelling he erected is shown in the following item from the *Mercury* of June 24, 1859:

"A NEW AND ELEGANT RESIDENCE.
. . . ."Among the constructions of the present season, we have observed the harmony of the elements of comfort and convenience most happily displayed in a residence erected for Mr. John Bonnell, on the north side of Broad-street, west of Mazyck-

street, by Mr. William Jones, contractor. The lot is ample, being of fifty feet front and two hundred and twenty-nine feet
depth, extending from Broad-street through the block to Short
street. The house has been located with its front recessed twen-
ty-one feet from Broad-street. The front of the house measures
thirty feet, and its depth forty-two feet. The walls are of well
culled brick, laid by Mr. Wm. Hutton, and the south and west
sides are faced with a broad piazza. The house is three stories
and an attic in height, and protected by a slate roof. At the foundation it is raised five feet above the ground for the purposes of
thorough ventilation . . . . Hot and cold water is led by pipes
to almost every room in the house . . . . The good qualities of
this house have so pleased a gentleman, about erecting for himself, that he has procured a design for a residence from Mr. William Jones, who is the designer as well as contractor of his
buildings" . . .

Mr. Bonnell's house no longer stands. The last sentence of the
description does not mean, as it sounds, that William Jones *always*
designed the buildings which he executed. His name appears frequently in records of the Ante-Bellum period simply as a contractor.
In 1850, he was given the contract for enlarging the College of
Charleston, according to plans drawn by E. B. White (qv), but was
unable to carry out the work.

LOUIS F. LEBLEUX. Working c. 1855-1860

Louis F. LeBleux (whose name was sometimes misspelled *Le-
Blue*) appeared in the directories of 1855 and 1859. The first termed
him architect; and the second, architect and civil engineer. His business address, 122 East Bay, was also that of Edward B. White, and
suggests that LeBleux may have been one of several young architects employed under White in building the Custom House.

In 1855, LeBleux was secretary of the patriotic "76 Association",[1]
and in 1856, secretary of the Vigilant Fire Engine Company,[2] a volunteer organization, for which he later designed a presentation
trumpet.[3]

JOHN A. MICHEL. Working by 1850

John A. Michel may have been related to the Michel family of
silversmiths who worked in Charleston during Ante-Bellum days.[1]

He attended the College of Charleston, leaving that institution in 1847.[2] He must then have studied architecture, perhaps in the office of Edward B. White, for in September, 1850, Michel inserted a card in the *Courier:*

"JOHN A. MICHEL,
Architect, Civil Engineer and Surveyor.
Office 52 East Bay, south of the Exchange.
Reference—E. B. White, Architect." [3]

Michel's office was in the notably quaint group of little houses long known as Coates Row, still at the corner of East Bay and Exchange Street.

By 1853, Michel had secured the position of city surveyor of the upper wards.[4]

In May, 1857, he announced that he had "returned to the city." [5]

He was practicing as a surveyor and civil engineer as late as 1867. His office was then on Broad Street and his residence on St. Philip Street.[6]

EDWIN J. WHITE AND WILLIAM M. RAMSAY. Working by 1859

Edwin J. White was a surveyor from 1843 at least as late as 1872.[1] The directory of 1859 listed him as architect. As his business address, 122 East Bay, was the same as that of Edward B. White, it seems likely that he may have been one of several professional men employed under the latter in building the Custom House.

By the end of 1859, Edwin J. White was a partner of William M. Ramsay in the firm of White & Ramsay, architects, civil engineers and surveyors, with offices at 9 Broad Street.[2]

White became a lieutenant in the Confederate army, and was engineer in charge at Fort Sumter when it sustained the last great bombardment.[3]

He was listed by the directory of 1867-68 as a partner of John K. Gourdin in the firm of White & Gourdin, civil engineers and surveyors.

JUSTICE WUHRMANN. Working 1855

Justice Wuhrmann appeared in the directory of 1855, listed as an architect. His address was the corner of Broad and Church, which was also that of Jones & Lee's office, so that it seems likely that he was in their employ.

He was probably related to "Wuhrmann J. H. liquors, 104 East Bay, cor. Wentworth and Anson."

JOHN HENRY DEVEREUX

July 26, 1840—March 16, 1920

J OHN HENRY DEVEREUX'S WORK BELONGS TO THE era which followed the Confederacy, but his interest in archi- tecture began before 1861, and he was a pupil of one of the best-known Charleston architects of the Ante-Bellum period. On the day following Devereux's death, the *News and Courier* published an article concerning him, which included the statement that he studied architecture under Edward Lee Jones, of Liverpool, England, and A. McConkey, of Edinburgh, Scotland." [1] "Edward Lee Jones" is evidently an error for Edward C. Jones (qv), the partner of F. D. Lee, though the mention of Liverpool is surprising, since Jones is generally termed a native Charlestonian.

Devereux was born in Wexford, Ireland, but was brought to this country by his parents, about 1843. [2] When still a small boy, he over- heard his father and mother discussing hard times, and determined to help. Without their knowledge, he went to work in the cotton mill. (This was the mill designed by Charles Tillinghast James. (qv)) At the end of a week, he presented his wages, $1.50, to his horrified parents, who promptly sent the youthful breadwinner to school. [3]

His amusement was modeling, and a bust of Preston S. Brooks, made after the Brooks-Sumner dispute, gained the attention of the South Carolina Institute which offered to have him trained as a sculptor in Italy, but his father declined the offer, and he studied architecture in Charleston. [4]

He was twenty when the War between the States began. He served as a captain of cavalry, and then as inspector of depots for the Confederate War Department. [5]

After the war, he became a practicing architect and builder. Structures designed by him include St. Matthew's Lutheran Church, built 1867-1872.

    ... "Mr. J. H. Devereux was the architect, and in turning over the building to the church authorities he presented the congre-

gation with a silver key attached to a gold cross. The congregation presented to him a sterling silver tea service. The building
measures 64 feet by 157 feet deep, capped by a tower and spire
that extend 297 feet above the sea" . . .[6]

About 1869,[7] Devereux designed the Academy of Music, made
by remodeling a large drygoods store at the northwest corner of King
and Market Streets. Here, with white and gold decoration and red
plush, he achieved something like the fussy but sincere playhouses
of provincial Europe, more akin to the old opera house at Nice, for
example, than to the usual American theatre. The Academy had extraordinarily good acoustics. It was torn down a few years ago.

The Masonic Hall, designed by Devereux, is a large brick and
stucco building, begun in December, 1871,[8] which still stands at the
southeast corner of King and Wentworth Streets.

Devereux entered the service of the treasury department, for
which he did a great deal of work, in Charleston and elsewhere,
of which the Charleston postoffice [9] is the most noticeable example.

The architect is recalled as a stout, jolly man. Fond of rowing
boats, he spent his summers on Sullivan's Island, where his gateway
was formed of a whale's jawbones, and a wooden lady, once the fig-
urehead of a ship, presided over the garden.

Stella Maris, the Roman Catholic church on the island, was
begun by his efforts, and he and the priest together worked with
their own hands on the foundations.[10]

Devereux married, June 27, 1863, Miss Agatha Eulalie Brandt,
who lived only a few years. They had three children. The architect
died March 16, 1920, at his home, 99 Wentworth Street, and was
buried in St. Laurence Cemetery.[11]

REFERENCE NOTES

NOTES

THE EARLY MEN

1. Statutes at Large of S. C., vol. 7, p. 17.
2. Lapham: A History of the Practice of Architecture in the State of South Carolina in General (etc.) Part I, p. 6.
3. Charleston Inventories, vol. 1732-46, p. 87—Inventory of John Fitch; and *Ibid.*, vol. 1732-36, p. 95-A—Inventory of Thomas Rose.
4. Wills, Inventories, and Miscellaneous Records, vol. 1729-31, p. 45—Inventory of Farmer Bull.
5. Inventories, vol. 1732-36, p. 229—Inventory of Thomas Bless or Bliss.
6. *Ibid.*, vol. 1732-46, p. 27-B—Inventory of John Rich.
7. *Ibid.*, vol. 1732-36, p. 194—Inventory of John Fowler.
8. South-Carolina Gazette, Sept. 28-Oct. 5, 1734.
9. *Ibid.*, Feb. 8-15, 1734/5.
10. *Ibid.*, Feb. 22-March 1, 1734/5.
11. *Ibid.*, Jan. 31-Feb. 7, 1735/6.
12. *Ibid.*, March 27-April 3, 1736.
13. *Ibid.*, Jan. 29-Feb. 5, 1737.
14. *Ibid.*, July 5-12, 1740.
15. *Ibid.*, Jan. 4-11, 1734/5.
16. Inventories, vol. 1732-46, p. 20-B—Inventory of John Wood.
17. *Ibid.*, p. 1-B.

FOUR ENGINEERS

GABRIEL BERNARD

1. Statutes at Large of South Carolina, vol. 7, pp. 17-22, Act of 1700. Mentions "half moon" at east end of Cooper Street.
2. *Ibid.*, vol. 7, pp. 28-33. For Rhett and the pirates, see McCrady's History of S. C. under the Proprietary Government, chap. 26.
3. Statutes at Large of S. C., vol. 7, p. 43.
4. Ichnography of Charles-Town at High Water. This shows the old walls and tells their story.
5. Rousseau: Les Confessions, première partie, livre 1.
6. *Ibid.*, livre 5.
7. SCHGM vol. 17, p. 129.
8. *Ibid.*
9. S. C. Gazette, June 12-19, 1736.
10. This battery is described in Peter Henry Bruce's Memoirs, p. 453.
11. SCHGM vol. 17, p. 129.
12. St. Philip's Register, vol. 1, p. 251.
13. S. C. Gazette, July 16-23, 1737 (executor's notice).

14. SCHGM vol. 17, p. 129.
15. Charleston Inventories, vol. 1736-1739, p. 132—Inventory of Gabriel Bernard.
16. Rousseau: Les Confessions, première partie, livre 5.

OTHNIEL BEALE

1. Tombstone of William Beale, in Circular Church graveyard, erected by his brother Othniel Beale, which mentions their parents.
2. Beale's advertisements of goods for sale may be found in the S. C. Gazette, July 11, 1743, Aug. 20, 1744, and other dates.
3. This anecdote is told in Mrs. St. Julien Ravenel's Charleston, the Place and the People, p. 91.
4. De Brahm: Historico-Politico-Hydrogeography, p. 205.
5. House Journal, p. 354.
6. S. C. Gazette, July 19-26, 1742; Ibid., Sept. 13-20, 1742.
7. Ibid., Nov. 15, 1742.
8. Ibid., June 20, 1744.
9. Peter Henry Bruce: Memoirs, p. 517.
10. Ibid., p. 518.
11. Tombstone of William Beale, Circular Church graveyard.
12. St. Philip's Register, vol. 1, p. 152.
13. Charleston Wills, 1771-1774, p. 432.
14. SCHGM vol. 1, p. 85.
15. Charleston Year Book of 1880, p. 273.

PETER HENRY BRUCE

This account is based largely on Bruce's Memoirs. The brief account of Bruce in the Dictionary of National Biography is founded almost entirely on the Memoirs.

1. Bruce's Memoirs, p. 5.
2. Ibid., p. 183.
3. Ibid., p. 449.
4. Ibid., pp. 442-443.
5. Ibid., pp. 452-454. The Vanderdussen plantation's location is mentioned in the S. C. Gazette, July 13, 1745.
6. Bruce's Memoirs, pp. 493-494.
7. Charleston Year Book of 1942, "Public Powder Magazines at Charleston," by Nora M. Davis.
8. S. C. Gazette, Sept. 17, 1744.
9. Bruce's Memoirs, p. 515.
10. S. C. Gazette, July 6, 1745.
11. Bruce's Memoirs, Advertisement.
12. St. Philip's Register, vol. 2, p. 146.

WILLIAM GERARD DE BRAHM

1. S. C. Gazette, Feb. 3, 1757—adv. for lost horses.
2. A. R. Huger Smith and D. E. Huger Smith: The Dwelling Houses of Charleston, p. 175.

3. Plowden C. J. Weston: Documents connected with the History of South Carolina, p. 157. (Weston's Advertisement to De Brahm's Philosophico-Historico-Hydrogeography).
4. A. J. Morrison: John G. De Brahm, in South Atlantic Quarterly, July, 1922, p. 257.
5. Ibid., p. 254.
6. De Brahm: P.-H.-Hydrogeography (Part relating to S. C. only, repub. by Weston, 1856, p. 196).
7. S. C. Gazette, May 6, 1756.
8. DAB., article on De Brahm.
9. De Brahm: P.-H.-Hydrogeography, pp. 205-206.
10. Ibid., p. 206.
11. Ibid., p. 197.
12. A Short Description of the Province of Carolina.
13. Year Book of 1882—map opp. p. 360 shows Revolutionary defenses.
14. De Brahm: P.-H.-Hydrogeography, p. 214.
15. S. C. Gazette, Feb. 3, 1757.
16. De Brahm: P.-H.-Hydrogeography, p. 169.
17. Ibid., p. 163.
18. DAB., article on De Brahm.
19. Ibid.
20. S. C. Gazette, Oct. 18, 1770; and Oct. 25, 1770.
21. DAB., article on De Brahm.
22. Ibid., for reinstatement; A. J. Morrison: John G. De Brahm, for London visit.
23. A. J. Morrison: John G. De Brahm, p. 254.
24. Ibid., S. C. & American General Gazette, Feb. 23-March 8, 1776—marriage notice.
25. DAB., article on De Brahm.
26. A. J. Morrison: John G. De Brahm, p. 255.
27. DAB., article on De Brahm.
28. A. J. Morrison: John G. De Brahm, p. 255.

SOME MID-EIGHTEENTH CENTURY NAMES

1. S. C. Gazette, April 29—May 6, 1751.
2. Ibid.
3. Ibid., March 8, 1770.
4. Ibid., Sept. 20, 1770.
5. Ibid., Feb. 28, 1771.
6. Stoney: Plantations of the Carolina Low Country, pp. 64-65.
7. Dalcho: An Historical Account of the Protestant Episcopal Church in South Carolina, p. 329.

ST. MICHAEL'S AND SOME NEIGHBORS

SAMUEL CARDY AND MR. GIBSON

1. Charleston Wills, 1774-79, p. 39, (Will of Samuel Cardy).
2. Ibid., 1752-56, p. 401, (Will of Andrew Rutledge).
3. Statutes at Large of S. C., vol. 7, p. 80 et seq.

4. MCO, vol. W-W, p. 324 (and various other indentures in this volume).
5. S. C. Gazette, Feb. 22, 1752.
6. Charleston Year Book of 1886, p. 285. (The Parish Church of St. Michael, by George S. Holmes.)
7. Charleston Library Society card index, giving reference to S. C. Gazette of Sept. 4, 1799.
8. The Carolina Backcountry on the Eve of the American Revolution, The Journal and other Writings of Charles Woodmason, Anglican Itinerant, Richard J. Hooker, ed., pp. 70-71.
9. DNB, article on Hawksmoor.
10. George W. Williams: St. Michael's, Charleston, 1751-1951, p. 141.
11. St. Michael's Vestry Book, vol. 1, p. 41.
12. George W. Williams: St. Michael's, Charleston, pp. 138-140.
13. Ibid., p. 20.
14. Rev. John Kershaw: History of the Parish and Church of St. Michael, p. 95.
15. Statutes at Large of S. C., vol. 4, p. 206.
16. Charleston Year Book of 1883, p. 491.
17. SCHGM, vol. 37, p. 25, and vol. 38, p. 131.
18. MCO, vol. L-6, p. 541.
19. SCHGM, vol. 25, p. 46, from City Gazette.
20. Ibid.
21. S. C. Gazette, March 29, 1773.
22. SCHGM, vol. 39, p. 84.

WILLIAM RIGBY NAYLOR

1. South-Carolina Gazette, March 19, 1744.
2. Journal of James Elerton, schoolmaster at Goose Creek Mansion, published in The Olden Times of Carolina, by Mrs. E. A. Poyas, p. 185.
3. Charleston Year Book, 1898, p. 364.
4. South-Carolina Gazette, Oct. 5-12, 1767.
5. South-Carolina and American General Gazette, Oct. 23-Nov. 2, 1769.
6. Fraser: My Reminiscences of Charleston, p. 101.
7. MCO, vol. L-6, p. 537, plat of glebeland, "Laid out 8th Decr. 1770 by Wrigby Nailor."
8. St. Philip's Register, vol. 2, p. 188.
9. Ibid., vol. 2, p. 82.
10. South-Carolina Gazette, Oct. 15, 1772.

MILLER AND FULLERTON

1. St. Michael's Vestry Books, vol. 1.
2. Johnson's Traditions and Reminiscences of the American Revolution, pp. 31-32.
3. Gibbes' Documentary History of the American Revolution, vol. 1, pp. 10-11.
4. Information from Samuel Gaillard Stoney.
5. Historical Society, Langdon Cheves collection—letter from William Simmons.
6. S. C. Gazette and Public Advertiser, Oct. 20-23, 1784.
7. State Gazette of S. C., Sept. 27, 1787.

PETER AND JOHN ADAM HORLBECK

1. Horlbeck monument, St. John's Lutheran Church graveyard.
2. Simons & Lapham: Charleston, S. C., p. 19.
3. Year Book of 1898.
4. *Ibid.*, p. 370 *et seq.*
5. *Ibid.*, p. 357.
6. Rev. William Way: The Old Exchange and Custom House, p. 5.
7. *Ibid.*, p. 6.
8. Year Book of 1898, p. 365.
9. Memoir of Josiah Quincy, Jr. (Feb. 28, 1773.)
10. Diary of William Dunlap, vol. III, p. 694.
11. Times, Oct. 13, 1801 (contract wanted.)
12. Mills: Statistics of S. C., p. 407.
13. Schirmer's Record, Sept. 19, 1835.
14. *Ibid.*, March 7, and Dec. 1846.
15. Horlbeck monument.
16. Simons & Lapham: Charleston, S. C., unpaged leaf near end of book.
17. SCHGM, vol. 25, p. 45 (James Steedman's obituary.) Charleston Wills, vol. 1793-1800-C, p. 482 (James Steedman's will.) Courier, July 28, 1854 (article based on minute books of Orphan House commissioners.)
18. Shecut: Topographical, Historical, and other Sketches of the City of Charleston, p. 30.
19. Yates Snowden: Notes on Labor Organizations in S. C., 1742-1861, p. 48.
20. Alston Deas: The Early Ironwork of Charleston, p. 72.
21. MCO, vol. F-4, p. 176.
22. Charleston Wills, vol. 1793-1800-C, p. 292 (George Fillhauer's will); and vol. 1818-1826-F, p. 95 (Catherine Horlbeck's will.)
23. SCHGM, vol. 20, p. 156 (H. A. M. Smith: The Upper Ashley and the Mutations of Families.)
24. Charleston Wills, vol. 1793-1800-C, p. 421 (Peter Horlbeck's will.)
25. Horlbeck monument.
26. State Gazette of S. C., June 2, 1788.
27. Horlbeck monument.
28. City Gazette & Daily Advertiser, April 4, 1812 (John Horlbeck's obituary.)
29. Horlbeck monument.

EZRA WAITE

1. S. C. Gazette & Country Journal, Aug. 22, 1769.
2. Samuel Lapham: A History of the Practice of Architecture in the State of South Carolina (etc.), p. 7.
3. Memoir of Josiah Quincy, Jr. (March 8, 1773).
4. Charleston Wills, vol. 1767-1771, p. 369 (Waite's will).
5. St. Philip's Register, vol. 2, p. 330.
6. Charleston Wills, vol. 1767-1771, p. 369 (Waite's will).
7. SCHGM, vol. 38, pp. 128-129.
8. S. C. & American General Gazette, Nov. 14-20, 1769.

GABRIEL MANIGAULT

1. The Manigault Family from 1665 to 1886, by Louis and Dr. Gabriel E. Manigault, grandsons of the architect, in Transactions of the Huguenot Society, No. 4.
2. Ann (Ashby) Manigault's diary is found in SCHGM, vol. 21.
3. The Manigault Family, p. 67.
4. *Ibid.*, p. 81.
5. St. Philip's Register, vol. 2, p. 7.
6. SCHGM, vol. 19, chart facing p. 121.
7. Charleston Probate Court, Inventories, 1751-53, p. 72.
8. S. C. Gazette, May 13, 1774.
9. Simons and Lapham: Charleston, p. 103.
10. Jones: American Members of the Inns of Court, p. 152.
11. Simons and Lapham: Charleston, p. 103.
12. Royal South Carolina Gazette, Sept. 21, 1780.
13. H. A. M. Smith: The Baronies of South Carolina, pp. 53 and 166.
14. Charleston Wills, E-1807-1818, p. 115. (Will of the architect.)
15. *Ibid.*
16. Easterby: A History of the College of Charleston, p. 261.
17. Easterby: South Carolina Society, p. 129.
18. S. C. Carpenter: Report of the Trial of Joshua Nettles and Elizabeth Cannon for the Murder of John Cannon, on the Night of the 24th October, 1804.
19. Louis Manigault's Family Records—copy of bill.
20. City Gazette & Daily Advertiser, November 21, 1809.
21. S. C. Weekly Gazette, May 4, 1785.
22. Mercury, May 20, 1824. (Mrs. Manigault's obituary.)
23. Charleston Wills, E-1807-1818, p. 115. (Will of the architect.)
24. St. Philip's Register, vol. 2, pp. 24, 26, 104, 107, 111, 117, 131.
25. *Ibid.*, p. 24.
26. Courier, Oct. 25, 1804.
27. Charleston Wills, E-1807-1818, p. 115. (Will of the architect.)
28. City Gazette & Daily Advertiser, November 21, 1809.
29. Courier, May 15, 1824.
30. Simons and Lapham: Charleston, p. 103.
31. *Ibid.*, unpaged leaf near end of volume. Date of house from Samuel Gaillard Stoney.
32. A. R. Huger Smith and D. E. Huger Smith: The Dwelling Houses of Charleston, p. 292.
33. Simons and Lapham: Charleston, unpaged leaf near end of volume.
34. Tablet in Orphan House Chapel.
35. Times, Sept. 18, 1802.
36. City Gazette & Daily Advertiser, July 26, 1800.
37. Easterby: South Carolina Society, p. 45. Also Simons and Lapham: Charleston.
38. The Manigault Family, p. 83.
39. Mills: Statistics of South Carolina, pp. 408-409.
40. City Gazette & Commercial Daily Advertiser, Jan. 31, 1817.

EDWARD MAGRATH AND JOSEPH NICHOLSON

1. City Gazette, Nov. 8, 1800.
2. St. Michael's Vestry Book, vol. II, p. 257.
3. Green: A History of the University of South Carolina, p. 18.
4. St. Michael's Vestry Book, vol. II, p. 303.
5. Year Book of 1898, p. 334 (history of the Second Presbyterian Church).
6. Rev. Mr. Brackett: Manual. (This contains a list of members of the Second Presbyterian Church. Magrath's name is absent.)
7. City Gazette, May 24, 1800.
8. *Ibid.*, Sept. 11, 1800.
9. *Ibid.*, Nov. 8, 1800.

WILLIAM DRAYTON

1. Courier, Aug. 20, 1853. The title in the paper is "My Reminiscences."
2. Charles Fraser: My Reminiscences of Charleston, p. 100.
3. City Gazette & Daily Advertiser, Dec. 11, 1792.
4. Wallace: The History of S. C., Vol. II, p. 338.
5. Emily Heyward Drayton Taylor: The Draytons of South Carolina and Philadelphia, in Publications of the Genealogical Society of Pennsylvania, vol. VIII, No. 1 (March, 1921).
6. DAB, article on William Drayton by James H. Easterby and Dumas Malone.
7. *Ibid.*
8. *Ibid.*
9. McCrady: South Carolina under the Royal Government, p. 335.
10. E. H. D. Taylor: The Draytons of South Carolina and Philadelphia.
11. John Belton O'Neall: Biographical Sketches of the Bench and Bar of South Carolina, vol. I, p. 314.
12. DAB, article on William Drayton.
13. E. H. D. Taylor: The Draytons of South Carolina and Philadelphia.
14. Charleston Wills, vol. B-1786-1793, p. 419 (William Drayton's will).
15. E. H. D. Taylor: The Draytons of South Carolina and Philadelphia.
16. *Ibid.*, and Charleston Wills, vol. B-1786-1793, p. 419.
17. DAB, article on William Drayton.
18. E. H. D. Taylor: The Draytons of South Carolina and Philadelphia.
19. Year Book of 1883, p. 457.
20. DAB, article on William Drayton.
21. Charleston Wills, vol. B-1786-1793, p. 419.
22. E. H. D. Taylor: The Draytons of South Carolina and Philadelphia.
23. *Ibid.*
24. *Ibid.*
25. Fraser: My Reminiscences of Charleston, p. 100. This states that Drayton lived "in Tradd-street, in the house now owned by Judge Frost." Judge Frost lived in the Humphrey Somers house. (See A. R. Huger Smith and D. E. Huger Smith: Dwelling Houses of Charleston, p. 233.)
26. E. H. D. Taylor: The Draytons of South Carolina and Philadelphia.
27. Fraser: My Reminiscences of Charleston, p. 101.
28. Charleston Wills, vol. B-1786-1793, p. 419.
29. E. H. D. Taylor: The Draytons of South Carolina and Philadelphia.

30. City Gazette & Daily Advertiser, Dec. 11, 1792.
31. William Gilmore Simms: Charleston (in Harper's New Monthly Magazine, June, 1857).

JAMES HOBAN

1. DAB, article on James Hoban by Fiske Kimball.
2. Prime, series 1, p. 295, from Pennsylvania Evening Herald, May 25, 1785.
3. Edwin L. Green: History of Richland County, p. 153.
4. Wallace: The History of S. C., II, p. 338.
5. Mills: Statistics of S. C., p. 700.
6. Courier, Aug. 18, 1847.
7. MCO, vol. B-6, p. 336. Vol. C-6, p. 16. Vol. U-6, p. 231.
8. Charleston City Gazette & Daily Advertiser, May 4, 1790.
9. Ibid., Aug. 14, 1792.
10. Office of County Clerk, McCrady Case, Plate 17.
11. Mills: Statistics of S. C., p. 423.
12. Schirmer's Record, 1833, Aug. 11.
13. Courier, Aug. 8, 1850 (bids invited for taking down theatre).
14. Letters and Recollections of George Washington (ed. Louisa Lear Eyre), p. 57.
15. Stoney: Plantations of the Carolina Low Country, p. 75.
16. DAB, article on Hoban by Fiske Kimball.

THOMAS BENNETT

1. Charleston Year Book of 1882, p. 392—Inscription on Thomas Bennett's monument.
2. A. R. Huger Smith and D. E. Huger Smith: The Dwelling Houses of Charleston, pp. 321-322.
3. John Drayton: A View of South-Carolina, p. 216.
4. City Gazette & Daily Advertiser, Nov. 14, 1792.
5. John Drayton: A View of South-Carolina, p. 216.
6. Courier, July 28, 1854, "The Orphan House", gives specifications taken from minutes of the Commissioners. A picture is in Courier, Oct, 1853.
7. Ibid., Sept. 18, 1819 (proposals for painting cupola).
8. Ibid., July 9, 1819 (repairs to roughcast).
9. Ibid., July 28, 1854, giving specifications taken from minutes of the Commissioners.
10. Ibid., October 18, 1853, based on minutes of the Commissioners.
11. Ibid.
12. Courier, July 28, 1854. Also, City Gazette & Daily Advertiser, Sept. 20, 1793.
13. Charles Fraser: My Reminiscences of Charleston, p. 23.
14. City Gazette & Daily Advertiser, Sept. 20, 1793.
15. Ibid., July 31, 1793.
16. Ibid., Sept. 20, 1793.
17. Ibid., Aug. 11, 1800 (proposals for building wall).
18. Columbian Herald or the Southern Star, Nov. 10, 1794.
19. Times, Aug. 31, 1802.
20. Courier, April 13, 1821.

21. Rev. George N. Edwards, History of the Independent or Congregational Church of Charleston, p. 45.
22. Courier, July 16, 1853—article on Circular Church.
23. Minutes of St. Michael's Vestry, vol. II, p. 304.
24. A. R. Huger Smith and D. E. Huger Smith: The Dwelling Houses of Charleston, p. 322.
25. Charleston Wills, vol. E-1807-1818, p. 388 (Will of Thomas Bennett the Elder.)
26. *Ibid.*
27. Tombstone, Circular Church graveyard.
28. Charleston Wills, vol. E-1807-1818, p. 388. (Will of Thomas Bennett the Elder).
29. O'Neall: Bench and Bar of South Carolina, vol. 1, pp. 78-79. This speaks of Sarah as the "eldest daughter" of Thomas Bennett, indicating that there were others.
30. Year Book of 1882, p. 392—inscription on monument.
31. Year Book of 1886—"The Public Schools of Charleston—Their Origin, Development and Present Status", p. 184.

JOHN CHRISTIAN SENF AND MINOR CONTEMPORARIES

JOHN CHRISTIAN SENF

1. SCHGM, vol. 25, p. 179.
2. Deutsche National-Litteratur, vol. 135, first part, p. 182. This mentions poet.
3. Wallace's History of S. C., vol. II, p. 399.
4. SCHGM, vol. 28, p. 8. The belief that Senf was a Swede, mentioned here, is erroneous.
5. *Ibid.*
6. H. E. Ravenel: Ravenel Records, pp. 231-232 (old diary).
7. Two Diaries from Middle St. John's, Berkeley, South Carolina, Feb.—May, 1865. (Pub. by the St. John's Hunting Club, 1921), p. 39.
8. SCHGM, vol. 30, p. 120 (quoting Courier).
9. Mills: Statistics of South Carolina, p. 53.

MR. EMES AND THOMAS HOPE

1. State Gazette of South Carolina, June 2, 1788.
2. The French Broad-Holston Country, A History of Knox County, Tennessee, pp. 428-429.
3. *Ibid.*
4. *Ibid.*

THOMAS WALKER AND JOHN BRUTON RICKETS

1. "Here Lyes Buried, Taste and Trade in Charleston Tombstones", in Antiques, March, 1942.
2. City Gazette, Oct. 31, 1793.
3. Charleston Wills, vol. H-1834-1839, p. 366. (Will of Thomas Walker).
4. City Gazette, July 2, 1799, and many times repeated.

5. St. Philip's Register, vol. 2, p. 361.
6. City Gazette, July 1, 1800. (Estate notice. This gives his middle name in full.)

DAVID BURN AND DEPRESSEVILLE

1. S. C. Gazette, July 18, 1785.
2. Charleston City Gazette & Advertiser, April 17, 1797.

MR. COX

1. St. Michael's Vestry Books, vol. 2, p. 242.
2. Directory of 1802.

FOUR FRENCHMEN

AUGUSTUS DE GRASSE

1. Agatha Aimar Simmons: Charleston, S. C., A Haven for the Children of Admiral de Grasse.
2. For Admiral de Grasse's defeat and subsequent conduct, see Mahan's The Influence of Sea Power upon History.
3. A. A. Simmons: Charleston, S. C., A Haven for the Children of Admiral de Grasse.
4. *Ibid.*
5. S. C. Gazette & Daily Advertiser, June 17, 1800.
6. *Ibid.*, July 9, 1800.
7. City Gazette & Daily Advertiser, Aug. 30, 1800.
8. *Ibid.*, Oct. 16, 1800.
9. Times, Jan. 10, 1801.
10. A. A. Simmons: Charleston, S. C., A Haven for the Children of Admiral de Grasse.

JEAN BAPTISTE AVEILHE

1. MCO, vol. X-6, p. 3.
2. Times, Sept. 26, 1803.

JOSEPH JAHAN

1. His tombstone, St. Mary's churchyard.
2. Directories of 1809 and of 1816 (call him "carpenter"); Directories of 1819 and of 1822 (call him "architect").
3. City Gazette, Dec. 29, 1815.
4. Courier, Jan. 31, 1833.
5. *Ibid.*, also Courier, Dec. 22, 1820.
6. Courier, Jan, 25, 1826.
7. His tombstone, St. Mary's churchyard.
8. Guilday; The Life and Times of John England, Bistop of Charleston, vol. 1, pp. 223-225.
9. Directories of 1819 and 1822; Courier, Jan. 31, 1833.
10. His tombstone, St. Mary's churchyard.
11. Courier, Jan. 31, 1833.

JAMES AND JOHN GORDON

1. The tombstone of Mary Gordon and her son, James Gordon, in the First (Scotch) Presbyterian churchyard gives the relationships. The DAB article on Andrew Gordon Magrath, son of James and John Gordon's sister, Maria, states that Maria "came to America from Scotland in 1792": She was a child at the time.
2. Courier, July 28, 1854, account of Orphan House based on minutes of the Commissioners.
3. City Gazette, Nov. 8, 1800.
4. MCO, vol. H-8, p. 25 (deed of partition and division of estate of Andrew Gordon.)
5. Times, July 2, 1802.
6. Tablet in vestibule of Second Presbyterian Church.
7. Mills: Statistics of S. C., p. 413 (mentions intended steeple.)
8. History of St. Paul's Church, Radcliffeboro', p. 19.
9. *Ibid.*
10. Mills: Statistics of S. C., pp. 413 and 415.
11. History of St. Paul's Church, Radcliffeboro', p. 22.
12. Tombstone of Master Charles Cleary in Unitarian churchyard.
13. City Gazette & Commercial Daily Advertiser, Jan. 4, 1816.
14. History of St. Paul's Church, Radcliffeboro', p. 23.
15. Courier, March 22, 1816.
16. Year Book of 1898—Historic Sketch of the Second Presbyterian Church, p. 335.
17. Tombstone of Mary Gordon and James Gordon, First Presbyterian graveyard.
18. *Ibid.*
19. Charleston Wills, E-1807-1818, p. 434—Indenture between James and John Gordon.
20. Statutes at Large of South Carolina, vol. 6, p. 154.
21. Ms. account book, "Estate of John Splatt Cripps Esq. in acct. with Danl. Ravenel, Administrator de bonis non", p. 6. This shows cash paid John Gordon for work on a house and outbuildings.
22. Courier, Dec. 16, 1823, quoting New York Christian Journal.
23. *Ibid.*
24. Courier, Sept. 30, 1823.
25. Courier, March 18, 1824.
26. Directory of 1840-41, "Fires in Charleston".
27. H. A. M. Smith: The Baronies of South Carolina, p. 176.
28. Mercury, Jan. 22, 1844.
29. H. A. M. Smith: The Baronies of South Carolina, p. 181.
30. Courier, March 4, 1826.
31. Courier, March 20, 1824.
32. Easterby: History of the St. Andrew's Society, p. 71.
33. Courier, March 27, 1819.
34. Termed colonel on his tombstone, First Presbyterian graveyard.
35. City Gazette & Commercial Daily Advertiser, Fed. 22, 1819.
36. City Gazette, April 14, 1812.

37. DAB, article on Andrew Gordon Magrath.
38. *Ibid.*
39. Charleston Wills, vol. H-1834-1839, p. 86 (Will of John Gordon).
40. Tombstone of John Gordon, First Presbyterian graveyard.
41. Schirmer's Record, May 11, 1835.
42. *Ibid.*, March 5, 1840.
43. Bennett lot, Magnolia Cemetery.

HUGH SMITH

1. Agnes Smith's tombstone in First Presbyterian Church graveyard. Also Hugh Smith's funeral notice, Courier, April 7, 1826.
2. Elevation at University of S. C. Museum. Also Green: A History of the University of S. C., p. 15.
3. Charleston Wills, vol. F-1818-1826, p. 615 (Will of Peter Smith).
4. Hugh Smith's funeral notice, Courier, April 7, 1826.
5. Courier, Feb. 21, 1857, quoting the printed "Rules of the Union Light Infantry Company".
6. J. Bachman Chisolm: St. Andrew's Society, in Year Book of 1894, p. 279.
7. Easterby: History of the St. Andrew's Society, p. 71.
8. Chisolm: St. Andrew's Society, p. 281, and p. 279.
9. Courier, Jan. 1, 1819 (notice to contractors).
10. Charleston Wills, vol. G-1826-1834, p. 25 (Will of Hugh Smith).
11. Mills: Statistics of S. C., p. 412.
12. City Gazette & Commercial Daily Advertiser, April 27, 1819.
13. Chisolm: St. Andrew's Society, p. 279.
14. Easterby: History of the St. Andrew's Society, p. 74.
15. Chisolm: St. Andrew's Society, p. 279.
16. Mary Boykin Chesnut: A Diary from Dixie, p. 30.
17. Wallace: History of S. C., Vol. III, p. 154.
18. Mercury, extra of Dec. 20, 1860.
19. Easterby: History of the St. Andrew's Society, p. 84.

WILLIAM JAY

1. Autobiography of the Rev. William Jay. (American edition, 1855). Vol. 1, pp. 99 and 106.
2. Dictionary of National Biography—article on William Jay (the Rev.).
3. Autobiography of the Rev. William Jay, vol. 1, p. 274.
4. *Ibid.*, p. 106.
5. *Ibid,* p. 104.
6. Georgia, A. Pageant of Years, p. 84.
7. J. Robie Kennedy, Jr.: Examples of Georgian and Greek Revival Work in the Far South (in the Architectural Record for March, 1907). This names Jay as architect of the Owens, Scarborough, Bulloch, and Telfair houses.
8. John Mead Howells: Lost Examples of Colonial Architecture, plate 2.
9. Georgia, A Pageant of Years, p. 84.
10. Tyrone Power: Impressions of America during the Years 1833, 1834, and 1835, vol. 2, p. 117.

11. Courier, Jan. 1, 1820.
12. Southern Patriot, Feb. 4, 1820. Less full account in Courier, Feb. 5, 1820, from Columbia Telescope of Feb. 1.
13. Fraser Account Book (ms.) (Accts. for 1820).
14. Dunlap: History of the Arts of Design in the United States, vol. 3, p. 58.
15. Directory of 1829, and Mills' Statistics of S. C., p. 411, describe the Academy of Fine Arts Building briefly.
16. Autobiography of the Rev. Wm. Jay, vol. 1, p. 107.
17. *Ibid.*
18. *Ibid.*
19. *Ibid.*
20. Courier, Dec. 29, 1847.
21. MCO, vol. T-11, p. 315. Daniel Cannon to Patrick Duncan, release.
22. MCO, vol. X-7, p. 197. Elizabeth Combe to Patrick Duncan, convey.
23. MCO, vol. P-10, p. 465. Patrick Duncan to James Nicholson, convey.
24. C. R. S. Horton, in an article, *Charleston, between Ashley and Cooper,* in *The Georgian Period, American Architect and Building News,* (1902) p. 41.
25. MCO, vol. V-8, p. 393 (John Robinson's purchase of the lot), and *Courier,* Sept. 21, 1825 (his adv. of the house for sale).

ROBERT MILLS

1. Mills: The Architectural Works of Robert Mills (unfinished), in Gallagher's Robert Mills, p. 170.
2. Times, April 5, 1802.
3. Courier, July 1, 1854, "Our Orphan House", quoting minute book of orphan house commissioners.
4. St. Philip's Register, vol. 2, p. 203.
5. Hutson: Introduction to second ed. of Mills' Atlas.
6. Gallagher: Robert Mills, p. 7.
7. *Ibid.*
8. City Gazette & Daily Advertiser, Oct. 8, 1795.
9. Virginia Historical Register and Literary Companion, Jan., 1853, article by Mills, "Architecture in Virginia", signed R. M.
10. *Ibid.*
11. Hutson: Introduction to second ed. of Mills' Atlas.
12. Charleston Wills, vol. D-1800-1807, p. 269. (Will of William Mills).
13. Tombstone of William Mills and George Lusher, First (Scotch) Presbyterian churchyard.
14. Green: A History of the U. of S. C., p. 19.
15. DAB, article on Robert Mills by Fiske Kimball.
16. Year Book of 1882, article on Circular Church.
17. Gallagher: Robert Mills, pp. 77-78.
18. Courier, July 16, 1853.
19. St. Michael's vestry minutes, vol. 2, p. 298.
20. Times, June 20, 1804.
21. MCO, vol. S-7, p. 478, and vol. T-7, p. 298.
22. Gallagher: Robert Mills, chap. III.

23. Courier, March 5, 1804.
24. *Ibid.*, March 15, 1814 (notice signed by Mills).
25. *Ibid.*, July 14, 1815.
26. SCHGM vol. 39 (Mills' letters).
27. Mills' Autobiography (unfinished).
28. City Gazette & Commercial Daily Advertiser, April 20, 1819.
29. *Ibid.*, Sept. 16, 1819.
30. Courier, Jan. 17, 1822.
31. City Gazette & Commercial Daily Advertiser, Jan. 6, 1821.
32. Courier, Nov. 30, 1822.
33. *Ibid.*, March 4, 1824.
34. Bess Glenn: Some Letters of Robert Mills, Engineer and Architect.
35. Letter of Eliza Mills to Robert Mills, dated Nov. 27, 1829 (in Gallagher's Robert Mills, p. 212).
36. Courier, Feb. 21, 1822.
37. C. C. Wilson: Robert Mills, Architect, p. 34.
38. Gallagher: Robert Mills, p. 43.
39. Mills: Statistics, p. 415, footnote (organ music); SCHGM vol. 39 (Mills' letters) (horn).
40. Courier, March 20, 1822.
41. Mills: Statistics, p. 420.
42. Basil Hall: Travels in North America in the Years 1827 and 1828, vol. 2, p. 205.
43. Mills' Autobiography (unfinished).
44. Courier, April 25, 1822.
45. Rep. & Res. 1827, p. 40.
46. Courier, Aug. 3, 1822.
47. *Ibid.*, Feb. 21, 1824.
48. Winyah Intelligencer (Georgetown, S. C.), Dec. 7, 1825.
49. Courier, Jan. 9, 1823.
50. Green: A History of the U. of S. C., p. 33.
51. Courier, May 19, 1824.
52. News and Courier, June 2, 1941, article on powder magazine, by H. W. C. Furman.
53. Mills' Autobiography (unfinished).
54. Mills: Statistics, p. 706 (description); Courier, Sept. 22, 1824 (Mills' authorship).
55. C. C. Wilson: Robert Mills, Architect, p. 34.
56. Hutson: Introduction to second ed. of Mills' Atlas.
57. DAB, article on Robert Mills.
58. Year Book of 1939, pages 175-176 (The Marine Hospitals of Charleston, by Joseph Ioor Waring, M. D.).
59. Roger Hale Newton: Bulfinch's Design for the Library of Congress, in Art Bulletin, Sept., 1941.
60. Glen Brown: History of the United States Capitol (Gov. Printing Office, 1903, vol. 1, pp. 97-98).
61. Courier, April 27, 1825.

62. Mercury, August 7, 17, 22, and 24, 1850.
63. Baltimore American Times, quoted in Courier, Sept. 8, 1853.

FREDERICK WESNER

1. Charleston Year Book of 1885, p. 343.
2. Directory of 1790.
3. Charleston Wills, vol. C-1793-1800, p. 191 (Will of Henry Philip Wesner).
4. City Gazette, Oct. 5, 1798.
5. Charleston Wills, vol. C-1793-1800, p. 506 (Will of Barbara Wesner).
6. Directory of 1813.
7. Bernheim: The Lutheran Church in North and South Carolina, p. 447.
8. *Ibid.*
9. Lionel H. Kennedy and Thomas Parker: An Official Report of the trials of sundry negroes charged with an attempt to raise an insurrection. (1822) p. 28.
10. *Ibid.*, p. 43.
11. *Ibid.*, pp. 124-125.
12. Bond: The Story of the Citadel, p. 7.
13. Gongaware: The History of the German Friendly Society of Charleston, p. 215.
14. Courier, Oct. 22, 1821.
15. Easterby: The South Carolina Society, p. 148.
16. *Ibid.*, p. 45.
17. *Ibid.*
18. City Gazette & Commercial Daily Advertiser, Nov. 18, 1824.
19. Ticket for admission to lectures, now in Library of the Medical College of the State of S. C. at Charleston. Shows picture of building, marked "F. Wesner, Architect".
20. Year Book of 1895, p. 397—Gen. E. McCrady: An Historical Address.
21. Directory of 1886, with photograph taken after the earthquake.
22. Mills: Statistics of S. C., p. 421.
23. Courier, June 28, 1828.
24. City Gazette & Commercial Daily Advertiser, Feb. 20, 1830.
25. Thomas: History of the South Carolina Military Academy, p. 24.
26. Bond: The Story of the Citadel, pp. 19 and 202.
27. Courier: Aug. 4, 1831—letter signed "One who has known Hard Work".
28. Year Book of 1881, p. 368 et seq.
29. Miller's Almanacs for 1822, '23, and '24.
30. *Ibid.*, for 1825, and '26.
31. Courier, Sept. 14, 1821.
32. *Ibid.*, Sept. 24, 1823.
33. Miller's Almanac for 1825.
34. Courier, Jan. 25, 1826.
35. *Ibid.*, March 4, 1824.
36. Schirmer's Record, Dec. 31, 1833.
37. Thomas: Protestant Episcopal Church in S. C., p. 493. This calls him "F. Wisner".
38. Miller's Almanac for 1831.

39. Miller's Almanac of 1832.
40. Charles Fraser: My Reminiscences of Charleston, p. 26.
41. Bernhard, Duke of Saxe-Weimar Eisenach: Travels Through North America during the Years 1825 and 1826, vol. 2, p. 9.
42. Times, Oct. 24, 1801 (and similar notices in newspapers of other years).
43. Bernhard, Duke of Saxe-Weimar Eisenach: Travels, vol. 2, p. 9.
44. Miller's Almanacs from 1832 through 1840.
45. Tombstone of Frederick and Elizabeth A. Wesner, St. John's Lutheran Church graveyard, from which birth date is also taken.
46. Schirmer's Record, March, 1848. (This states that Wesner died March 12, but his tombstone has March 11.)
47. Reeves family records (mss.) and Charleston Wills, Box 114, No. 15 (Will of Elizabeth A. Wesner).
48. Tombstone, graveyard of St. John's Lutheran Church.

JOHN HORLBECK JR., AND HENRY HORLBECK

1. Schirmer's Record, Oct. 13, 1836.
2. Gongaware: The History of the German Friendly Society. Appendix A.
3. *Ibid.*, p. 37.
4. *Ibid.*, p. 38.
5. *Ibid.*, p. 40.
6. Bernhard, Duke of Saxe-Weimar Eisenach: Travels Through North America, during the Years 1825 and 1826, Vol. II, pp. 12-13.
7. Schirmer's Record, Sept. 17, 1864.
8. Bernheim: The Lutheran Church in North and South Carolina, p. 447. (This speaks of "Mr. J. F. H. Horlbeck's" contract, an obvious error for J. & H. Horlbeck, probably the result of misreading a difficult ms.)
9. Schirmer's Record, Dec. 26, 1835; and Oct. 24, 1836.
10. Directory of 1822; and MCO, vol. D-20, p. 243.
11. News and Courier, Jan. 26, 1939, "Old House Bows to the Automobile Age."
12. Investigator, Oct. 13, 1812.
13. Horlbeck monument, St. John's Lutheran graveyard.
14. Elizabeth Lindauer's dates from Horlbeck monument. Marriage notice, from City Gazette, Dec. 17, 1795.
15. SCHGM vol. 20 (H. A. M. Smith: The Ashley River, Its Seats & Settlements).
16. Horlbeck monument.
17. Schirmer's Record, Feb. 26, 1846.
18. MCO, vol. W-11, p. 249.
19. Easterby: A History of the College of Charleston, p. 281.
20. Yates Snowden: Notes on Labor Organizations in South Carolina, 1742-1861, p. 48.
21. Miller's Almanac of 1823.
22. *Ibid* of 1824.
23. City Gazette, Feb. 24, 1798 (marriage notice).
24. Horlbeck monument.

25. Stoney: Plantations of the Carolina Low Country, p. 83.
26. Schirmer's Record, Dec. 17, 1837.
27. Miniature owned by Henry H. Lowndes of Charleston.

RUSSELL WARREN

1. DAB—article on Russell Warren by William M. Emery.
2. Antoinette Forrester Downing: Early Homes of Rhode Island, p. 463.
3. MCO, Q-9, p. 262.
4. Directory of 1822.
5. MCO, Q-9, p. 270.
6. MCO, Q-9, p. 262.
7. Directory of 1840-41, article on "Fires in Charleston".
8. Charleston City Ordinances—"An Ordinance to close up and discontinue Ellery Street as a Public Highway", ratified Sept. 2, 1840.
9. A. R. Huger Smith and D. E. Huger Smith: Dwelling Houses of Charleston, South Carolina, p. 155.
10. Information from Charleston Historic Foundation.
11. Downing: Early Homes of Rhode Island, p. 401.
12. The Wentworth Street house was advertised for rent in the Courier of March 7, 1842, as "recently built".
13. Downing: Early Homes of Rhode Island, p. 457 and Plate 205.

CHARLES FRASER

1. O'Neall: Bench and Bar, vol. II, p. 313.
2. SCHGM vol. 5, p. 58, from Fraser family Bible.
3. A. R. Huger Smith and D. E. Huger Smith: Charles Fraser, p. 1.
4. Notes by Wilmot G. DeSaussure, interleaved in his copy of Fraser's "My Reminiscences of Charleston", now owned by the Charleston Library Society. Mr. DeSaussure had access to records of the St. Cecilia Society, since lost when the St. Andrew's Hall burned in 1861.
5. Ibid.
6. Journal of Josiah Quincy, Junior (March 3, 1773).
7. A. R. Huger Smith and D. E. Huger Smith: Charles Fraser, p. 2.
8. Courier, Oct. 18, 1853—article on Orphan House, founded on old minute book of the Commissioners of the Orphan House.
9. Charles Fraser: My Reminiscences of Charleston, p. 23.
10. Ibid., p. 100.
11. A Charleston Sketchbook, p. 13.
12. O'Neall: Bench and Bar, vol. II, p. 313.
13. Wallace: The History of S. C., vol. II, p. 394.
14. A. R. Huger Smith and D. E. Huger Smith: Charles Fraser, p. 28.
15. Ibid., p. 23.
16. Ibid., pp. 12, 15, 17, 25.
17. Charleston Wills, Box 137, No. 2 (Will of Charles Fraser).
18. G. S. Bryan: Biographical Sketch of Charles Fraser.
19. Charleston Wills, vol. I and J-1839-1845, p. 353 (Will of Isaac Bateman).
20. O'Neall: Bench and Bar, vol. II, p. 314.

21. William L. King: The Newspaper Press of Charleston, S. C., p. 22, footnote.
22. William Gilmore Simms: Charleston (in Harper's New Monthly Magazine, June, 1857).
23. The tower as it was before Fraser's cupola was added is shown in Hill's Birdseye View of Charleston, printed 1851.
24. Mercury, June 20, 1859.
25. Ms. Letterbook of Daniel Ravenel. Letter of Oct. 6, 1860, to Rev. Mr. I. R. G. Peck.

HYDE, REEVES AND SOME LESSER LIGHTS

JOSEPH HYDE

1. McCrady: A Sketch of St. Philip's Church, p. 38.
2. *Ibid.*, p. 39.
3. MCO, vol. R-10, p. 472 *et seq.*
4. Joseph B. Hyde: History of Union Kilwinning Lodge No. 4, p. 13. The similarity of Mr. Hyde's name to that of the architect is coincidental.
5. Schirmer's Record, Aug. 10, 1837.
6. *Ibid.*, Aug. 23, 1837.
7. *Ibid.*, April 27, 1838.

ABRAHAM P. REEVES

1. Circular Church Register.
2. Alston Deas: The Early Ironwork of Charleston, p. 30.
3. Courier, May 5, 1819.
4. *Ibid.*, Dec. 2, 1820.
5. *Ibid.*, Jan. 1, 1828.
6. *Ibid.*, Oct. 16, 1829.

THE CURTIS FAMILY OF MASTER BUILDERS

1. Courier, Jan. 8, 1819.
2. *Ibid.*, Aug. 2, 1827.
3. Stoney: Plantations of the Carolina Low Country, p. 81.
4. E. M. Seabrook: The History of the Protestant Episcopal Church of Edisto Island, pp. 53-54, 56.
5. Special Services Held at St. Philip's Church, Charleston, S. C., on the 12th and 13th of May, 1875, Appendix, p. 147.
6. Courier, Jan. 25, 1840 (Proceedings of Council).
7. *Ibid.*, Dec. 18, 1837.
8. *Ibid.*, Aug. 25, 1851.
9. Schirmer's Record, Sept. 13, 1858.
10. Courier, April 21, 1859.
11. Information from Albert Simons.

JAMES DUPRE

1. Shecut: Topographical, Historical, and other Sketches of the City of Charleston, p. 25.
2. Fraser: My Reminiscences of Charleston, pp. 25-26.

TWO GREEK REVIVAL GIANTS

WILLIAM STRICKLAND

1. DAB, article on William Strickland by Alfred Mansfield Brooks.
2. Photo. of bust is in Joseph Jackson's Development of American Architecture, p. 211.
3. DAB, article on Strickland.
4. Courier, March 17, 1829.
5. *Ibid.*, Dec. 14, 1829.
6. *Ibid.*, April 3, 1840 (Proceedings of Council).
7. Easterby: History of the College of Charleston, p. 163.
8. *Ibid.*, p. 199.

THOMAS USTICK WALTER

1. DAB, article by William Sener Rusk on Walter.
2. *Ibid.*
3. *Ibid.*
4. Year Book of 1901, Sketch of the Hibernian Society.
5. *Ibid.*
6. Courier, March 22, 1839.
7. Schirmer's Record, May 4, 1840.
8. Minute Book of the Hibernian Society, minutes of February 2, 1841 (quoted in News & Courier, January 21, 1941).

CHARLES F. REICHARDT

1. Mercury, Dec. 26, 1836.
2. Hamlin: Greek Revival Architecture in America, p. 61.
3. Courier, July 18, 1842.
4. MCO, vol. Z-10, p. 587.
5. Schirmer's Record, July, Sept., Nov., 1839.
6. Irving: History of the Turf in S. C., p. 148.
7. For pictures of Schinkel's Royal Theatre and Reichardt's theatre, see Enc. Brit., 11th ed., article "Architecture", fig. 87, and News & Courier, March 24, 1940, respectively.
8. Courier, Dec. 18, 1837.
9. Schirmer's Record, Dec. 21, 1837.
10. Mercury, Sept. 9, 1837 (to contractors).
11. Year Book of 1884, "Sketch of the Charleston Port Society", pp. 323-324.
12. Mercury, Sept. 29, 1837 (to contractors).
13. Courier, Nov. 7, 1837 (to contractors).
14. Southern Rose, Sept. 1, 1838, p. 1.
15. Schirmer's Record, July 29, and Aug. 1856.
16. Alston Deas: The Early Ironwork of Charleston, p. 32.
17. Courier, March 14, and May 2, 1839.
18. Mercury, March 2, 1840 (proceedings of council).
19. Courier, April 23, 1840 (proceedings of council).
20. Schirmer's Record, April 13, 1840; and Jan. 13, 1841.
21. Courier, March 25, 1840.

EDWARD BRICKELL WHITE

1. SCHGM vol. 36, p. 43. Records from the Blake and White Bibles.
2. S.-C. Gazette & Country Journal, July 23, 1771 (Blake Leay White's adv.)
3. DAB—article on John Blake White by Leila Mechlin.
4. *Ibid.*
5. Annual Reunion of the Association of Graduates of the U. S. Military Academy, West Point; Philadelphia, 1882, pp. 102-104.
6. Allan Nevins: Frémont, the West's Greatest Adventurer, vol. 1, p. 24 (quoting Frémont's Memoirs, p. 24).
7. Cullum: Biographical Register of the Officers and Graduates of the U. S. Military Academy, vol. 1, p. 292. Also, Report of a Reconnaissance for the Charleston, Georgetown and All Saints Rail Road.
8. Mercury, June 5, June 18, and June 25, 1840 (proceedings of council).
9. Courier, July 17, 1840 (proceedings of council).
10. *Ibid.*, April 12, 1841.
11. Mercury, Sept. 4, 1840 (proceedings of council).
12. Census of Charleston (for 1848; pub. 1849), p. 57.
13. Courier, Feb. 16, 1850 (to contractors).
14. Mercury, Feb. 3, 1844 (adv. of a house "nearly opposite the New Arsenal (now building)").
15. Schirmer's Record, Aug. 31, 1844 and May 11, 1845. Also, Courier, Aug. 5, 1845.
16. Courier, July 19, 1845 (to contractors).
17. Courier, Oct. 1, 1845. *Ibid.*, June 28, 1847. Curtis' name is on steps of Huguenot Church as its builder.
18. Courier, June 28, 1847.
19. Receipts and Expenditures of City Council, 1850 (April). Also, Schirmer's Record, Aug. 23, 1849.
20. Courier, June 18, and Aug. 17, 1847. Schirmer's Record, Nov. 28, 1848.
21. Courier, Sept. 2, 1847 (to contractors). Schirmer's Record, Jan. 1848, and March 31, 1850. Gospel Messenger, July 1850.
22. Carson: Life of James L. Petigru, p. 67.
23. Courier, June 15, 1850 (to contractors).
24. St. Michael's Vestry Minutes, vol. IV, p. 100.
25. Courier, Aug. 26, 1847 (proceedings of council).
26. *Ibid.*, Feb. 15, 1850 (to contractors). *Ibid.*, Oct. 15, 1852 (Werner's bill for fence).
27. *Ibid.*, Feb. 16, 1850 (to contractors).
28. *Ibid.*, April 25, and Sept. 29, 1851.
29. *Ibid.*, Sept. 2, 1850.
30. *Ibid.*, Nov. 8, 1850.
31. Easterby: History of the College of Charleston, pp. 111-112.
32. Courier, March 7, 1851.
33. Simms: Charleston (in Harper's New Monthly Mag., June, 1857), p. 12.
34. Courier, Feb. 13, 1851 (to contractors). Evening News, Feb. 14 (letter from "Salnitre"). Courier, March 18 (letter from "A Member"). *Ibid.*, April 4 (letter). *Ibid.*, April 8, editorial paragraph.
35. *Ibid.*, Aug. 27, 1853.

36. *Ibid.*, July 1, 1854 (to contractors).
37. SCHGM, vol. 25, p. 94.
38. Directory of 1855, appendix, pp. 32-33.
39. Courier, March 21, 1857.
40. *Ibid.*, April 16, 1856.
41. Signature on monument. Date from Schirmer's Record, May 5, 1858.
42. Charleston Evening News, June 18, 1856.
43. Cullum: Biographical Register of the Officers and Graduates of the U. S. Military Academy, vol. 1, p. 292.
44. SCHGM, vol. 36, p. 115, footnote.
45. SCHGM, vol. 36, p. 120.
46. *Ibid.*, vol. 37, p. 68 *et seq.*
47. Directory of 1867-68.
48. St. Michael's Vestry Minutes, vol. IV, p. 155.
49. Simons & Lapham: Charleston, unpaged leaf near end of volume.
50. Ceremonies at the Unveiling of the Bronze Bust of William Gilmore Simms (pamphlet).
51. SCHGM, vol. 36, p. 115, footnote.

EDWARD C. JONES

1. Bylaws and Register Book of Marion Lodge, I.O.O.F. (ms).
2. Courier, June 1, 1848.
3. Schirmer's Record, Feb. 3, 1850.
4. Mercury, Nov. 20, 1849.
5. Officers of the S. C. Institute, 1849 (pamphlet, in vol.° A.PM, Ser. 4, vol. 22, at Charleston Library Society).
6. S. C. Institute, List of premiums at 1849 Fair.
7. Courier, Nov. 8, 1849.
8. Receipts and Expenditures of City Council (from July 1, 1849 to July 1, 1850).
9. Courier, Oct. 1, 1849. Description of hotel in Courier, March 26, 1855.
10. *Ibid.*, Sept. 5, 1850.
11. *Ibid.*, Jan. 16, 1850. Also tablet from Old Roper Hospital, now in the present Roper Hospital.
12. Tablet from Old Roper Hospital, now in present Roper Hospital.
13. *Courier*, July 1, 1853, letter signed "Justice", praising work by Jones: "Col. Ashe's residence, South-Bay, is a gem".
14. Courier, Jan. 1, 1850.
15. *Ibid.*, July 20, 1850.
16. Receipts and Expenditures of City Council (from July 1, 1849 to July 1, 1850).
17. *Ibid.*
18. This old photograph, said to have been taken about 1865-68, appeared in the News & Courier, April 21, 1939.
19. Courier, May 27, 1854 (proceedings of council).
20. *Ibid.*, Aug. 22, 1850. Also, Journal of the Diocesan Convention of S. C., 1851, p. 30.
21. *Ibid.*, June 14, 1850.

22. *Ibid.*, Aug. 5, 1850.
23. Schirmer's Record, March 6, 1850.
24. Courier, March 8, 1851.
25. *Ibid.*, May 23, 1851.
26. *Ibid.*, Feb. 6, 1852.
27. *Ibid.*, Aug. 27, 1853.
28. McGlothlin: Baptist Beginnings in Education, pp. 110-111.
29. Courier, March 3, 1853, quoting Baltimore American of Feb. 28.
30. Courier, March 4, 1853.
31. *Ibid.*, Aug. 27, 1853.
32. Schirmer's Record, March, 1854, and Dec. 27, 1854.
33. Courier, March 7, 1853, ascribes the State Bank to the firm. Simms (Harper's New Monthly Mag., June, 1857) says that it was "designed by Jones, one of the most popular of the Palmetto architects".
34. Courier, March 7, 1853.
35. Tablet in hall of Orphan House, says remodeling was done by Jones and Lee. The editorial on Lee's death, News & Courier, Aug. 29, 1885, states that Lee assisted Jones in the remodeling.
36. Courier, June 15, 1853 (meeting of council).
37. Tablet in Orphan House hall.
38. Courier, July 16, 1853, says that the committee for repairing the Circular Church "procured an architectural plan from Messrs. Jones & Lee, and engaged them as architects to superintend the projected improvements." But the Courier of Aug. 8, 1853, speaks of a "well-merited tribute to the Architect"; and "Justice", praising Jones in the Courier of July 1, 1853, says: "the Circular Church, interior, just completed, is a beautiful effort."
39. Schirmer's Record, Aug. 7, 1853.
40. Courier, Aug. 2, 1854.
41. *Ibid.*, Jan. 5, 1857.
42. *Ibid.*, Feb. 26, 1859 (to contractors).
43. *Ibid.*, April 4, 1859.
44. The Journal of Cadet Tom Law, pp. 245-246.
45. Year Book of 1886 (Henry P. Archer: The Public Schools of Charleston—Their Origin, Development, and Present Status), p. 187.
46. Mary Taylor: A History of Memminger School, p. 5.
47. Schirmer's Record, May 20, 1859.
48. Year Book of 1886, pp. 187-188.
49. Charleston News, November 23, 1871 (editorial on death of John Russell): "For several years Mr. Russell had as copartners his two half-brothers, Edward and James Jones." Dates of Russell's birth and death from this editorial; date of James C. Jones' death from stone in E. C. Jones lot, Magnolia Cemetery, where he and Russell are buried.
50. Courier, Feb. 20, 1857.
51. *Ibid.*, May 11, 1854.
52. *Ibid.*, Dec. 11, 1861.
53. MCO, vol. N-15, p. 405.—"I Edward C. Jones heretofore of Charleston . . . and now of Memphis in the State of Tennessee."
54. MCO, vol. L-17, p. 605; and vol. B-20, p. 306.

FRANCIS D. LEE

1. Samuel Lapham: (Part I) A History of the Practice of Architecture in the State of South Carolina in General (etc.), p. 8.
2. Simons & Lapham: Charleston, S. C. (However, an editorial in the News and Courier, Aug. 29, 1885, stated that Lee was born in 1827.)
3. Charleston Wills, vol. L-1851-56, p. 358 (Will of Eliza Lee). Times, Feb. 23, 1803 (marriage of William Lee and Elizabeth Markley).
4. S. C. Gazette, March 2, 1767 (marriage of William Lee, watchmaker, to Anna Theus, daughter of Jeremiah Theus, limner). O'Neall's Bench & Bar, vol. 1, has an account of the watchmaker's son, Judge Thomas Lee, uncle of the architect.
5. Easterby: A History of the College of Charleston, p. 308.
6. Courier, Aug. 6, 1845.
7. Easterby: A History of the College of Charleston, p. 308.
8. Courier, Sept. 29, 1847.
9. Joseph B. Hyde: History of Union Kilwinning Lodge, No. 4.
10. Easterby: South Carolina Society, p. 126.
11. Russell's Magazine, vol. 2, p. 467.
12. Courier, April 25, 1848; and Mercury, Jan. 1, 1849.
13. S. C. Institute Fair catalogue for 1849.
14. News and Courier, Aug. 29, 1885.
15. Courier, Nov. 8, 1850.
16. *Ibid.*, April 26, 1853.
17. Year Book of 1882, p. 417.
18. Courier, Aug. 27, 1853.
19. *Ibid.*, Feb. 14, 1853.
20. *Ibid.*, July 1, 1852.
21. Samuel Lapham: (Part I) A History of the Practice of Architecture in the State of South Carolina in General (etc.), p. 8, credits bank to Lee. Courier, June 13, 1853, stated that plans could be seen at office of Jones & Lee.
22. Dates from Schirmer's Record, Sept. 1853, and March, 1854.
23. Mercury, June 30, 1853.
24. Courier, Aug. 27, 1853.
25. Simms, in Harper's New Monthly Magazine, June, 1857.
26. Courier, Aug. 27, 1853.
27. *Ibid.*, List of foundries is in Courier, Sept. 3, 1853.
28. *Ibid.*, Oct. 17, 1856.
29. *Ibid.*, Oct. 19, 1853.
30. News and Courier, Aug. 29, 1885.
31. Courier, Nov. 22, 1856.
32. *Ibid.*, Jan. 5, 1857.
33. Directory of 1855; and Courier, Jan. 6, 1857 (Lee's card).
34. MCO, vol. E-14, p. 77 (building contract).
35. Courier, March 26, 1860.
36. MCO, vol. F-15, p. 169 (building contract).
37. Courier, May 13, 1859.
38. The War of the Rebellion, A Compilation of the Official Records of the Union and Confederate Armies, series I, Vol. VI, p. 18.

39. *Ibid.*, p. 16.
40. John Johnson: The Defense of Charleston Harbor, p. 31.
41. *Ibid.*, p. xxix *et seq.* and p. clix *et seq.*
42. *Ibid.*, p. 31.
43. News and Courier, Aug. 29, 1885.
44. Simons & Lapham: Charleston, S. C. (Unpaged leaf near end of book).
45. Letter of March 8, 1941, to Albert Simons from John A. Bryan, research associate in American Architecture.
46. News and Courier, Aug. 29, 1885.
47. Letter of March 8, 1941, to Mr. Simons from Mr. Bryan.
48. *Ibid.*

LOUIS J. BARBOT AND JOHN H. SEYLE

1. Courier, Aug. 2, 1852.
2. South Carolina Institute Fair catalogue, 1849.
3. Easterby: South Carolina Society, p. 107.
4. Courier, Dec. 5, 1853.
5. Charleston Wills, vol. C-1793-1800, p. 191—will of Henry Philip Wesner (mentions son Frederick, daughter Mary Susanna, etc.) Times, March 8, 1802 (marriage notice of Samuel Seyles (sic) and Mary Susanna Wesner). Charleston Wills, vol. L-1851-1856, p. 465—will of Samuel Seyle (mentions son John H. Seyle, wife Mary S. Seyle, etc.)
6. King: The Newspaper Press of Charleston, S. C., p. 22, footnote.
7. South Carolina Institute Fair catalogue, 1849.
8. Directory of 1855, appendix, p. 29.
9. Charleston Evening News, July 11, 1855.
10. Schirmer's Record, Oct. 16, 1860.
11. Courier, Aug. 27, 1853.
12. Schirmer's Record, June, 1854.
13. Proceedings of the Constitutional Convention of South Carolina, held at Charleston, S. C., beginning January 14th and ending March 17th, 1868.
14. A Sketch of Charleston (pamphlet, 1870).
15. Year Book of 1882, p. 174 (record of fires).
16. Courier, Aug. 27, 1853.
17. Schirmer's Record, Nov. 22, 1858.
18. Courier, June 18, 1853 (to contractors).
19. *Ibid.*, Aug. 27, 1853.
20. *Ibid.* Also, *Ibid.*, Oct. 29, 1853.
21. *Ibid.*, Dec. 15, 1853.
22. *Ibid.*, July 11, 1854.
23. Charleston Evening News, Dec. 6, 1855.
24. Courier, Dec. 20, 1855.
25. *Ibid.*, May 6, 1856 (to contractors).
26. MCO, vol. Z-12, p. 627.
27. Courier, July 21, 1856 (to contractors); and News and Courier, August 23, 1937.
28. Courier, April 5, 1856 (to contractors).
29. Year Book of 1887, p. 357 (The Methodist Church in Charleston).
30. Mercury, May 24, 1859.

31. Courier, March 8, 1859.
32. Year Book of 1893, p. 251.
33. Directories of 1855, 1859, 1867-68.

MR. YOUNG

1. For Young and the Boston Custom House, see John Mead Howells: Lost Examples of Colonial Architecture, plate 13. For Young and Rogers and the Boston Custom House, see Thomas E. Tallmadge: The Story of Architecture in America, p. 114.
2. Schirmer's Record, Dec., 1848.
3. Ibid., July, 1849.
4. Courier, Feb. 19, 1850.
5. Ibid., March 1, 1850 (White). Ibid., March 2, (Hammarskold). Ibid., March 7 (Jones; and Norris).
6. Ibid., March 7, 1850, and March 8.
7. Ibid., Aug. 27, 1853.

P. H. HAMMARSKOLD

1. South Carolina Institute 1852 Fair catalogue.
2. Courier, Oct. 21, 1850 (proceedings of council).
3. Fredrika Bremer: The Homes of the New World, vol. I, p. 267.
4. Courier, Aug. 23, 1851 (to contractors).
5. Ibid., July 20, 1850.
6. Ibid., March 16, and March 24, 1853.
7. Ibid., Aug. 15, 1853 (to contractors).
8. Ibid., March 7, 1853 (to contractors). Also, A. R. Huger Smith and D. E. Huger Smith: The Dwelling Houses of Charleston, p. 255—this speaks of the addition of balconies and fence after the house had changed hands in 1853.
9. MCO, vol. Z-12, p. 350.
10. Courier, Dec. 13, 1861.
11. Ibid., Feb. 27, 1854.
12. Green: A History of the University of South Carolina, p. 155.
13. Courier, June 22, 1854.
14. Ibid., Aug. 5, 1854.
15. Ibid.
16. Ibid., May 27, 1856, from Columbia Times of May 26.
17. Schirmer's Record, Jan. 15, 1856.
18. Tennessee, A Guide to the State, pp. 161 and 224.

GEORGE EDWARD WALKER

1. Courier, March 20, 1851 (to contractors).
2. Schirmer's Record, June 29, 1852.
3. Walker, Evans & Cogwell's map of Charleston, revised 1879.
4. "H" in Courier, June 30, 1853.
5. Courier, April 28, 1853 (Walker's notice).
6. Ibid., Sept. 6, 1853.
7. Ibid.

8. *Ibid.*, April 28, 1853.
9. A. S. Salley: The State Houses of South Carolina 1751-1936, p. 18.
10. Courier, Feb. 20, 1854 (to contractors).
11. *Ibid.*, June 19, 1854 (to contractors).
12. Easterby: A History of the College of Charleston, p. 116.
13. Courier, August. 5, 1854.
14. Salley: The State Houses of South Carolina, p. 18.
15. G. E. Walker: Exposition of the Proceedings of Commissioners of the New State Capitol, Columbia, S. C. (Pamphlet, at Charleston Library Society, SC Pm. Misc. v. 4, No. 3).
16. Courier, Jan. 14, 1856 (to contractors).
17. S. C. Women in the Confederacy, vol. 1, p. 305.
18. History of the Evangelical Lutheran Synod of S. C., Rev. S. T. Hallman, D.D., ed., pp. 69-77.
19. Information from Clarence McK. Smith, formerly of Newberry College.
20. Charleston Evening News, Nov. 5, 1856 (quoting the South Carolinian).
21. Year Book of 1885, p. 353.
22. MCO, vol. T-10, p. 340, Vol. B-12, p. 626. Vol. E-11, p. 487.
23. Directory of 1831.
24. Courier, Dec. 2, 1850.
25. Schirmer's Record, Sept. 19, 1863.
26. MCO, vol. S-11, p. 43.

MID-CENTURY MODERNS

CHARLES TILLINGHAST JAMES

1. DAB—article on James by Harold U. Faulkner.
2. *Ibid.*
3. Schirmer's Record, Oct. 2, 1847; Courier, Oct. 4, 1847.
4. Courier, Oct. 4, 1847.
5. Schirmer's Record, April 12, 1848.
6. *Ibid.*, May 17, 1852.
7. DAB—article on James.

JOHN E. EARLE

1. Schirmer's Record, Nov. 3, 1853; and Courier of same date.
2. Courier, Nov. 7, 1853.
3. *Ibid.*, Aug. 13, and Nov. 7, 1853.
4. *Ibid.*, March 7, 1853.
5. *Ibid.*, Dec. 17, 1861.
6. *Ibid.*, Aug. 13, 1853.
7. *Ibid.*, Nov. 7, 1853.
8. *Ibid.*, Aug 13, 1853.
9. *Ibid.*
10. For plumbing, see chapter on Russell Warren; also Mercury, Aug. 1, 1844 (petition granted to lay salt water pipe to William Ravenel premises, East Bay); also advertisements in the following: Courier, May 14, 1850 (97—now 119—Broad Street); Courier, Feb. 28, 1851 (41 Montagu Street). For furnace heat, see adv. in Courier, Aug. 12, 1852 ("four large Furnaces,

for heating apartments, together with several hundred feet of Piping");
report of meeting of council, in Courier, Feb. 16, 1853.
11. Courier, Aug. 13, 1853.
12. *Ibid.*, Aug. 27, 1853.
13. *Ibid.*, April 25, 1856.

JAMES A. LONGLEY AND JOSEPH H. LONG

1. Courier, Jan. 26, 1856.
2. *Ibid.*, March 12, 1840 (proceedings of council).
3. *Ibid.*, Aug. 27, 1853.
4. *Ibid.*, Dec. 15, 1839.

CHURCHES AND CHURCH SCHOOLS

PATRICK CHARLES KEELY

1. Monsignor Joseph L. O'Brien: A Chronicle History of St. Patrick's Church, Charleston, South Carolina. Also (anonymous pamphlet), Cathedral of St. John the Baptist, Charleston, S. C.—Its Consecration and History.
2. Courier, April 6, 1854.
3. *Ibid.*
4. *Ibid.*
5. *Ibid.*, May 20, 1854.
6. Cathedral of St. John the Baptist, Charleston, S. C.—Its Consecration and History.
7. Richard J. Purcell: P. C. Keely: Builder of Churches in the United States— in Records of the American Catholic Historical Society of Philadelphia, vol. 54, p. 208 *et seq.*

MINOR ANTE-BELLUM ARCHITECTS

EDWARD BENJAMIN BRYAN

1. Cullum: Biographical Register of the Officers and Graduates of the U. S. Military Academy, Vol. II, p. 216.
2. *Ibid.*, also Bryan's adv. in Courier, Dec. 13, 1848.
3. Cullum (for cotton planting); Mercury, April 29, 1861 (for reading and study).
4. Mercury, April 29, 1861. Also, Carolina Art Asso., catalogue of An Exhibition of Miniatures owned in S. C. and Miniatures of South Carolinians owned elsewhere painted before the year 1860 (1936).
5. Cullum, vol. II, p. 216. Also Mercury, April 29, 1861.
6. Cullum, vol. II, p. 216.
7. Mercury, April 29, 1861.
8. Charleston Wills, vol. M, 1856-62, p. 470 (Will of Edward Benjamin Bryan). *Ibid.*, vol. N. 1862-68 (Will of Julia Grace Bryan).
9. Miniature, owned by Richard Bryan of John's Island.

CHRISTOPHER C. TRUMBO

1. Courier, Feb. 29, 1840.
2. Directory of 1849 (mason); *Ibid* of 1852, and *Ibid* of 1855 (bricklayer); *Ibid of* 1867-68 (contractor).
3. Courier, Aug. 27, 1853.
4. *Ibid.,* July 13, 1853.
5. News and Courier, Sept. 21, 1892.

WILLIAM BELL

1. Courier, Oct. 15, 1847.

LOUIS F. LEBLEUX

1. Directory of 1855.
2. Courier, Aug. 19, 1856.
3. Mercury, Feb. 8, 1860.

JOHN A. MICHEL

1. The Michel silversmiths are listed in Burton's South Carolina Silversmiths 1690-1860, p. 120.
2. Easterby: A History of the College of Charleston, p. 312.
3. Courier, Sept. 5, 1850.
4. *Ibid.,* Dec. 7, 1853.
5. *Ibid.,* May 7, 1857.
6. Directory of 1867-68.

EDWIN J. WHITE AND WILLIAM M. RAMSAY

1. MCO, Index to John McCrady plats.
2. Mercury, Dec. 6, 1859.
3. Johnson: The Defense of Charleston Harbor, p. 231.

JOHN HENRY DEVEREUX

1. News and Courier, March 17, 1920.
2. *Ibid.*
3. Information from his great-niece, Mrs. James N. Stedman.
4. Typescript owned by Mrs. Stedman.
5. News and Courier, March 17, 1920.
6. History of the Evangelical Lutheran Synod of South Carolina (Rev. S. T. Hallman, D.D., ed.), p. 167.
7. Charleston, S. C., in 1883, p. 18.
8. Thomas P. Lesesne: 150 Years of Orange Lodge, No. 14, A.F.M., p. 21.
9. News and Courier, March 17, 1920.
10. *Ibid.*
11. *Ibid.*

BIBLIOGRAPHY

MANUSCRIPTS

Charleston Mesne Conveyance Records.

Charleston Probate Court Records (wills, inventories, miscellaneous).

Wilmot G. de Saussure, notes interleaved in his copy of Fraser's *My Reminiscences of Charleston*. Owned by Charleston Library Society.

John Henry Devereux, typescript concerning. Owned by Mrs. James N. Stedman, of Charleston.

Charles Fraser's *Account Book*. Collection of Alwyn Ball, deposited at Carolina Art Association.

Marion Lodge, I.O.O.F., *Bylaws and Register Book*. Odd Fellows, Charleston.

Robert Mills, plans and specifications for enlarging St. Michael's Church, Charleston. Owned by the vestry.

Daniel Ravenel (1787-1873), *Letterbooks and account books*. Owned by the writer.

St. Michael's *Vestry Minutes*. Owned by the vestry.

Jacob F. Schirmer's *Record*. Owned by South Carolina Historical Society, Charleston.

Letter from William Simmons in Cheves collection, South Carolina Historical Society.

Albert Simons, letters and papers on architects.

NEWSPAPERS

Charleston, S. C., newspapers:

Charleston Courier. (Name changed to Charleston Daily Courier, July 1, 1852).

Charleston Daily News.

Charleston Evening News.

Charleston Mercury.

Charleston News.

Charleston Times.

City Gazette. (Subject to frequent changes of name—Charleston City Gazette and Advertiser, City Gazette and Commercial Daily Advertiser, City Gazette and Daily Advertiser).

Columbian Herald, or the Southern Star.

Investigator.

News and Courier.

Royal South Carolina Gazette.

South Carolina and American General Gazette.

South Carolina Gazette.

South Carolina Gazette and Country Journal.

South Carolina State Gazette.
South Carolina Weekly Gazette.
Southern Patriot.
Georgetown, S. C., newspaper:
Winyah Intelligencer.

MAGAZINES

Gospel Messenger, July, 1850, article on St. Philip's Church.

Kennedy, J. Robie, Jr.: "Examples of Georgian and Greek Revival Work in the Far South", *Architectural Record*, March, 1907.

Lapham, Samuel, Jr.: "Architectural Specifications of a Century Ago, Being a Copy, with Commentary, of the documents and drawings for a Church on John's Island, S. C., by Robert Mills, Architect." *Architectural Record*, March, 1923.

R. M. (Robert Mills): "Architecture in Virginia", *Virginia Historical Register and Literary Companion*, January, 1853.

Manigault, Louis, and Dr. Gabriel Manigault: "The Manigault Family from 1665 to 1886", *Transactions of the Huguenot Society of South Carolina*, No. 4, 1897.

Mills, Robert: "The Daily Journal of Robert Mills", *Maryland Historical Magazine*, vol. XXX, No. 3, Sept., 1935.

Monthly Review, December, 1782, review of Peter Henry Bruce's Memoirs.

Morrison, A. J.: "John G. De Brahm", *South Atlantic Quarterly*, July, 1922.

Newton, Robert Hale: "Bulfinch's Design for the Library of Congress", Art *Bulletin*, Sept., 1941.

Purcell, Richard J.: "P. C. Keely: Builder of Churches in the United States", *Records of the American Catholic Historical Society of Philadelphia*, vol. 54, p. 208 *et seq.*

Ravenel, Beatrice St. J.: "Here Lyes Buried—Taste and Trade in Charleston Tombstones", *Antiques*, March 1942.

Russell's Magazine, vol. 2, p. 467, item on E. C. Jones.

Simms, William Gilmore (attributed): "Charleston", *Harper's New Monthly Magazine*, June, 1857.

Simons, Albert, and Samuel Lapham: "The Development of Charleston Architecture", *Architectural Forum*, Oct., 1923 through Jan., 1924.

South Carolina Historical and Genealogical Magazine, Pub. by South Carolina Historical Society.

Southern Rose, Sept. 1, 1838, leading article.

Taylor, Emily Heyward Drayton: "The Draytons of South Carolina and Philadelphia", *Publications of the Genealogical Society of Pennsylvania*, vol. VIII, No. 1, March, 1921.

Tolman, Ruel P.: "The Technique of Charles Fraser, Miniaturist", *Antiques*, Jan. and Feb., 1935.

BOOKS AND PAMPHLETS

Babcock, J. W.: *Robert Mills*. (In South Carolina Department of Agriculture, Commerce and Immigration, *Handbook of South Carolina*. Columbia, 1907.)

Bernard, Duke of Saxe-Weimar Eisenach: *Travels through North America, during the Years 1825 and 1826.* Philadelphia, 1828. 2 vols.

Bernheim, G. D.: *History of the German Settlements and of the Lutheran Church in North and South Carolina.* Philadelphia, 1872.

Boddie, William Willis: *History of Williamsburg; Something About the People of Williamsburg County, South Carolina.* Columbia, 1923.

Bond, Oliver James: *The Story of the Citadel.* Richmond, 1936.

Brackett, Rev. Gilbert P.: *Manual for the Use of Members of the Second Presbyterian Church, Charleston, S. C.* Charleston, 1894.

Bremer, Fredrika: *The Homes of the New World.* New York, 1858. 2 vols.

Brown, Frank P.: *London Buildings.* London, 1933.

Brown, Glenn: *History of the United States Capitol.* Washington, 1900-1903. 2 vols.

Bruce, Peter Henry: *Memoirs of Peter Henry Bruce, a Military Officer in the Services of Prussia, Russia, and Great Britain.* Dublin edition, 1783.

Bryan, G. S.: *Biographical Sketch of Charles Fraser.* (In Fraser Gallery catalogue. Charleston, 1857.)

Burton, E. Milby: *South Carolina Silversmiths, 1690-1860.* Richmond, 1942.

Carolina Art Association: *Catalogue of an Exhibition of Miniatures owned in South Carolina, and miniatures of South Carolinians owned elsewhere painted before the Year 1860.* Charleston, 1936.

Carpenter, S. C.: *Report of the Trial of Joshua Nettles and Elizabeth Cannon for the Murder of John Cannon on the Night of the 24th October, 1804.* Charleston, 1805.

Carroll, B. R.: *Historical Collections of South Carolina.* (A collection of early source material.) New York, 1836. 2 vols.

Carson, James Petigru: *Life, Letters, and Speeches of James Louis Petigru, the Union Man of South Carolina.* Washington, 1920.

Cathedral of St. John the Baptist, Charleston, S. C., Its Consecration and History. (Charleston?) 1907.

Census, Committee on, for 1848: (Report) *exhibiting the condition and prospects of the city . . . .* Charleston, 1849.

Ceremonies at the Unveiling of the Bronze Bust of William Gilmore Simms, at White Point Garden, Charleston, S. C., June 11, 1879. Charleston, 1879.

Charleston *Directories,* of 1790, 1801, 1802, 1806, 1807, 1809, 1813, 1816, 1819, 1822, 1829, 1831, 1837-38, 1840-41, 1849, 1852, 1855, 1859, 1867-68, 1886.

Charleston *Year Books,* 1880 through 1942. Charleston.

Chesnut, Mary Boykin: *A Diary from Dixie.* New York, 1905.

Cullum, George Washington: *Notices of the Biographical Register of Officers and Graduates of the United States Military Academy at West Point . . . .* New York, 1879. 3 vols.

Cunningham, Clarence, ed.: *A History of the Calhoun Monument at Charleston, S. C.* Charleston, 1888.

Dalcho, Rev. Frederick: *An Historical Account of the Protestant Episcopal Church in South Carolina . . . .* Charleston, 1820.

Deas, Alston: *The Early Ironwork of Charleston.* Columbia, 1941.

Deutsche National-Litteratur, vol. 135, first part. (Historische kritische Ausgabe.) Stuttgart.

Dictionary of American Biography. New York, 1928-36.

Dictionary of National Biography. London, 1885-1900.

Digest of the Ordinances of the City Council of Charleston, A. Charleston, 1844.

Downing, Antoinette Forrester: *Early Homes of Rhode Island*. Richmond, 1937.

Drayton, John: *A View of South Carolina, as Respects her Natural and Civil Concerns*. Charleston, 1802.

Dunlap, William: *Diary*. (Historical Society Publications, vols. LXII, LXIII, LXIV.) New York, 1930.

History of the Arts of Design in the United States. (New edition). Boston, 1918. 3 vols.

Easterby, J. H.: *A History of the College of Charleston*, New York, 1935.

History of the St. Andrew's Society of Charleston, South Carolina, 1729-1929. Charleston, 1929.

South Carolina Society. Baltimore, 1937.

Eyre, Louisa Lear, ed.: *Letters and Recollections of George Washington*. New York, 1906.

Fraser, Charles: *My Reminiscences of Charleston*. Charleston, 1854.

Gallagher, H. M. Pierce: *Robert Mills, Architect of the Washington Monument, 1781-1855*. New York, 1935.

Georgia, A Pageant of Years. (Pub. by Georgia Society of the Colonial Dames of America.) Richmond, 1933.

Giedion, Siegfried: *Space, Time, and Architecture*. Cambridge, Mass., 1941.

Glenn, Bess, ed.: *Some Letters of Robert Mills, Engineer and Architect*. With Notes by A. S. Salley. Columbia, 1938.

Gongaware, Rev. George J.: *The History of the German Friendly Society*. Richmond, 1935.

Green, Edwin L.: *A History of Richland County*. Columbia, 1932.

History of the Buildings of the University of South Carolina. Columbia, 1909.

A History of the University of South Carolina. Columbia, 1916.

Guilday, Rev. Peter: *The Life and Times of John England, First Bishop of Charleston*. New York, 1927. 2 vols.

Hall, Basil: *Travels in North America in the Years 1827 and 1828*. Philadelphia, 1829. 2 vols.

Hallman, Rev. S. T., ed.: *History of the Evangelical Lutheran Synod of South Carolina, 1824-1924*. Columbia, (1925?)

Hamlin, Talbot: *Architecture Through the Ages*. New York, 1940.

Greek Revival Architecture in America. New York, 1944.

History of St. Paul's, Radcliffeborough, Made up from Such Records and Traditions as Still Survive the Ravages of the War. Charleston, 1878.

Howells, John Mead: *Lost Examples of Colonial Architecture; Buildings that Have Disappeared or Been so Altered as to be Denatured*. New York, 1931.

Hutson, Francis Marion: (Introduction to) Second edition of Mills' *Atlas of the State of South Carolina*. Columbia, 1938.

Hyde, Joseph B.: *History of Union Kilwinning Lodge, No. 4, Ancient Free Masons of South Carolina.* Charleston, 1930.

Irving, John Beaufain: *History of the Turf in South Carolina.* Charleston, 1857.

Jackson, Joseph: *Development of American Architecture, 1783-1830.* Philadelphia, 1926.

Jay, Rev. William: *Autobiography.* (American edition.) New York, 1855.

Johnson, John: *The Defense of Charleston Harbor.* Charleston, 1890.

Jones, E. Alfred: *American Members of the Inns of Court.* London, 1924.

Journal of the Diocesan Convention of South Carolina, 1851. Charleston, 1851.

Kennedy, Lionel H., and Thomas Parker: *An Official Report of the Trials of Sundry Negroes Charged with an Attempt to Raise an Insurrection.* Charleston, 1822.

Kershaw, Rev. John: *History of the Parish and Church of Saint Michael, Charleston.* Charleston, 1915.

Kimball, Fiske: *American Architecture.* Indianapolis, 1928.

King, William L.: *The Newspaper Press of Charleston, S. C.* Charleston, 1872.

Law, John Adger, ed.: *Citadel Cadets, the Journal of Cadet Tom Law.* Clinton, S. C. 1941.

Lee, Mary Elizabeth: *Poetical Remains; with a Bibliographical Memoir by S. Gilman.* Charleston, 1851.

Lesesne, Thomas Petigru: *150 Years of Orange Lodge No. 14 A. F. M.* Charleston, 1939.

Mazÿck, Arthur: *Guide to Charleston Illustrated.* Charleston, 1875.

McCrady, Edward: *The History of South Carolina under the Proprietary Government, 1670-1719.* New York, 1896.
The History of South Carolina under the Royal Government, 1719-1776. New York, 1899.
A Sketch of St. Philip's Church, Charleston. Charleston, 1901.

McGlothlin, William Joseph: *Baptist Beginnings in Education; a History of Furman University.* Nashville, 1926.

Miller, A. E.: Miller's *Almanac,* for 1822 through 1826; and 1831 through 1840. Charleston.

Milligan, Dr. George (attributed): *Short Description of the Province of South Carolina . . . written in 1763.* (In Carroll's Historical Colls. of S. C. New York, 1836.)

Mills, Robert: *Statistics of South Carolina.* Charleston, 1826.

Mumford, Lewis: *The South in Architecture.* New York, 1941.

Nevins, Allan: *Frémont, the West's Greatest Adventurer.* New York, 1928.

O'Brien, Monsignor Joseph L.: *A Chronicle History of St. Patrick's Parish, Charleston, South Carolina, 1837-1937.* Charleston, 1937.

O'Neall, John Belton: *Biographical Sketches of the Bench and Bar of South Carolina.* Charleston, 1859. 2 vols.

Patton, Sadie S.: *Story of Henderson County, the.* Asheville, N. C., 1947.

Power, Tyrone: *Impressions of America During the Years 1833, 1834, 1835.* London, 1836. 2 vols.

Poyas, Mrs. E. A.: *The Olden Time of Carolina.* Charleston, 1855.

Prime, Alfred Coxe, ed.: *The Arts and Crafts in Philadelphia, Maryland, and South Carolina.* Topsfield, Mass. 1929 and 1932. 2 vols.

Proceedings of the Constitutional Convention of South Carolina, held at Charleston, S. C., beginning January 14th and ending March 17th, 1868. Charleston, 1868.

Quincy, Josiah, ed.: *Memoir of the Life of Josiah Quincy, Junior, of Massachusetts Bay: 1744-1775.* (Third edition, ed. by Eliza Susan Quincy, Boston, 1875.)

Ramsay, David: *Memoirs of the Life of Martha Laurens Ramsay.* Philadelphia, 1811.

Ravenel, Henry Edmund: *Ravenel Records.* Atlanta, 1898.

Ravenel, Mrs. St. Julien: *Charleston, the Place and the People.* New York, 1906.

Receipts and Expenditures of City Council from July 1, 1849 to July 1, 1850. (Charleston?)

Reichardt, C. F.: *Centro-Amerika.* Braunsweig, 1851.

Nicaragua. Braunsweig, 1854.

Rothrock, Mary V., ed. *The French Broad-Holston Country, A History of Knox County, Tennessee.* Knox County History Committee, East Tennessee Historical Society. Knoxville, 1946.

Rousseau, Jean-Jacques: *Les Confessions.* Paris edition of 1817.

Salley, A. S.: *The State Houses of South Carolina, 1751-1936.* Columbia, 1936.

St. Philip's *Parish Register, 1720-1758.* Charleston, 1904.

St. Philips *Parish Register, 1754-1810.* Charleston, 1927.

Scott, Robert N., ed.: *The War of the Rebellion, A Compilation of the Official Records of the Union and Confederate Armies,* series I, vol. VI. Washington, 1882.

Seabrook, E. M.: *The History of the Protestant Episcopal Church of Edisto Island.* (Charleston?) 1853.

Shecut, J. L. E. W.: *Topographical, Historical, and Other Sketches of the City of Charleston from Its First Settlement to the Present Period.* Charleston, 1819.

Simmons, Agatha Aimar: *Charleston, S. C., A Haven for the Children of Admiral de Grasse.* Charleston, 1940.

Simons, Albert, and Samuel Lapham, Jr.: *Charleston, South Carolina.* (The Octagon Library of American Architecture.) New York, 1927.

Smith, Alice R. Huger: *A Charleston Sketchbook.* (Charles Fraser's sketchbook.) Carolina Art Association, 1940.

Smith, Alice R. Huger and D. E. Huger Smith: *Charles Fraser.* New York, 1924.

The Dwelling Houses of Charleston, South Carolina. Philadelphia, 1917.

Smith, Henry A. M.: *The Baronies of South Carolina.* Charleston, 1931.

Snowden, Yates: *Notes on Labor Organizations in South Carolina, 1742-1861.* Columbia, 1914.

South Carolina Institute, *catalogues* for 1849 and 1852 fairs. Charleston, 1849 and 1852.

South Carolina *Reports and Resolutions,* for 1827.

South Carolina Women in the Confederacy, 2 vols. Columbia, 1903 and 1907.

Special Services Held at St. Philip's Church, Charleston, S. C., on the 12th and 13th of May, 1875 . . . . Charleston, 1876.

Statutes at Large of South Carolina, The. Columbia, 1836-1841.

Stoney, Samuel Gaillard: *Plantations of the Carolina Low Country*. Charleston, 1938.

Tallmadge, Thomas E.: *The Story of Architecture in America*. New York, 1927.

Taylor, Mary: *A History of the Memminger Normal School, Charleston, S. C* Charleston, 1941.

Tennessee, A Guide to The State. New York, 1939.

Thomas, Bishop Albert S.: *A Historical Account of the Protestant Episcopal Church in South Carolina, 1820-1957*. Columbia, 1957.

Thomas, John P.: *History of the South Carolina Military Academy*, Charleston, 1879.

Treasurer's Report to the Honorable the Board of Trustees of the South Carolina College, Nov. 1, 1859. (Columbia?)

Two Diaries from Middle St. John's, Berkeley, South Carolina, February-May, 1865. Pub. by the St. John's Hunting Club, 1921.

United States Census Bureau: *Heads of Families at the First Census of the United States taken in . . . 1790*. Washington, 1907-1908.

Walker, G. E.: *Exposition of the Proceedings of Commissioners of the New State Capitol, Columbia, S. C.* (R. M. Shokes, printer. No place or date.)

Wallace, David Duncan: *Life of Henry Laurens . . .* New York, 1915.
History of South Carolina, The. New York, 1934. 4 vols.

Washington, George: *Diaries*. Vol. 4 (1789-1799). Ed. by John C. Fitzpatrick. Boston, 1925.

Way, Rev. William: *The Old Exchange and Custom House, 1767-1942*. Revised edition. Charleston, 1942.

Weston, Plowden C. J., ed.: *Documents Connected with the History of South Carolina*. (A collection of source material.) London, 1856.

White, Edward B.: *Report of a Reconnaissance for the Charleston, Georgetown, and All Saints Rail Road; between Charleston, S. C., and the North Carolina Line . . . .* Charleston, 1839.

Wilson, Charles C.: *Robert Mills, Architect*. Columbia, 1919.

Wilson, Charles C. and Samuel Lapham: *A History of the Practice of Architecture in the State of South Carolina in General and of the South Carolina Chapter of the American Institute of Architects in Particular*. 1938.

MAPS AND VIEWS

Charleston, Mesne Conveyance Office plats, including the John McCrady plats.

Delin and Toms: *The Ichnography of Charles-Town at High Water*. London, 1739.

Hill, John William: *View of Charleston*. London, 1851.

Mills, Robert: *Atlas of the State of South Carolina*. 2nd edition. Columbia, 1938.

Walker, Evans & Cogswell: *Map of Charleston, Revised, 1879*. Charleston, 1879.

TOMBSTONES AND TABLETS

Tombstones in churchyards of the Circular (Congregational), First (Scotch) Presbyterian, St. John's Lutheran, St. Mary's Roman Catholic, St. Michael's Protestant Episcopal, St. Philip's Protestant Episcopal, and Unitarian churches, and in Magnolia Cemetery, Charleston.

Tablets in First (Scotch) Presbyterian Church, Orphan House, Orphan House Chapel and Roper Hospital, at Charleston, and on the old library building, University of South Carolina, at Columbia.

INDEX

Buildings are listed under the names of the towns or districts to which they belong. Plantation names are grouped together under "Plantations"